MW01705915

Alpha

Alpha

A Strategic Review

Cliff Leach

Prentice Hall
New York London Toronto Sydney Tokyo Singapore

First published 1994 by
Prentice Hall International (UK) Limited
Campus 400, Maylands Avenue
Hemel Hempstead
Hertfordshire, HP2 7EZ
A division of
Simon & Schuster International Group

Printed and bound in Great Britain by
Redwood Books, Trowbridge, Wiltshire

Library of Congress Cataloging-in-Publication Data

Leach, Cliff.
Alpha: a strategic review / Cliff Leach.
p. cm.
Includes index.
ISBN 0-13-327925-1
1. Alpha (Microprocessor) 2. Digital Equipment Corporation.
I. Title.
QA76.5.L3748 1994
338.4'7004165–dc20 93–45758
CIP

British Library Cataloguing in Publication Data

A catalogue record for this book is available from
the British Library

ISBN 0–13–327925–1

1 2 3 4 5 98 97 96 95 94

Contents

Preface

Digital Equipment Corporation (DEC) made a great difference to the world of computing with the introduction of the PDP and then the VAX range of highly successful minicomputers. No other hardware supplier in the mainstream of commercial DP had done as much to change the conditions prevailing in the market up to that point. With the advent of the personal computer and its clones, IBM for once looked like they had the leading edge and soon the market was turned into a more competitive place altogether. In this period, Digital continued to be a success, though at a slower rate than in the past. Soon the corporation's fortunes looked decidedly rocky, and by 1990 things looked black indeed. UNIX systems, based on off-the-shelf hardware from a myriad of suppliers, were hitting the corporation hard and DEC's refusal fully to commit to UNIX in the way that, say, HP had done was starting to spell trouble for the corporation.

Alpha was the response. Digital made a truly huge investment in the development of a technology that has now put them back in the lead, ahead of the competition today and ahead even of the next generations of microprocessor from many of their competitors. This book is aimed at the strategic decision makers in organizations, it is not a technical reference manual but is intended to guide the reader through many of the issues surrounding the decision on platform choice. I have attempted to make the sections as standalone as possible so that the reader can select as much information as required from any section that takes their fancy.

The choice of platform hardware is never simple, and this book looks at the problem from the perspective of existing DEC users or developers and also from the point of view of the non-DEC user or developer. It is clear that the performance of the hardware is excellent, the best in the world today. What I am trying to address with this book is the likely commercial impact of the adoption of this technology. The opportunity that the Alpha microprocessor brings is significant, and applications can now become the repositories of real added value. Data that has sat in inaccessible mountains for so long can now be thoroughly analysed, turning a liability into an asset. My warning message is that the hardware must not be used simply to reduce the value of systems on the market today. To do this is not just a waste of a powerful technology, it is also a suicidal move for the industry.

This book would not have been possible without the help and advice of many of my friends at DEC and I would like to pay a special thanks to Alan Blank for his assistance and advice.

Despite some of my reservations, I think DEC will win with Alpha. Let us hope that the applications can keep up!

Andover, Hampshire Cliff Leach
May 1994

Acknowledgements

3Com is a registered trademark of 3Com Corporation.

Apple and Macintosh are registered trademarks of Apple Corporation Inc.

DEC, PDPII, VAX, VMS, ULTRIX, RSX are registered trademarks and DECnet, MicroVAX and Alpha_AXP are trademarks of Digital Equipment Corporation.

Intel is a registered trademark and Intel386, Intel 486 and Pentium are trademarks of Intel Corporation.

Microsoft, MSDOS and XENIX are registered trademarks and Windows and Windows NT are trademarks of Microsoft Corporation.

NetWare and Novell are registered trademarks of Novel Inc.

UNIX is a registered trademark of Unix Syatels Laboratories.

Hewlett Packard and HPUX are trademarks of Hewlett Packard Corporation.

DGUX and Data General are trademarks of Data General Corporation.

IBM, OS/2, RS6000, OS400, SNA and AS400 are registered trademarks of International Business Machines Corporation.

NCR is a trademark of NCR Corporation.

Microfocus is a registered trademark of Microfocus Ltd.

This book is dedicated to my wife Gill
for her patience and encouragement

CHAPTER 1

Introduction

1.1 Introduction

In the last five years the computer and information technology industry has undergone massive change even by its own standards. Small, influential companies have risen fast, some to become major players, others to disappear overnight. Large, previously dominant corporations like IBM, Data General and Digital have seen their traditional positions and market shares threatened and eroded by the impact of alternative technologies, innovation and a change in the buyer purchasing criteria of their market sectors. In the face of this, the corporate decision makers have had to take a tough and difficult line on personnel, technology and commercial strategy. It was under these difficult and testing conditions that Digital had to define a competitive strategy which would determine their future survival.

By early 1990 it looked as if Digital was on its way down, ready for acquisition under threat on market share and producing a lacklustre performance financially. Many in the industry believed that Digital were trapped by a strategy of proprietary systems based on VMS and had missed the UNIX bandwagon. Certainly they seemed to have ignored the industry trends for a very long time. When the change of mood came in the form of the 5000 series, Digital seemed even then to be committing half-heartedly to the UNIX market. By comparison, HP and DG had both moved much earlier and more aggressively into UNIX systems and were developing a good market share in the sector. To all those that were concerned with strategy based on Digital hardware, be it as user, developer or reseller, the future looked gloomy for Digital and they certainly seemed to have mistimed the market initiatives. One could see a rerun of the abortive attempts to make headway in the desktop PC market looming on the horizon. To many the tacit question was 'Is it time to abandon Digital as a serious contender in open systems?'

Since relations with Digital were part of my job I began to wonder if they were going to pull out of this downwards spiral. Technically I believed they could, commercially I had my doubts. Having worked for Digital in the past I knew they had to make the company far more commercially responsive and aware. This was a philosophy change which could not be allowed to impact their excellent technology record. Alpha was Digital's response to this challenge, and how Alpha fits into the strategy of Digital, those who develop software and those who use software, are the subjects of the rest of this book.

Alpha is not just a remarkably fast microprocessor or the product of state-of-the-art semiconductor design and manufacture, it is a quantum leap in computing power. Digital have put their future on the line with Alpha and in this book I cover all the aspects that relate to the technology and how it is likely to perform in the market. The view that I have formed is that the industry will now be trying to catch up with the potential of Alpha-based technology in all areas: applications, systems design, services, etc.

The readership will be those with an interest in the future of Digital as a company and those presently involved with existing systems from Digital, i.e. developers of software and end users of systems as well as larger distributors of Digital's products. This book gives an overview of the technology and puts it in context with the market and strategy of today. It is not intended as a technical reference manual for the Alpha_AXP microprocessor but does go into some detail on specific areas of the technology that are key to the main objective of setting a technology in a strategic context.

1.1.1 Structure of this Chapter

In this introduction I will give a general overview of the book, its structure and its contents and guide the reader to the central issues of the subject matter. In some respects, this first chapter is a management overview or executive summary of the rest of the book. The basic structure is:

- **Introduction** covering this chapter and the book in outline as well as looking at where and how the book is relevant and summarizing the questions that are addressed by the book overall.
- **Setting the scene in the business** is all about the context, in the widest sense, within which the Digital Alpha strategy exists. The recession, the effects of open systems and competition and the heritage of the legacy systems in the user base are all considered.
- **Digital under threat** looks at the central technology threats to Digital which the Alpha program will have to rebuff. These include the future for VMS, the effects of UNIX (and of ULTRIX), Microsoft and Windows as well as NT and its implications for the Digital market. Finally I consider the strengths, weaknesses, opportunities and threats for Digital as it launches into the Alpha program.

- **Technology needs** is a section that summarizes the main issues to be addressed by the Alpha technology if it is to be a world beater. Central to this are the issues of the systems platform and of client server architectures. The needs of the computing power for existing and future applications and of the central problems with the architectures is also summarized in this section.
- **What is Alpha?** summarizes the Alpha technology in terms of its history and the hardware itself (this is only one part of the overall program). Alpha operating systems and the changes in market approach by Digital conclude this section.

1.1.2 Issues Covered in this Book

I am not often impressed or surprised in this industry. I have seen great innovation and miraculous, as well as disastrous, business performances. The Digital Alpha technology and the supporting commercial programme do impress me, though. I recall being in Scotland visiting a friend of mine, Bill Laing, early in 1992. Bill worked at the Digital facility at South Queensferry, overlooking the River Forth. I had seen the Alpha technology some time earlier. I had read a lot on the power, the methods of production and likely commercial implications for Digital from the technology, but when I met Bill Laing I really understood, in that short time, that Digital had changed. Suddenly I was talking to people in a company with one mission and one focus. All the people I spoke to, from Piere Carlo Falotti and Geoff Shingles down to the humblest software engineer, struck me as being 110% committed to making the Alpha program work.

Over the following months, the need to manage a radically different salesforce in innovative and more focused ways also manifested itself. All the old practices that had stood in the way of Digital's progress for the past four or five years were on the mend. At that time I was working as the Technical Strategy Director for one of AT&T's subsidiaries in England, part of my job being the evaluation and assessment of new technologies. I recall the reaction of the community to my news on Alpha. This could be summarized as '... technically interesting, but can they make the commercial strategy happen?...' I was then, and am now, convinced that the answer is yes, although not without risk.

To begin with, this book gives a brief history of Digital as a corporation then considers the reasons for changing the approach and technology that had made Digital so successful over the years with the VAX and VMS. In Chapter 4 I look in some detail at what Alpha is, both at a technology level and also at a programme level (covering sales, marketing, complementary products, etc.). Chapter 5 looks in some considerable detail at the hardware and leads on to Chapter 6 which deals with the operating systems components of the Alpha program including OpenVMS, UNIX and Microsoft Windows NT.

Naturally, the only reason to have any of the hardware is so that software can be written to run on it and solve the problems for end users. Therefore in Chapter 6, I will assess the issues for the software developer, for both migration and new development. In Chapter 5 I also look from the perspective of the end user, the developer and the systems builder at the Alpha technology and its implications technically and commercially. Finally in Chapter 6 I take three examples - the discrete manufacturing industry, the process manufacturing industry and the warehousing and distribution industry and look at these key players and how and when Alpha might affect them and the information technology they depend upon.

The last three chapters of the book cover a review of Alpha and its likely chances of success, a vision of possible future directions for the Alpha technology programme and Digital.

1.1.3 Questions Raised by Digital Alpha

So what? Digital have developed a hot new microprocessor and launched a range of hardware based on this. How will this change Digital's commercial performance or the industry? These are just a few of the questions I am regularly asked when I talk to the senior decision makers in large banking, insurance and government agencies or developers of applications. Digital raise a lot of questions with the Alpha programme, although the central ones to consider are relatively straightforward and are set out below:

1. What about the userbase? Digital have a huge base of users. These users are set out on a range of systems, the primary ones being VAX and VMS, followed by PDP and RSX and lastly RISC/MIPS and ULTRIX (I chose to leave out the PC ranges and the small SCO presence since they are relatively small). How will Alpha affect them? Will they all be easily able to migrate up to this platform, for instance?
2. What kind of company are Digital? This used to be a pet question of mine when I worked for Digital. I received a whole bunch of different answers, often not matching the actions of the person making the statement. 'A software company' used to be fashionable for a while, then it was neat to say 'number one in services'. *All* of this while still shifting proprietary systems! Digital are now a different, better and more focused company. It will also change as the Alpha technology gets a hold.
3. What changes did and do they still have to make? Clearly Digital have had a traumatic time, like all of the players in the information technology business. It is important to understand what these changes have been and what further changes still need to occur so that the business matches the opportunity in the market.
4. Is the Alpha programme achievable? A good question. Obviously at the technology level it is, but at the programme level it is one hell of a big task. Has Digital been realistic or will this whole thing sink the corporation forever?

5. Why bother with Alpha? What's wrong with the competition? Both for the new systems from Digital and for the existing customer who is, say, looking to change over to a UNIX system, this is a key question. Is Alpha just reinventing another wheel or has it something special to offer?

These, then, are the central issues to look at and are tackled at length in this book. There are no simple answers. All the factors that impact the end decision that Digital has taken, the decision to stake its whole future on the Alpha programme, have to be properly explored so that the reader understands the answers to these deceptively simple questions. By exploring the issues surrounding these questions I hope that the broader issues in the industry will also come to light.

1.1.4 The Readership of this Book

The object of this book is to highlight the issues surrounding Digital's Alpha programme, the Alpha_AXP hardware and the strategic decisions, both technical and commercial, that relate to the users or prospective users of the hardware. This is not a detailed technical manual on Alpha but gives a comprehensive technical overview.

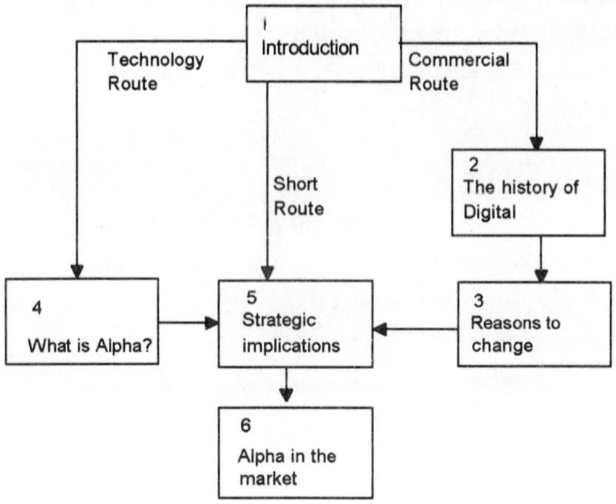

Figure 1.1

The book is intended to be used as a source of reference. To make the chapters stand alone and be suitable for this purpose I have had to repeat some material, and the avid reader who goes from cover to cover will have to excuse this. In Figure 1.1 I have shown the routes through the book based on the reader's background and interests.

The first group at which this book is aimed are the existing Digital customer base. Typically the reader will be in the role of technical strategist for the user, either openly or by default. I regularly work with a number of clients at present advising them on the likely impact that Digital Alpha will and should have on their present and future technical strategy decisions. Much of the research for this area was done with them in mind.

Second, the book is aimed at the decision makers of companies developing software and applications for the present Digital markets. This covers VAX, and MIPS hardware and includes those working on VMS and ULTRIX. I have not restricted the view to those developing in 3GL code. I have also looked at the 4GL/RDBMS side of the business as well as the application of the Alpha systems to knowledge-based applications and neural networking. There are likely to be potential users of the Digital Alpha systems, either direct from Digital or using Digital Alpha processors in other systems (Cray or Olivetti, for example). These people will need a good understanding of the technology aspects and of the likely effect of the business on the parent company for the processors, Digital, in such a commercial strategy.

Finally, those who are just interested in the commercial effects on the Digital corporation of this programme, such as financial analysts, stockbrokers and the like, will find that this book looks from both the technology and the commercial strategy levels into the future for Digital and Alpha. As such, the views given are based on the best information at the time, and I would like to express my thanks to all at Digital for their help and assistance in producing this book. It should, however, be remembered that this is an independent view of a consultancy and not a sponsored publication by Digital. Therefore, the criticism and analysis of risk are unbiased.

1.1.5 Questions to be Addressed

In brief, the kind of questions that this book addresses will be of the type:

- 'Is Alpha for me or my organization?'
- 'What are the risks with Alpha?'
- 'What does Alpha give me?'

The book is an aid to those evaluating their own technical strategy at the moment. This naturally presupposes that there is an adequate technical strategy in place today. It is likely that for many organizations, the technology they have is seen as their strategy rather than as part of some thoughout, longer-term plan to fit needs with solutions for the business. To those in this position I hope that this book will form the basis of a proper investigation into some of the key aspects of technical strategy that any organization needs to consider.

1.2 Setting the Scene in the Business

There is an old adage: 'Question: What is the difference between a recession and a depression? Answer: When my neighbour loses his job it's a recession, when I lose mine, its a depression!' Certainly the business community around the world has been hit by a severe economic storm and the information technology business, so long seemingly immune from the ravages of the economy, has been hit hard.

Digital, like many others, has had to cope with this change. In some ways I think that the organization that comes out of the process is likely to be much closer to the real philosophy of Digital than it was in the mid-1980s. Certainly it needs to be. In the 1980s Digital seemed lost and adrift. Management of the corporation seemed to have ignored many of the vital signs of the industry and the UNIX movement was eroding their market share fast. It was the change in the climate of business that, as we shall see later, was to be the catalyst for a shake-up in the information technology business in general and in Digital in particular and which resulted in the Alpha programme.

1.2.1 The Recession

When I first entered the information technology business the cost of the products relative to the turnover of the companies buying them was large, much larger than now. Furthermore, the margin on all of the products, hardware, software or service was very large indeed. The ability to charge such high prices and make such significant margins was dependent upon a big shortfall in skills and an associated lack of product for a market that had just woken up to the benefits of information technology with the advent of the mini computer.

The recession in the late 1980s made the market price sensitive and reduced the level of commitment to the individual systems vendors. As with all economic downturns, the fittest had to survive while the weakest went to the wall. Like other recessions, the greatest danger for those that survived the worst was that of under-investment.

If one goes through the worst of a downturn in business the upturn demands the same tactics that it always did; competitive advantage and innovation. The real survivors, those who will go on to win the upturn, are those able to continue research and development of products during the hard times.

1.2.2 Open Systems and All That

In the times of the most severe value-for-money judgements, UNIX began to look like a good move for a number of companies. Digital were slow to realize that this was the case and tried to gain lost ground with the introduction of their 5000 series systems based on RISC technology from MIPS CO. These systems were good and running ULTRIX (Digital's flavour of UNIX) they kept a business going in new sales while also serving their base with good and improving VAX/VMS systems. Openness was the real issue, though UNIX was seen as open and despite all Digital's attempts to convince the market of the rightness of going to VMS with its open interfaces and standards, the corporation continued to slow up.

The choice of ULTRIX was also a poor one. ULTRIX is a long way from standard System V UNIX. It has many peculiarities and porting between the two can be a fraught business. To move more in line with the industry, Digital attempted, via OSF/1, to get back on track. Unfortunately this policy took a long time to bear fruit. The simple fact of the matter was that Digital should have gone to the market with a fairly vanilla version of System V UNIX. Not doing so was a really big mistake and typical of the arrogance of the organization in the 1980s.

1.2.3 The Competitive Edge

The information technology industry is changing fast. The pace of market competition has significantly speeded up, especially from Open Systems, with a collapse in the proprietary systems markets around the world. Clearly there can be only a few winners and Digital's Alpha programme is designed to make Digital not just one of the few but the leader of that few. This is an all or nothing strategy. If it fails then this will be the end of Digital as a force in the industry. As you will see later, I think it will succeed, but there are many risks and a great deal of attitudinal change is required from Digital to cope with them.

1.2.4 Legacy Systems

Legacy systems are all around us. They are large, installed systems and software that require maintaining and support and will not disappear overnight. Many of these systems reside on proprietary systems at the moment and any technology path that offers real power to move and maintain them will be seen as positive. Alpha is designed in such a way that Digital are able to position the systems ready for downsizing operations in the market, empowering legacy systems by protecting the investment in the software and data and then adding value to this.

1.3 Digital under Threat

Digital grew fast for 38 years to become the acknowledged leader in the mid-range systems market, and it did this largely on the basis of technology innovation.

Technology has always been Digital's strength and it quickly realized the power of interconnection. Soon Digital VAX systems became well known for the openness that they allowed between different systems in wider solutions. In this respect, from the standards point of view, Digital have been a leading Open Systems player.

Despite this, Digital, with its reliance on CISC processors and a proprietary architecture, were hit badly by commodity hardware and UNIX. They had to respond to this threat and Alpha was their answer. As we will see, it is a fundamental change for Digital not just in technology but in marketing and sales operations as well.

1.3.1 VMS

VMS, Digital's premier operation system, was designed close coupled to the VAX CISC processor. With 10 million users and around $3 billion per annum in maintenance revenues resting on this, Digital are not about to walk away. However good VMS was, the new sales were all happening on UNIX. This problem, how to keep VMS, develop UNIX and get back on top in the market, was the cause of Digital's move to Alpha. The big problem for Digital was that VMS could not move easily to another microprocessor architecture (like MIPS R4000).

1.3.2 UNIX

UNIX is older than VMS. Clearly it has been significantly rewritten over the years and finally, after more than 20 years, it has begun to take off as the operating system in commercial applications environments. Interestingly, UNIX is itself now threatened by the rising star of Microsoft Windows NT. Within a very few years it is likely that one or the other will dominate. My view is that Microsoft Windows NT will be that operating system.

1.3.3 Microsoft and All That

So what of Microsoft? In the last analysis, Microsoft MS-DOS and MS-Windows are the most open of all operating systems since, purely on numbers, they have dominated the market as a whole. Neither are true multi-user systems, however, and it is this issue that Microsoft are addressing with NT.

Microsoft Windows NT is a full, pre-emptive multitasking operating system capable of multi-user support in a server mode. Furthermore, it is based on Object Technology and has an excellent graphical interface, putting it years ahead of either VMS or UNIX in many areas, especially in the eyes of the non-technical end user. Digital have moved into the arena with Alpha_AXP systems running Microsoft Windows NT. However, at the time of writing this book, Microsoft Windows NT is still not a mature operating system, though it is gaining ground.

1.3.4 SWOT for DEC

In summary, the main strengths, weaknesses, opportunities and threats (SWOT) for Digital as it moves off with Alpha are as follows:

- **Strengths** Innovation, especially in technology. Open to change at all levels. Large user base generating significant revenues.
- **Weaknesses** Tied in to VMS and VAX. New business for VAX and VMS poor. Never really succeeded on desktop, Digital is not the strongest selling organization.
- **Opportunities** Alpha could sweep the board in power RISC architectures. Excellent standards compliance in products. Technology lead of Alpha exceeds all others.
- **Threats** Alpha introduces a level of confusion. Digital's late commitment to UNIX may give the opposition time to gain market share. Alpha is new but not an industry standard like Intel. It might get sidelined.

1.4 Technology Needs

The past five years have seen the focus in the market move more towards the technology than at any other time in the past. This is largely as a result of the debate on open systems. The market desire has been to move towards networked systems in client-server architectures using commodity hardware and a UNIX-based operating system. The hardware architecture debate has settled on RISC as the basis of platforms for the foreseeable future.

The biggest desire is for longevity and investment protection from technology. The market has seen a lot of change, much of it traumatic, and it is keen to avoid a similar situation. This book shows how Digital will be able to achieve these ends with Alpha in a way that no other manufacturer can..

1.4.1 The Platform Concept

Platforms are the base of systems development. A platform consists of layers of software and hardware, and in each case the move in the industry is towards greater degrees of standardization of these components and a greater drive towards commodities. In such a market, Digital have developed a hardware architecture that can exploit these conditions while allowing the consistent development of high value added systems for the market. This is achieved by a hardware system that is second to none and one with Open Systems engineering as its design focus.

1.4.2 Computer Power

Computing power has increased dramatically in the past five to ten years. However, there have been two major problems on the horizon. First, the limitations of processor performance have restricted the ultimate capabilities of many applications to use computationally intensive methods in general. Second, there is the reliance of hardware architectures on 32-bit implementations with the restriction on directly addressable memory that this implies. Digital Alpha breaks the mould on both counts. Its processor performance starts well beyond the best capabilities of the industry, and its true 64-bit architecture allows the applications of tomorrow to be written and used today (remember, 64-bits is 4 billion times larger than 32-bits). Alpha is an order of magnitude jump on the opposition. All that remains is for Digital to make this a sound commercial success.

1.4.3 Applications Needs, Now and in the Future

Applications have, in many cases, not changed much in the last five to ten years. One reason for this is the issue of legacy systems, the other is the lack of affordable power to provide facilities to the great mass of mid-range users. In the future visualization will be high on the agenda. The users of applications in the next five years will require a significant improvement in the human-computer interface, and this innovation is realistically achievable in the case of Alpha-based systems.

1.5 What is Alpha?

Alpha or, to use the proper name the DECchip 21064A microprocessor, is a new microprocessor from Digital. It is a full 64-bit implementation of the Alpha RISC architecture and is based on CMOS semiconductor technology. In addition to the technology, Alpha is also a full programme of sales, marketing and services to support this technology and its introduction into the market.

1.5.1 Simple History

The Alpha programme started in 1988. Now 5 years on and several billion dollars later the technology is launched (to be precise, was launched in 1992) and already the first

Alpha systems are shipping to the wide world and making revenues. Alpha grew out of the realization that unless Digital made a dramatic change it was going to lose market share slowly and decline from its leading position. Alpha was not just a response to the market and technology changes, it was a bid to turn round the fortunes of the corporation in the longer term.

1.5.2 Overview of Hardware

The Alpha Microprocessor implementation supports some 1.7 million transistors on the microprocessor. It is a full RISC architecture, load-store system producing today around 200 MIPS and clocked at 200 MHz. The architecture operates in true 64-bit mode and can be configured into multiprocessing environments. The production of the Alpha 64-bit microprocessor pushes back the limits of semiconductor manufacturing technology and takes place both in the USA and Scotland. Alpha 21064 chips retail at around $1600 each.

The Alpha hardware is sufficiently well designed to support VMS (now known as OpenVMS) and a number of other operating systems as well.

1.5.3 Operating Systems Issues

VMS is supported (OpenVMS) on the complete Alpha_AXP implementation range of computers. However, this is not the limit to the range of operating systems, UNIX in the form of OSF/1 is supported as is Microsoft Windows NT. For the first time Digital have a true range of operating systems running on a consistent platform in the market.

1.5.4 A Change in the Market Approach

As significant as the technology is the change in the commercial operations policy of Digital in the Alpha programme. Digital are now licensing a number of different manufacturers to include Alpha microprocessors in their hardware range. The list includes Cray, Kubota Pacific, Olivetti and Raytheon. It is expected that semiconductor manufacturers will, in time, also be licensed to produce the microprocessor.

This is a move that only three years ago seemed impossible for the corporation. Many have seen this change to very open business practices as a sound indication of Digital's commercial resolve. From my own point of view, I am clear that it is an essential component of the future for Digital and other major manufacturers.

CHAPTER 2

A History of Digital Equipment Corporation

2.1 Introduction

Of all the corporations that rose in the 1970s and the first big wave of computer business, Digital is, in my opinion, one of the most remarkable. I worked for Digital Equipment in the 1980s having dealt with them from the outside for a long time. The technology was impressive, the ethos of 'engineer as king' was one that governed the company, but I think it is fair to say that, in those heady days, Digital succeeded in spite of itself. At a commercial, selling level, Digital were unable to match their record of technical superiority. Couple this with an attitude sometimes unworldly and arrogant towards the market and one begins to see the basis for the problems that beset the corporation later on. From proud and inspiring beginnings, Digital rose fast on a seemingly unstoppable tide of innovation. However, this mismatch between technical and commercial skills was eventually to put the corporation in jeopardy.

Digital was the best company I have ever worked for. They tried hard to do all the right things by the workforce and managed their resources in a way that was really good. Unfortunately, the real tide of events in the outside world often seemed to be dismissed or ignored until decisions were forced on them. In this respect Digital was similar to IBM and some of the other major players in the market, innovative technically but carrying on without really taking notice of the market threats. Now, in the early 1990s, Digital is a changed and still-changing corporation. Alpha is the programme that is the focus for this and is far more than the excellent microprocessor or high-value systems. Alpha, in my opinion, is a new beginning, a catharsis for Digital. This chapter outlines the history of Digital to date, and no review of a major technology such as Alpha can be put into context without understanding the economic and commercial drivers that led up to its inception. Technologists reading this book may be tempted to skip this section, but I would urge them not to do so. The economic history of Digital is, in many ways, just as fascinating as the technological history, and Digital's future will certainly be a function of both.

2.1.1 Structure of the Chapter

In this chapter I will look at several main issues. The chronicle is a summary of events from the birth of Digital in 1957 up to the present day, covering the management, financial and product highlights in each year. These events are then analysed to show the main themes in Digital's history. Product proliferation is a feature of the corporation, and the pros and cons of this are reviewed, as is the move to a more service-focused culture. The trends in the business are reviewed in detail to put the move to Alpha in perspective. This is done from four points of view:

- Technology
- Commercial
- Services
- Philosophy

In the summary section at the end of the chapter, the key themes of the chapter are reviewed as are the reasons why Digital is the company it is together with the options for the future.

2.1.2 Issues Covered in this Chapter

The computing industry has changed enormously in the 35 years since Digital was formed. Similarly, Digital as an organization has adapted to changing circumstances and markets. Generally, this adaptation was in the form of technology advances and many of these technical innovations, such as the PDP and the VAX, have become influential components of the computing industry over the years and have generated large revenues for Digital. The key issues covered in this chapter are:

- What is Digital's history?
- What does it look like now?
- What is its likely future?

To begin to answer such questions it is first essential to look at the past of the corporation, to see how rapidly it grew and why it was, for so many years, one of the most successful computer manufacturers in the world. That world has now changed both economically and technically. Fashion and desire in the consultancy business now predicate towards UNIX-based systems as the key growth area, and for proprietary platforms like VAX/VMS this makes the market tough. Digital's response to this could have taken many forms. Like Hewlett Packard, Digital could have abandoned its proprietary systems in favour of UNIX. Like NCR, Digital could have moved to a processor strategy based entirely on commodity third-party processors (in NCR's case the Intel i86 processor family). However, Digital chose to move to its own processor, building on the strength of its history in microprocessor and semiconductor production technology gained in the design, development and production of the VAX. This chapter's main themes are the history of events leading up to this decision and the likely outcome of the decision itself.

2.1.3 Questions Likely to be Answered

Digital's history is full of legendary systems and people like the VAX and Ken Olsen, for instance. The fact of Digital is no less impressive than the legend. This chapter cannot be a full history of a corporation with a 35 year pedigree but it does answer some of the key questions about where Digital came from, why it did so well, what its present problems are and how it is, given its past, likely to succeed in the future. Perhaps the one key question to ask, which I hope this chapter adequately addresses, is 'given Digital's aims and objectives for the next 25 years, does its past performance and present behaviour lead us to believe that this is achievable?'

2.2 The Chronicle

The history of a corporation as complex as Digital could fill a book in its own right (see Pearson,1992). In this section I am setting down an overview of the history to date in order that the present positioning and strategy can be put into context. As you read this section you will see the rise and rise of a remarkable organization through the 1950s to the 1990s. Products like the PDP and the VAX have long and successful histories and have been the driving force for the corporation to date. Now at the birth of a new technology, the Alpha microprocessor, Digital is, I believe, set to grow as fast in the next ten years as it did in the last 30.

2.2.1 1957 to 1992

This section gives a year by year breakdown of the main trends in the business. This is shown under three categories for each year: Management, Financial and Products. Digital have changed a lot over the years in all respects as this summary clearly illustrates.

1957
Management: Digital Equipment opens for business in Maynard, Massachusetts, operating out of a converted wool mill and just 8500 square feet of space.
Financial: $55,000 sales
Products: Systems module

1958
Management: Founding team
Financial: $95,000 sales
Products: Systems modules

1959
Management: Founding team
Financial: $776,000 sales
Products: System modules

1960
Management: Founding team
Financial: $1.3 million, sales
Products: PDP-1 launched in November, the first commercially available small, interactive computer.

1961
Management: Founding team
Financial: $2.65 million sales
Products: System modules

1962
Management: Founding team, still USA based
Financial: $6.5 million sales
Products: PDP-1

1963
Management: Three-person office added in Munich, two-person office added in Ottawa.
Financial: $9.9 million sales
Products: PDP-5 launched as the first real minicomputer in the world (April). PDP-1 operating system launched as the first timesharing operating system in the world (September).

1964
Management: Manufacturing facility set up in Canada. UK and Australian subsidiaries formed. European customer training centre opens in Reading, UK.

Financial: $10.9 million sales
Products: PDP-6 announced (October), the first 36-bit computer.

1965
Management: Growing rapidly
Financial: $14.9 million sales
Products: PDP-8 is introduced as the first mass-produced minicomputer in the world.

1966
Management: Growing rapidly
Financial: First public stock offering. $22.7 million.
Products: PDP-8 range of systems

1967
Management: Manufacturing facility set up in Reading, UK, for PDP and peripherals.
Financial: $38 million sales
Products: PDP-10 is introduced, PDP-8 being made in Reading, UK.

1968
Management: Puerto Rico manufacturing plant opens, Japanese headquarters opens in Tokyo. Workforce increases 68% and tops 2600 headcount located in 11 countries.
Financial: Digital stock starts trading on the American Stock Exchange. $57.3 million sales.
Products: PDP-8/I - Integrated Circuit version of PDP-8 launched.

1969
Management: European headquarters opens in Geneva, Switzerland.
Financial: Digital stock is split three-for-one, $87.8 million sales.
Products: PDP. Note that this is the year that Bell Laboratories use a PDP-7 to write the UNIX operating system.

1970
Management: New production facility opens in Westfield, Massachusetts, for peripherals. New production facility opens in Westminster, Massachusetts. Production facility opens at Mountain View, California, for the production of disks.
Financial: Digital stock begins trading on the New York Stock Exchange. Installed base of Digital Computers exceeds 8000, 1800 are installed in Europe. $135 million sales.
Products: PDP 11/20 is delivered, the first of the famous range of 16-bit minicomputers.

1971
Management: The tradition of annual customer satisfaction surveys is established. A manufacturing facility is set up in Galway, Ireland.
Financial: $146.8 million sales
Products: The DECsystem-10 is introduced to the market.

1972
Management: Springfield, Massachusetts, facility opens for the production of power supplies and sub-assemblies. Parker Street offices open in Maynard, Massachusetts. New production plant in Kanata, Canada, is completed. Plant opens in Taiwan for core memory production. Headcount now exceeds 7800 world-wide.
Financial: $188 million sales.
Products: PDP and DECsystem

1973
Management: Marlboro, Massachusetts, facilities open. Facility opens in Hong Kong for core-memory production.
Financial: $265 million sales.
Products: PDP and DECsystem

1974
Management: The Maynard Industrial Park, known and loved as 'The Mill' is acquired.
Financial: $421 million sales. Installed base of computer systems reaches 30,000. Digital Corporation ranks 475th in the *Fortune 500* sales league.
Products: PDP and DECsystem

1975
Management: No significant changes.
Financial: $533 million sales. Installed base reaches 50,000, world-wide.
Products: The LSI-11, Digital's 16-bit microcomputer and the PDP-11/70 are both introduced. Digital's Networking Architecture is announced heralding a new strategic weapon in the market.

1976
Management: Manufacturing plants in Ayr, Scotland, and Burlington, Vermont, begin production.
Financial: $736 million, sales. Digital stock splits three-for-one.
Products: DECsystem-20 is introduced as the lowest-price 36-bit, timesharing machine on the market.

1977
Management: Manufacturing facilities open in Kaufbeuren, Germany, Augusta, Maine, Merrimack, New Hampshire, and Clonmel, Ireland. Colorado Springs facility opens for remote diagnostics, an industry first. Headcount exceeds 36,000.
Financial: $1 billion sales. Digital stock trades on the Pacific Stock Exchange.
Products: The VAX is born and the VAX 11/780 is introduced to the market.

1978
Management: Facilities open in Colorado Springs, Tewksbury, Massachusetts, and Digital opens its first retail outlet in Manchester, New Hampshire.
Financial: $1.4 billion sales. Customer installed base exceeds 100,000 systems.
Products: PDP, VAX, DECsystem.

1979
Management: Continued globalization of the corporate business.
Financial: $1.8 billion sales.
Products: VAX 8600 project starts.

1980
Management: Facilities opened in Hudson, Massachusetts, for semiconductor manufacture, cooperative venture with Intel and Xerox on Ethernet. Manufacturing plant opens in Boston, Massachusetts. Software engineering facility opens in Nashua, New Hampshire. Production facility opens in Tempe, Arizona.
Financial: $2.3 billion sales. Installed base exceeds 200,000 systems.
Products: ULTRIX Engineering founded. VAX 11/750 LSI 32-bit system released.

1981
Management: Customer support centre opens in Atlanta, Georgia.
Financial: $3 billion sales.
Products: PDP11/24 announced to the market.

1982
Management: Facilities opened in Greenvile, South Carolina, Andover, Massachusetts, Singapore and Tokyo. Headcount is 67,000.
Financial: $3.9 billion sales. Ranking 137th in the *Fortune 500* sales league.
Products: RA60 and RA81 disks and, VAX 11/730 announced. Digital launch a range of personal computers (the DECmate II, Professional 325 and 350 and the Rainbow 100).

1983
Management: No specific changes.
Financial: $4 billion sales. Ranking 95th in *Fortune 100* sales league.

Products: VAXclusters announced allowing VAX systems to be coupled together. VAX 11/725, MicroVAX I and the VT200 family of terminals introduced. DECtalk is announced (this is a text-to-speech system).

1984
Management: Systems research centre opened in Palo Alto, California. Centre for storage systems opens in Shrewsbury, Massachusetts. Headcount exceeds 85,600.
Financial: $5.6 billion sales.
Products: VAX 11/785 introduced as the most powerful VAX to date. MicroPDP 11/73 released. ULTRIX 1.0 released as Digital's implementation of the UNIX operating system. VAX 8600 announced bringing a new generation of computers to the market. VAXstation I, Digital's first 32-bit workstation announced. DECmate III announced primarily as Digital's desktop word-processor system.

1985
Management: Digital facilities world-wide now number over 900. A new applications centre for technology (ACT) aimed at the automotive sector is opened in Turin, Italy. This is the year that Digital starts aggressive advertising with the 'Digital has it now...', campaign.
Financial: $6.7 billion sales. Ranking 65th in the *Fortune 100* sales league. MicroVAX II (launched this year) sales exceed 2000 systems.
Products: MicroVAX II (known as the 'VAX-on-a-chip') is introduced in May as is the high-performance VAXstation II workstation. The PDP range goes on with the introduction of the MicroPDP 11/83. The VAX 8650 is introduced to the market with 44% more power than the 8600 model.

1986
Management: Network Centre opened in Littleton, Massachusetts. 'Arguably the most successful entrepreneur in the history of American business.' This is how Ken Olsen, the founder of Digital was described by *Fortune* magazine in this, Digital's 29th year of operation. The corporation now employs some 94,000 people around the world.
Financial: Stock is split two-for-one, $7.6 billion sales. Company ranks 55th in the *Fortune 100* sales league.
Products: VAXstation II/GPX, a very high-performance UNIX workstation, is introduced. VAX 8800, 8200, 8300, 8500, 8550 and 8700 models are introduced. DECconnect, Digital's wiring architecture for all products, is announced to back up its position in networking. VAXmate, Digital's latest PC, is introduced running MS-DOS and able to work closely with a VAX. Local Area VAXclusters (LAVC) are introduced extending Digital's cluster capability to the workgroup level of the market.

1987
Management: Links established with Cray Research Inc. to allow both companies to jointly market and develop products linking each other's systems together. Headcount

of Digital now tops 110,500. The corporation operates in 64 countries around the world, and at the 9-day DECWORLD 87 exhibition in Boston, Massachusetts, Digital attracts over 48,000 people.

Financial: $9.39 billion, a 24% rise on the previous year. Net income is now a staggering $1.14 billion representing an 84% rise, return on shareholder value is 19%. Digital is considered America's most valuable company with a market valuation of $21.6 billion representing a massive 128% increase in just one year. VAX shipments now exceed 100,000 systems.

Products: VAX is still the mainstay with new 8978 and 8974 models coming in at the top end (over 50 times the power of the VAX 11/780). MicroVAX 200 and VAXstation 2000 low-cost system and workstation introduced. ULTRIX version 2.0 is released. VT330 and 340 terminals are announced. MicroVAX 3500 and 3600 models are introduced as a new generation in the MicroVAX line and associated VAXstation 3200 and 3500 models are introduced to the market. Phase V Digital Network Architecture (DNA) which allows DECnet products to migrate and become fully OSI compliant is announced.

1988

Management: Digital agree relationship with Apple Computer Inc. to link Apple systems and Appletalk networks with DECnet/OSI and VAX computer systems. Digital enter the Indian market by forming a joint venture with Hinditron to manufacture and market. The Open Software Foundation (OSF) is formed between Digital and six other manufacturers with the aim of agreeing on a single Open Software Environment. Digital now also open up in China but, most significantly, this is the year when Digital announce a technology exchange agreement for RISC (Reduced Instruction Set Computing) technology with MIPS Computer Systems Inc.

Financial: $11.5 billion sales, net income up to $1.3 billion. Digital rank 38th in the *Fortune 100* sales league.

Products: Digital's Network Application Support (NAS) extended to include MS-DOS, OS/2 and UNIX, VAX now supports symmetric multiprocessing with the VAX 8800 model announcement. The VAX 6200 systems are announced and these combine symmetric multiprocessing with a microprocessor technology known as CMOS (Complementary Metal Oxide Semiconductor) giving very high performance. VMS version 5 is released as is ULTRIX version 3. To support the market needs these systems will address DECtp is announced integrating required capabilities for large-scale transaction-oriented environments. MicroVAX 3300 and 3400 systems are also introduced.

1989

Management: Headcount in the company is 125,800 people world-wide, *Manufacturing Magazine* announces Digital as one of the top 10 companies in the USA to work for.

Financial: $12.7 billion sales, net income at $1.07 billion, 55% of sales now outside the USA. Digital now ranks 30th in the *Fortune 100* sales league.
Products: This is the year for a big push for the desktop market with the announcement of DECwindows software allowing VMS, UNIX and MS-DOS applications to be accessed anywhere on the system or network. DECstation 3100 is introduced as the fastest UNIX/RISC workstation in the world. VAXstation 3100, 3520 and 3540 multiprocessor workstations announced. DECstation 210, 316 and 320 PCs introduced. VAX goes on with the introduction of the 6300 and 6400 systems. DECstation 2100 UNIX workstation (RISC), the DECsystem 5400, 5810 and 5820 UNIX sytems running the MIPS RISC chips all introduced. VAX 9000 introduced after some problems, bringing VAX into the mainframe class.

1990
Management: Digital invest in a joint venture in Hungary. Operations centre opened in West Berlin to take advantage of the unification of Germany and new climate in the East. South Queensferry plant opened in Scotland and is one of the most advanced facilities in Europe and the biggest investment Digital has ever made outside the USA. Financial services section of Data Logic Ltd acquired by Digital getting them into the UNIX-based applications for trading and dealing operations. Digital takes over Kienzle from Mannesman in Germany to form Digital-Kienzle, specializing in selling and developing UNIX-based solutions to small and medium-sized enterprises throughout Europe. Digital announces intention to make VMS open by the adoption of POSIX standards and by X/Open branding.
Financial: $12.9 billion sales. Digital ranks 27th in the *Fortune 100* sales league but second on the basis of annual compound growth rate which has averaged 21.7%. More than 600,000 PDP systems have now been installed.
Products: To augment its growing position in transaction processing, Digital announces the VAXft 3000 system which runs VMS. Digital's Easynet computing network adds its 50,000th node and 20 new RISC-based systems and peripherals are announced. The PDP lives on and on this 20th anniversary of the first PDP-11 system the MicroPDP-11/93 and PDP-11/94 are introduced. The VAX 4000 server systems are introduced. Over 1000 applications are announced for the ULTRIX/RISC systems. ULTRIX version 4 is released. Digital announces the DEC 433MP systems using an Intel i486 microprocessor and running SCO UNIX and aimed at small to medium-sized enterprises (SME).

1991
Management: Digital opens a subsidiary in Czechoslovakia. Strategic agreement signed with MasPar to work on massively parallel computer systems research. EA Information systems formed with Asea Brown Boveri Inc. (ABB) in the 3-D design, documentation management and manufacturing systems markets. Open Advantage announced. This is Digital's strategy for becoming the industry leader in delivering open solutions. A Morocco subsidiary is opened and a joint venture with Sonda targets logistics and

marketing support for 14 Latin American countries. A subsidiary is opened in Poland. Microsoft and Digital collaborate to allow Microsoft Windows to exchange data with VAX systems using Pathworks software. Digital acquire the Information Systems division of Philips Electronics aimed at strengthening their operations in the SME sector in Europe. Plans announced for offices and operations in Russia.
Financial: $13.9 billion sales. Digital now ranks 30th in the *Fortune 100* sales league, the first time in 15 years the position has slipped.
Products: Digital introduce additions to their PC range with the introduction of notebook, portable, desktop and deskside systems all using Intel technology. DECnet phase V is announced. DECmpp 12000 series systems introduced under agreement with MasPar. VAX continues with the introduction of the 4500, the VAXstation 4060 and the VAX 6600 systems. User-based licensing introduced allowing a sort of 'pick-and-mix' for users on more open environments and 19 new RISC hardware, service and software products announced.

1992
Management: Cray Research Inc. and Digital agree for Digital to sell and distribute the CRAY Y-MP EL supercomputer world-wide. Digital and Intel Corporation announce a range of joint software projects and Digital will also sell MPP systems based on the Intel technology. A 52,600 square-foot facility for research and semiconductor manufacture is planned for Hudson, Massachusetts. Digital acquire BASYS Automation Systems from Independent Television News bolstering their strategy in the media industry. 800-SOFTWARE in California, one of the largest PC software and accessories distributors in the industry, are acquired by Digital. A subsidiary is opened in the Ukraine. Olivetti and Digital announce that Olivetti will be using the new Alpha processor in its next generation of systems. Digital now operates in 96 countries. In October 1992, 35 years after the company was formed, the founder Ken H. Olsen retires and Robert B. Palmer is made Chairman and CEO of Digital Equipment Corporation. The company now has 108,500 employees.
Financial: $13.93 billion, Net income shows a $2.79 billion loss after a $1.5 billion restructuring charge and a $485 million charge for accounting changes. Digital rank 28th in the *Fortune 100* sales league. VAX systems break the 500,000 mark.
Products: Digital announces the new Alpha processor, the most significant event in its history since the VAX. Digital announce that with Microsoft's Windows NT operating system the Alpha systems will better integrate Microsoft offerings into the Digital Enterprise Environment. A full range of Alpha APX systems from desktop to data centre is announced running VMS, OSF-1 (UNIX from the open software foundation) and NT at the low end.

2.2.2 Analysis of the Main Events

In its 35-year history, Digital has had many great successes and a few dismal failures. Today there are changes, some due to the introduction of new technologies, some to the prevailing economic climate, some to the retirement of the charismatic founder Ken Olsen. This section looks at the key events of the history of Digital and seeks to show the trends in the business at three levels:

1. Management
2. Financial
3. Products

As you will see, there are some definite reasons why Digital survived in the past and why they are likely to continue to survive in the future.

Management

Charisma describes much of Digital, from the technology through the real estate to the management. The driving force for the corporation was its founder, Ken Olsen, now recently retired. At Digital, the management philosophy has always been to value people for what they can do rather than by the position they hold. This philosophy extends to the physical things like offices and car-parks, eating space in the restaurants and user names on the systems, as well as to that most important area: responsibility and authority.

At Digital the meritocracy rules all (in theory at least), and elevation in that meritocracy is entirely dependent on achievement. Furthermore, goal setting is a real two-way exercise with a great deal of emphasis put on the individual's contribution. The general principle is that everyone has something to contribute and that effective decisions only take place when all the participants in the discussion, or at least the overwhelming majority, sign up to a commonly agreed position. In this respect Digital has something of the Japanese philosophy of production management about it, but it seeks to use such a philosophy in a highly egotistical and individualistic culture. This makes for some interesting and sometimes long meetings. For most of the 35 past years this approach seems to have worked well.

The chronicle I have set out is full of world firsts, continued growth and global expansion, all of which are evidence to the fact that Digital got things right for a long while. Much of the credit for this has to go personally to Ken Olsen, who *was* Digitl for so long and to so many people. As the company expanded his influence continued, if diluted, to exert a very real effect on the day-to-day operations of the organization.

The two real trends that mark the success of the management philosophy used by Digital over the past 35 years are:

- Technology lead
- Global expansion

Digital's commercial success is based entirely on its technology lead in the business, of being consistently the first, the best, the fastest, the most innovative computer company in the world over that period. The management at all levels and certainly at the most senior ones reflects generally a technology bias. In Digital the engineer is King. The effects of this in the early days from 1957 to 1980 clearly show a phenomenal growth entirely based on the product technology lead in the market. In those days Digital could almost do without a salesforce but from 1977 when the VAX was introduced Digital continued to drive forward still led largely by the views and opinions of engineering. While the company continued to grow fast and make revenues based on the VAX products, it had, to some extent, failed to start laying down the basis for a long-term sales-led culture. This was going to be essential at the inevitable point when computer hardware and operating systems fell in price to become a commodity market. In the late 1980s the problems caused by this lack of a sufficiently strong sales and marketing culture made Digital difficult to deal with from the outside. The Digital salesforce were often not highly regarded by their external counterparts and inside Digital there was a view that the products were bought because engineering made them so attractive rather than the salesforce selling them. There was some truth in this. The sales success in the 1980s was largely due to the massive expansion in global operations, the watershed being in 1989, when the revenues from the US market were overtaken by those from the rest of the world.

This globalization created many management and structural problems for Digital. As an employee, one seemed to spend an awful lot of time on airlines, going from one continent to another and servicing the needs of the fast-growing global operation. This trend to expand all over the world also changed the senior management focus of the corporation. The needs of the domestic US market had to be put into perspective and Maynard, Massachusetts, started to look to the wide world as the real growth area.

The 1980s were the time when Digital also started to become acquisitive, most recently through the acquisition of part equity in companies like MIPS and Olivetti and also through outright purchase (for instance, with Kienzle and Philips). This move to buy rather than invent marked a healthy broadening of the management attitude in the corporation. One might think that this has been a move that should have been more aggressive and wide-ranging to broaden Digital's base more quickly at a time of higher earnings and better share price.

In conclusion then, the trends in management for Digital have been to keep the technology lead and globalize the organization. At the end of the 1980s the last big market, the old Eastern bloc, was being penetrated as was the People's Republic of China, but both are likely to be slow growth markets in the next five to ten years. Technology lead was flagging in some respects with the rise of UNIX in many traditional Digital markets. It is true to say that Alpha is a technology lead that will help to develop the organization but in the late 1980s and early 1990s Digital started to understand the need for a more sales-led culture with visible positive results. As we look forward to the next ten years in Digita'ls life it is going to be essential for them to reach the same innovative level of excellence in sales and marketing that they have achieved in management and technology over the last 35 years.

Financial

The growth of Digital has been continuous and remarkable. From humble beginnings it achieved a quotation on the market and rose, in just 20 years, to a $1 billion corporation rising to $9.39 billion in the next ten years and standing now at well over $13 billion per annum. Figure 2.1 shows graphically this rise in revenues over time .

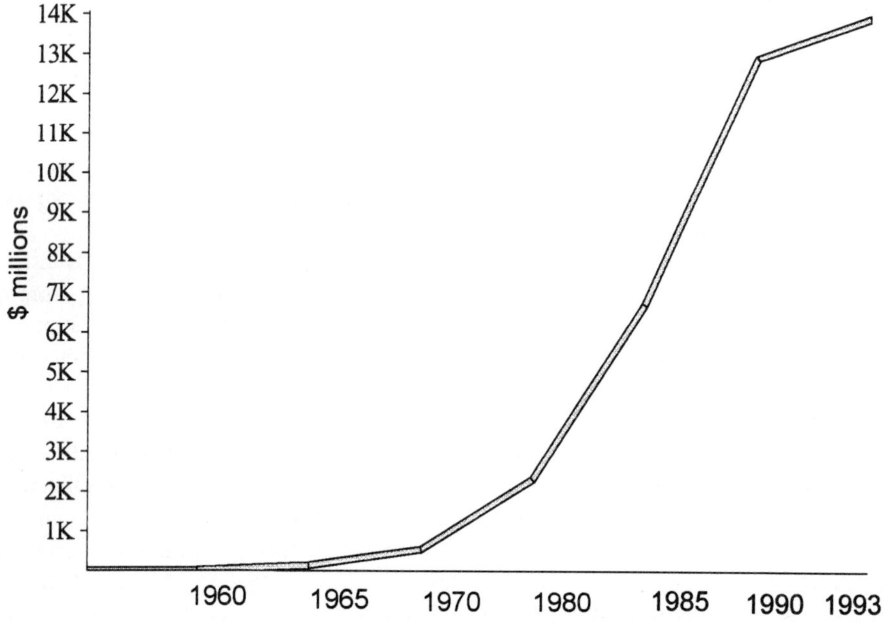

Figure 2.1

This market growth has continued in times when the proprietary system has fallen from fashion and the open system has become a price-sensitive commodity. Since 1989 the greatest volume of the corporation's business has come from outside the domestic USA, giving a high level of resilience to the business. High volumes have been the base for the business and the early quotation of the corporation gave it the sound financial base required to fund expansion around the world.

The recent move to acquisitions has ensured that the corporation's growth could include a customer base increase and the shift of emphasis to services as a key element of the business in the late 1980s has been fundamental to maintaining the corporation's income. The big change of late has been the level of restructuring. This has cost the corporation as it slims down by many thousands of people. But for these costs Digital would have been in profit recently, albeit a small one.

The key issue in the financial history of Digital was the sale of very high margin hardware, software and services. This situation has now gone forever and hardware margins have been squeezed throughout the industry. Digital has sought to replace this lost margin partly by increasing the service element in the business mix and partly by cost reduction. Yet more focus has to be brought to bear on Digital's cost of sales, which is still too high for the volumes.

Products

Digital's product lead history shows that innovation, when coupled with high-quality production, can drive a company forward with truly outstanding results. Digital's two big product successes were the VAX and the PDP, for many years exploited as hardware platforms and only later used as vehicles for the sale of software and services in any major way. The Digital approach was to lead with the base hardware and to back this up with a wide range of peripherals compatible across the systems over time.

Competition was on the basis of proprietary features for a long time, with a move to Open Systems coming only later in the 1980s. Power and price performance are two of the mainstays in the Digital armoury. Interestingly, one of the key features of the Alpha launch has been the emphasis on the thousandfold increase in power and performance of the processor likely over the next 25 years. Only comparatively recently has Digital really got into the area of joint technology agreements. One of the poorest elements of the Digital history was its failure in the desktop PC business. True, some of the systems it produced were excellently engineered. Unfortunately they were, by the standards of the industry, too expensive and also sold in a cumbersome and restricted way. PC salesmen are fast on their feet and willing to do a deal. If Digital had, say, acquired a large PC distributor/producer like Amstrad, then they might have been in a much stronger position with respect to the office revolution than they now are. In essence, the present product strategy almost seems to skip the last phase of the market, that of the 1 to 5 MIP desktop or deskside system and appears to be going for the next generation 6 to 50 MIP systems based on Alpha.

Because of the technical nature of the Digital management, the products tend to be good in technology markets and not so well focused in less technical areas. One example might be that of the workstation market, in which Digital has done reasonably well based on very high-performance systems at a low price on VMS and UNIX systems.

The other would be in office systems where ALL-IN-1 did very well initially only to get bogged down in reliability and functionality problems. What could here have been a very big market was restricted due to the lack of empathy between the Digital style and the customers' requirements, which were generally much more service and style based and less concerned with technology. Links with companies like Cray Research, Apple, Intel and Microsoft are now ensuring that Digital's products are begging to penetrate other manufacturers' product ranges, and that Digital's own product range is augmented by offerings from outside the corporation.

The burden of servicing such a wide range of products will have to be closely reviewed by Digital. They have to get tough and chop out older product lines in order to focus the resources and reduce overhead costs.

To conclude, Digital's products have been its greatest asset to date. This is now augmented by the huge customer base they have, a ready market for new products. Services have been a comparatively recent focus for the corporation and recently became an equal source of revenue in the business. The history of Digital and UNIX goes back a long way and it is a UNIX derivative (OSF/1) on which many of Digital's new sales will be made. VMS is far from dead, however. In the long term it is likely that VMS will move to a full Open System, possibly being fronted by Microsoft NT or some similar friendly front end.

2.2.3 Products and More Products

The proliferation of products and services is apparent in the history of Digital. There are thousands of individual products and these are going to be increased in number as the corporation acquires yet other businesses with other products and services to offer. The proliferation of products throughout Digital happens at all levels: Hardware, Software and Services. In the long term, though, there are a few major lines that can account for the main events in the corporation's long and successful history.

In hardware the key products have been as follows:

- PDP. The PDP-1 computer was launched in November 1960 and was the first, commercially available compact, interactive computer. In 1963 the PDP-5 was launched along with the PDP-1 operating system. This was to be the first real minicomputer and the first commercial timesharing operating system in the world. In 1964 the PDP-6 showed Digital's understanding of power requirements by being the first 36-bit system in the world. It was the PDP-8 launch in 1965 that really saw Digital move into the volume market position that it has occupied for so long. The PDP range carried the corporation along until the advent of the VAX in 1977 and even long after the launch of the VAX the PDP went on making great revenues for the business. Even as the Alpha systems were being launched the PDP processor family continued to be sold.
- VAX. The VAX came to the market in 1977 as Digital's latest offering to the world. The future growth of the corporation from the $1 billion mark in 1977 to the present turnover of over $13 billion was largely fuelled by the VAX and the operating system designed for it; VMS. In its first form, the 11/780, the VAX was a

low-power system by today's standards, but when it was launched back then it was one of the most powerful minicomputer systems in the world. Only 3 years later, the VAX was on an LSI (Large Scale Integrated) microprocessor and was out as the 11/750, a true 32-bit system. In 1982 the VAX 11/730 was launched to be followed every year by a new and more powerful successor. Often the performance increases were several fold like the massive jump in power from the VAX 8600 to the 8650, bringing an increase of 44% more processing power to the market. Today the VAX range is still growing. Now there is the option to switch the VAX processor for an Alpha processor, just a few hours' work and a new processor up and running in the same cabinet but with massively more power than the older VAX architecture and still capable of running VMS.

- MicroVAX. In the move to take up more of the systems range in the market, the MicroVAX was launched in 1983 as the early MicroVAX I system. MicroVAX completed the lower end of a range of truly scalable systems that stretch today from the small MicroVAX systems up to the massive 9000 systems running at the datacentre level. All the software is scalable up from the smallest to the largest systems without any level of recompilation required. 1985 saw the introduction of the MicroVAX II, a VAX on a single microprocessor chip and a great innovation in the industry. In 1987 the corporation introduced the MicroVAX 3500 and 3600. This line of systems went from strength to strength until the present day, where the power and sophistication of the systems is truly incredible
- Workstations. In many ways, Digital never did as well in the workstation market as they might have done. It is interesting to speculate on what would have happened if they had purchased Sun Microsystems back in the 1980s. Perhaps they would have mopped up a market share more representative of their technical lead than they did. Workstations first hit the road in the form of the 32-bit VAXstation I in 1984. The year 1986 saw the introduction of the VAXstation II GPX, a high-performance UNIX-based workstation. In 1987 the VAXstation 2000, a low-cost workstation, was introduced and in 1989 the range was further extended to include Multiprocessor support in the 3100, 3520 and 3540 systems.
- Personal computing. It is one of those sad peculiarities of history that Digital failed to take the personal computer market by storm. This is not because they were slow to start or that the hardware was poor but simply because they never got the sales and marketing right. In some ways they seem to have completely misunderstood the market strategy for this product, which needed to be seen as the commodity it was rather than a smaller version of the VAX sale. Digital entered the personal computing arena with the DECmate in 1982, with the Professional 325 and 350 and the Rainbow 100 also being launched that year. However, the full IBM compatibility issue never really sank in. This caused DEC to be very slow off the mark and pricing was often unrealistic. In 1984 the DECmate III (based on a PDP processor) aimed at word processing made a niche for itself among the existing Digital user community and 1986 saw the introduction of the VAXmate. It was not until 1989 that the market for the desktop system was really targeted by Digital with the DECstation

range of PCs. This was Digital's first really serious contender for the market but in a market where they had lost the chance for the channels for volume system sales at this level, a mistake that was to be balanced by the acquisition in 1992 of 800-SOFTWARE, the California-based PC sales outfit. 1990 saw the introduction of the 433-mp system but this is a higher value 486 SCO system. The next real move on the desktop was in 1992 with the introduction of a desktop Alpha-based system and the equity purchase by Digital of part of Olivetti. (Available in 1993.)

- Peripherals. Digital have manufactured a massive range of high quality peripherals for a very long time now and these have amassed significant revenues for the business (certainly several billion dollars). 1983 saw the introduction of the VT200 family of terminals replacing the older VT100 terminals that had set a standard in the industry while a year earlier in 1982, the RA 60 and RA 81 disks were hailed as significant advances in storage technology. In 1987 the VT 300 series of terminals was introduced with higher power and function than the 200 series. It is important to realize that within Digital the peripherals business is almost a corporation on its own. The peripherals themselves are capable of running with almost any Digital hardware and the rigorous enforcement of standards ensures that this will always be the case.
- RISC (MIPS). The introduction of RISC (Reduced Instruction Set Chip) technology followed on from the market requirement for more power at lower cost coupled with the prevailing view of many in the industry that the RISC technology route had a lot to offer by way of technology edge. When Digital were buying into the MIPS corporation, they had already started to look at the development of their own RISC chip, and that project became Alpha. The time required to develop the Alpha chip was long relative to the needs of the market. One can see therefore that the buy-in of the MIPS technology was a stop-gap measure aimed at buying time while the Alpha chip was being designed and developed. There was, however, one big problem with the MIPS chip: it could not run native VMS. This is not to say that the MIPS RISC chip could not be used in the wider VAX architecture. Indeed the 4000 range VAX systems use MIPS RISC technology in controllers, but the CPU requirements of VMS had been tuned to the VAX chip and, for instance, the number of different levels of Interrupt needed by VMS would alone exclude the MIPS chip. The alternative, to rewrite VMS, was completely unrealistic and if followed would almost certainly have caused massive upgrade issues for the existing VMS community, Digital's biggest asset. So in 1989 Digital introduced the DECsystem 5000 range of computers and DECstation 5000 range of workstations, all based on MIPS RISC technology. These systems ran ULTRIX, Digital's own version of UNIX, and at that time it was hoped that the systems would be used in conjunction with the OSF operating system, indeed OSF-1 was made available on the 5000 range. The confusion within the Open Software Foundation at this time stopped this going ahead. The launch of the 5000 was a really interesting thing to see. At the time I was working for AT&T and recall being constantly bombarded by Digital advertisements and marketing material for 'UNIX from Digital' all on the 5000

systems, a marketing effort that was far higher profile at the time than anything from AT&T! Within 2 years I watched business change from 95% VMS, 5% UNIX to 90% UNIX, 10% VMS and almost all of this on the 5000 systems running ULTRIX.

On the software front Digital's operating systems policy has been much simpler (although its application portfolio has been as complex as its hardware range). In summary, the operating system history is as follows:

- RSX and RSTS. The PDP, more than any other product, was the foundation of Digital. The first real achievement in the operating system history for the PDP was the release in 1963 of the PDP-1 operating system. This release marked the availability of the first timesharing operating system in the world and it is from this base that Digital were able to penetrate so many organizations with true, interactive computing power. Following on from this, RSTS, the timesharing operating system was initially released in 1970. RSX with real-time monitoring and control functionality was released in 1973 as was RSTS/E, a timesharing operating system aimed at education and computing environments.
- VMS. In 1977 VMS was launched along with the VAX systems that then fuelled the massive growth in the corporation, a growth that would average $1 billion per annum for the next 12 years. Functions and features were added thick and fast to VMS. Two of the major events in the history of this excellent operating system were the addition of DECnet, the networking architecture, in 1980 and of VAXclustering in 1983, allowing higher-resilience systems to be configured. Of later times the advent of DECtp in 1988 addressed the needs of more mission-critical systems in the transaction processing field. 1992 brought the announcement of OPEN VMS and the move of VMS into a market presently dominated by flavours of UNIX system. The intention to do so was first made public in 1990, showing that by this time the final intentions for VMS to compete with UNIX on the Alpha architecture systems had been well thought out.
- UNIX. It has to be remembered that UNIX goes back a long way (see later) and that initially the UNIX operating system was written on a PDP system by a team at Bell Labs. For a long while, the VAX and the PDP were pretty standard systems for running UNIX, especially in the academic and technical environments. It soon became apparent that Digital had to take UNIX more seriously and they did so with ULTRIX. In 1980 ULTRIX engineering was founded and from this start ULTRIX was released to the world in 1984 and was to be the mainstay of Digital in the UNIX world until the release of OSF-1 in 1991. In the early days ULTRIX was engineered to run on the VAX, only later becoming available on the 5000 series systems at ULTRIX version 4.0, later superseded by OSF/1.

2.2.4 Summary

Digital has been and I think will continue to be a technology-led corporation. From the brief summary of products above, it is clear that there has been a shift of late from the proprietary to the Open Systems market requirements. However, Digital's strong position in the market based on both the VAX and PDP cannot be sacrificed, the VAX position especially. For this reason, Digital have decided to take the Open Systems market on at its own game and all levels: hardware, operating system and services.

Without doubt, Digital's prolific product range has to change to some extent, at a minimum by slimming down the number of older products that are now to be supported on the latest hardware. I think this is likely to be a replacement exercise. Digital's need to produce more service revenues will undoubtedly result in an increase in the number of Alpha-based services as this technology drives the next phase of the corporation's growth.

2.3 Trends in the Business

The information technology industry is on the edge of major change. First, the recession that has hit all industries hard is taking its toll on the expertise of the biggest organizations in the industry, including IBM, AT&T, HP, DEC and many others. Competition has increased dramatically as has the rate of technical innovation. Price performance of systems is dropping so fast that no sooner has a new system been purchased and installed than its price in the market has dropped by up to 20%. The major manufacturers are worried and each is responding differently to the challenges before it. UNIX has finally started to really gain ground in the commercial arena, fulfilling a prediction that has been made and then failed every year for the past ten years to my knowledge, that of really massive growth in the penetration of UNIX into a wide range of markets with a significant level of system switching going on.

It is at such a moment of turmoil and change that Digital have sought to release a new hardware architecture and to back this up with a massive marketing, sales, service and software programme. The information technology industry exists to serve the needs of commerce and government and in these areas there is a desire for richer functionality and more powerful facilities than can be supported by Digital's VAX and RISC/MIPS hardware today. The price of such things as image processing, high-resolution graphics and good user interfaces has had to fall to keep pace with the market. The sticking point has been the limitations of the 32-bit hardware and operating system and the facilities that these would support. With the Alpha programme Digital have entered the arena with a system that provides the facilities needed at a cost low enough to make them available to the mass market and with an architecture capable of servicing the needs of the next 25 years.

The market for Open Systems now regards processor power and mass storage as so cheap as to be no longer a significant factor in the systems design equation. The ability to make good use of them is, however, a different issue. While Digital have been developing a hardware architecture that brings a system capable of supporting the next two generations of applications technology to the market with winning price and performance, the applications development community has, by and large, been singularly lacking in any kind of imaginative use of facilities such as multimedia or true object technology. I refer to the thousands of industry-focused applications that are intended to provide the functionality for the great number of companies that will be the customers for Digital, Alpha-based systems, many of them presently using VMS and VAX or ULTRIX and RISC/MIPS 5000 series hardware.

In short, the Alpha hardware will show up the lack of skill and imagination in many of the applications I have seen to date. A key question is going to be: 'OK, so what are you guys going to do with all of this power?' The problem of strategic analysis and of the positioning of UNIX gets more complex, the more often one think about it. On one side of the argument there is the very important issue of the relationship with Digital and the Open Systems community, the whole area of standards and the hype on openness. On the other side there is the huge VMS installed base and the problems Digital would face if they went down the route followed by many in the industry and put all of their eggs in the UNIX basket. Digital are looking to solve this problem by a very smart strategy indeed.

Digital had a need to gain market share in the face of wins against VMS by UNIX-based opponents on a range of cheap, fast machines. The trick for Digital was first to understand the market rationale behind a move to a new Open operating system, then balance the relationship issues with the suppliers and finally get to grips with the applications software suppliers and have them sign up to the new Alpha-based platforms, either on VMS or OSF-1 in the mainstream Digital base and for Microsoft NT in some other areas. This has been done and the process of signing-up of applications vendors has begun and is moving apace.

There are a lot of gross misconceptions about UNIX, operating systems in general and Open Systems engineering in particular. People have been sold a line that once you buy a UNIX system, any software written for UNIX would run on it and changing suppliers of the hardware was going to be like changing socks. This line, I have to say, has not come from AT&T or the individual UNIX suppliers but is a bad representation of the facts from the press coupled with over-zealous promotion of the real concepts of Open Systems by some of its more vociferous apostles.

The prospective customers for new systems want to have more power in the trading situation. For a long time they had been aware that the suppliers of systems, applications and services in the information technology industry have been making very high margins at their expense. This relationship was further unbalanced by the locking in of the customers by the proprietary nature of the systems with high associated transition costs for the software. The desire so often stated to associate with software portability is really a requirement to have power in such a relationship and reduce costs.

In addition, there has now been a move by many applications developers to provide their offerings only on UNIX platforms, thereby further forcing the end users' hand in favour of UNIX systems.

This desire for power in the relationship came mainly from the proprietary systems side of the business in general, where the operating systems were specific to the hardware platform and therefore the vendor. The whole proprietary systems side of the business was thrown into stark contrast by the introduction of desktop systems and both DOS and Windows. These systems, highly functional and very low in cost, caused questions to be asked about the real and justified value of other, larger systems.

Digital, like all other vendors of proprietary systems, have had to take a long, hard look at customer wants and needs in order to justify the move to a more open strategy but not a solely UNIX-based one.

Last of all and possibly most importantly, performance and functionality have come to the fore. UNIX-based systems appeared to promise much higher price performance, and, despite some very misleading statements in the early days, there can be no doubt that the latest UNIX systems, especially those running on RISC type processors, are providing much higher performance than their proprietary counterparts. It has to be stressed, however, that the raw performance of the system, when considered without the issues of sophistication of facilities and the resilience of the overall architecture, is a very bad example to choose as an indicator of overall worth. It is unfortunate that these issues are so often ignored.

UNIX can only do so much to resolve the issues from the customer's perspective. For instance, the diversification in UNIX variants due to its history (dealt with later in this book) causes problems for the application developer when moving from one UNIX system to another. These problems may be quite trivial, but they can, and in my experience often are, difficult and complex to resolve.

The time was right, then, for a new contender to take account of the moves in the industry that were providing rapid increases in power and storage capacity and to leap ahead with a really bold technology move. It was this situation that Digital took advantage of to develop the Alpha technology and by so doing enable themselves both to compete with the fast RISC technology on the hardware front and to provide a platform for other operating systems and vendors on the software and value-added fronts (see Figure 2.2).

Things in the industry have changed at the hardware level and Digital's powerful new Alpha microprocessor is allowing this advanced technology to be made widely available to other hardware vendors who can include the processor in their own offerings. To date, Cray, Kabota Pacific, Raytheon and Olivetti are four manufacturers that have taken up the offer. IBM have moved down this route to some extent, providing RS6000 hardware to the likes of Bull as a base for their range of hardware.

UNIX is no longer in its infancy, some of us would say that it is starting to look well into its old (or at least late middle) age (and has indeed been subject to extensive engineering change during its life) but, like the hardware, it is another example of a component provided by a specialist supplier.

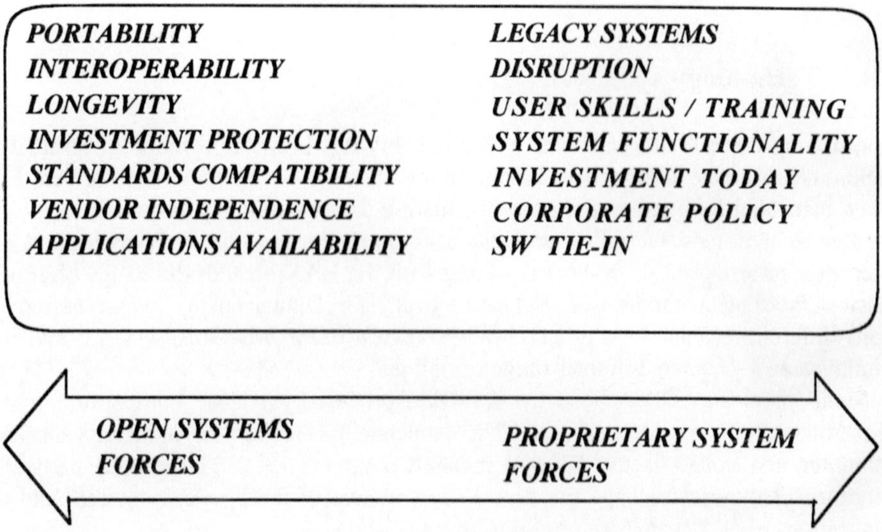

Figure 2.2

Applications developers also have a big technology challenge on their hands, that of object technology, and they are looking very closely at the operating system market to see who is going to do what to help them achieve this goal. Microsoft NT provides a level, albeit a proprietary one, of object technology with Microsoft NT (and in MS Windows 3.1). Furthermore, those who are Digital application vendors at the moment and who need to look at Alpha for a platform to move forward with, have to begin thinking very seriously about the facilities of the hardware.

The level of power can mean two things: either the systems price will shrink almost to zero and the applications will just be the same old things on a fast box. On the other hand, the applications vendors will begin to use the power they are seeing for the first time to include functionality and features that, to date, have been outside the scope of affordability, such as true, interactive multimedia or artificial intelligence methods such as neural computing.

The pace of change is increasing, and the investment of the major players in the development and the augmentation of microprocessors is massive. Intel spent in excess of $2 billion on the development of the Pentium microprocessor. Digital has spent a similar amount in the development of the Alpha AXP chip and the investments are continuing to increase. Of all the contenders, Digital is in the strongest position to make the future technology substantially different today on a pure technology basis. The one thing they lack is Intel's size and volume. Should Digital be able to get Intel to sign up to the Alpha programme at some level, then we really would be about to see some changes in the business. Whether this happens in the long term or not remains to be seen.

2.3.1 Technology

One driving force for the changes in the industry has been the technology itself. It is impossible to define all the changes that, in the 35 years since Digital was formed, have taken place and have led to the present situation. In this section I am going to look at the key technologies that influenced Digital to make the decision to develop the Alpha microprocessor. After all, what was wrong with the VAX or with the MIPS offerings? Answer, nothing in themselves, but strategically for Digital change was required for many different reasons. First of all, I want to review RISC, what it is, why it is and how Digital came to include it in their range of options.

Some years ago IBM chose the Intel i86 processor in close competition to the Motorolla 68000 microprocessor. They launched this in the revolutionary desktop computer and called it the IBM Personal Computer (PC). This fateful choice of microprocessor was to shape the future development of the operating system and the applications upon it from then until now.

The Intel chip was, in one major respect, not unlike the microprocessors in the mainframes from IBM or in the machines used by DEC, ICL and the other major systems vendors. It was what is known as a SISC (or CISC) chip. This is a 'Sophisticated Instruction Set Chip' (or Complex Instruction Set Chip). In this architecture the applications source code is compiled into a number of assembly level instructions that call macro routines on the chip (there are a number of other differences in SISC/RISC). These instructions are then executed as the program runs. In the mid-1980s there was a revolution in microprocessor design, known as RISC (Reduced Instruction Set Chip). In this design there were far fewer instructions on the chip and the chip stored its results on each cycle of the microprocessor clock. The end result was a massive improvement in raw performance and the RISC architectures were born.

The influence of RISC has been profound indeed and, although the RISC chips of today are streets away from their humble academic origins, they have influenced the designs of the microprocessors in IBM, DEC and ICL. The mighty Intel itself proclaims proudly that the i486 and Pentium have a number of RISC features. One thing is certain, RISC is here to stay.

Because of the influence of the RISC movement in the industry, Digital had no option but to buy or make this new technology architecture. If they brought in the technology they would have to change the face of VMS and would also have to say goodbye to a level of control that until now had remained within the corporation. If they did their own technology, there was a danger that it would be seen as marginal rather than mainstream and it was going to cost a lot of money and take a long time to do this.

Given the size and value of the VMS user base, Digital had only one sensible option: to get the Alpha chip developed and out as fast as possible and to make sure that they could bridge with shorter-term technologies while this was happening.

Open Systems and VMS

In 1990 Digital made the decision to make VMS officially an Open System. Before I go into what this means, I think it is worth taking some time to look at the issues surrounding Open Systems and their concepts.

Platforms are a real issue in the software and systems engineering community of today. Often the term is used in many varied contexts and with different meanings. It is important, then, that I start this section with some specific definitions which happen to fit the needs of this book.

Take a look at Figure 2.3. In this you can see a schematic representation of a system. At the top there is the applications software. This talks to the operating system, although there is a level which probably talks to or at least 'sees' the firmware on either the machine or, more likely, its peripheral devices. Below this there is the operating system itself. This makes the hardware usable and is itself a complex piece of software providing a range of facilities, functions and interfaces. Next in the cake comes the firmware. This is an intelligent component of the hardware, containing permanently encoded software instructions. Last comes the hardware itself.

It is important to understand that this schematic implies certain things. First, the interfaces between all the components should remain the same 'shape'. Shape in this context relates broadly to the syntax and the grammar of the interface between the components. If (as is often the case) the 'shape' of the interface changes between one pair of components, then there are three likely outcomes as follows:

- No effect.
- A change only between the two interfacing components.
- A change that implies a secondary effect. For instance, the hardware changes, and this needs the operating system to change and in turn that causes the application to change.

Now look at Figure 2.3. In this figure I have tried to explain the view of the world as required by an application developer. It should be noted that while the view I have proposed here represents good engineering practice, many (possibly most) applications do not follow this structure since they have their roots in earlier engineering practices (like witchcraft!).

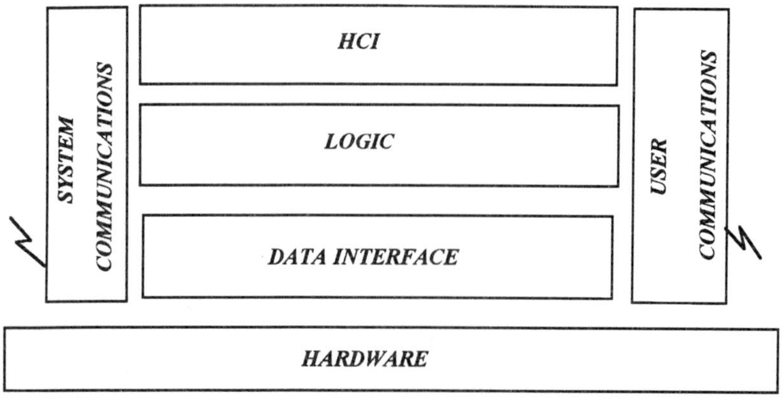

Figure 2.3

In Figure 2.3 the software is split into five logical units composed of three main units (HCI, Logic and Data Interface) and two secondary units (System communications and User communications). These components have the following functions:

- HCI (human computer interface). This is the place where the flesh and silicon meet! In general terms it can be thought of as all those things required to make a computer usable by the human being: keyboard, mouse, screen, printer etc. In this diagram I am implying the software element only. At the software level the HCI is interesting: we all need our glass window on the soul of the machine. Our interface to this has historically been a command line, typed text input, and I would argue that for many applications this is likely to remain so for the near future. However, when Apple entered the scene things changed a lot. The interface to the system now consisted of a point and shoot system, driven by a hand-held mouse or tracking ball. Furthermore, the iconic syntax (not unreminiscent of the hieroglyphics of the Pharaohs) has made a significant impact on the way we view and interact with the system. A picture they say is worth a thousand words and icon-based interfaces have now become common. Take a look at your desktop. If it is like mine you will be looking at a number of sheets of paper, some visible, some part covered, some invisible. It is interesting to note that this clutter is the way most of us work. The computing ability to allow this level of presentation and electronic clutter is known as windowing. In a windowing system the terminal you use can display a high-resolution picture which can be smoothly scrolled in all directions on the screen. Now the advantage of this kind of electronic interface is obvious. It allows a number of images to remain on the screen at the same time, thereby enabling the user of the system to jump between jobs and use the different items on the screen as and when they need to. Furthermore, the tablet of icons that comes with such systems presents a whole mass of alternative applications available at the click of a key. In a well-designed HCI the functions relevant to the interface with the user are all handled in that level of system. For instance, passwords and privileges, data validation, output formatting and terminal type detection, to name but a few. Most operating systems have some level of functionality to assist the HCI designer in the task of development and design, but some are better than others. For instance, in Microsoft NT there is a closer union of the ideas that surround the HCI and those that are associated with the management and manipulation of data through object orientation (covered later). These are powerful concepts for the HCI designer to use. In the Digital Alpha processor range we see the full functionality of operating systems like Microsoft NT, UNIX (OSF-1) and VMS empowered by the sheer speed and flexibility of a true 64-bit RISC architecture, thus allowing the HCI designer the real freedom from price and performance required to move computing on a generation.

- Next, in Figure 2.3 there is the functional logical of the application. This handles the rules of the application that are specific to the problem domain in which it operates. For instance, the rules: PRICE:= [COST+MARGIN]*LOCAL TAX or TIME TO DESTINATION:= DISTANCE/AVERAGE SPEED are simple rules that might then be encoded in the logic section of the software. (It must be noted that there are various approaches using artificial intelligence techniques such as neural networking in which rules can themselves be deduced, but this is outside the scope of this book.) In order for the rules to work, the facilities of the operating system and the platform must be adequate for the job. It is a fact that software and systems are becoming more and more complex as time goes by. In order for systems to keep pace with this the tendency is to distribute elements of the functionality to more than one machine, thereby allowing a job to be shared by several units and reducing the time taken to process the information or apportioning the functionality to the systems with the appropriate capability. In any operating system it is an essential capability to be able to communicate quickly and efficiently between applications and to let applications share data in a real-time manner in some circumstances. Data is everywhere, and the key to good applications design is to make the interface to the data as smooth and efficient as possible. So that this may take place the data handling has to be controlled and separated from the logic and the HCI in the system. This separation of the elements allows the data interface to be matched to a variety of conditions. This is important if the source of the data is going to change over the expected life of the application. For instance, data that is today held on a remote site and sent down using an IBM 3270 protocol to your PC might one day be held on a relational database and be transmitted after having received an SQL request. These two highly different approaches to the data interface (although the data may well be unchanged itself) would be easier to implement if the data handling interface was neatly separate. Also, it may be that there are elements of the data interface that might be put on a completely different machine, dedicated to the acquisition of the data, its sorting and storage. These are all functions that should be relegated to the data interface in a well-designed system.

- On the left in Figure 2.3 you will see a block marked 'system communications'. This is the interface from any of the three main layers to other systems functions. It is important to understand that the different elements of the system need to communicate and exchange control and data in either a single system or in a distributed system. However, this issue of systems distribution will be covered later in the book. End users want to send electronic messages to one another, be it mail, EDI messages or whatever. In the figure I have shown this as user communications, the level at which the system will support the routing, manipulation, storage and delivery of user-generated messages within the boundaries of the system or network.

These, then, are the main functional blocks that have to be considered by the would-be applications engineer. The problem is that many systems exist and most of them have their own ways of approaching these issues. This has created a nightmare world for the engineers and the businesses that use the software, a world of uncertainty, change and wastage on a vast scale. In the domain of proprietary systems the users are locked into the hardware and the specific operating systems that have been designed for this in a way which produces high cost to migrate to other platforms All this is good news if you are in the hardware business but it is not so good from the end user's perspective.

A platform, then, has a number of components, which may be considered from the systems or the applications developer's point of view, but the main components are as shown in the figure. The importance to the user is the thing that changes. It is true to say that there are a massive number of systems in the world today and that these systems have, by and large, been developed in very unstructured ways.

It is one aim of this book to get the reader into a position to understand the implications on their business of the Digital Alpha hardware architecture and associated programme and how this might fit into such an environment. However, in order to do this there are a number of related areas which must first be understood. In this section I have introduced the concept of the platform, and earlier I spoke of the need for the interfaces between the components to be well defined and that changes could have a number of effects. In the following section I will explore the dichotomy of the standards and the standardization school of thought in determining the future of systems engineering.

If there were only one operating system then there would be few of the problems that I mentioned earlier in this chapter. This (in principle at least) is the standardization argument. For a long time this was the argument put forward by the UNIX school, and that which is still felt to be valid by some in the POSIX camp. UNIX does have many of the special attributes that make it a strong contender for the role as the standard operating system. On the other hand, it has attributes that do not put it in a strong position either. In the arena of the desktop computer there was only one real contender and that was DOS now supplemented by Windows from Microsoft. It was Microsoft who were the darlings of IBM when the fortunes of the PC looked good back in the heady days of the early 1980s. Since then things have changed and IBM has tried to develop its own contender in the personal operating system market. Known as OS/2, it has singularly failed to make any significant impact on what has become one of the great multi-billion dollar industries of the twentieth century. Microsoft brought MS-DOS to market and then extended this with Icons and Windowing to become MS-Windows.

Both operating systems were constrained by the legacy of the chip for which they were originally designed, the Intel i86 family of microprocessors (both are written in assembly language), and therefore could be easily moved across to other systems platforms or extended to become true multi-user operating systems. Furthermore, this was a single-user environment for single-microprocessor machines, and the multi-user market was therefore denied to Microsoft.

The standards argument takes a more diverse line. In this view of the world there is always room for diverse operating systems and hence accommodation for innovation and change. All that is required is that there be correctly defined standards for the interfaces, functions and facilities offered to the end user and the applications developer.

This is a line that now has the backing of the major players in the industry to some greater or lesser extent, as each sees the ability to corporately attack the userbase of the others by the application of sufficiently robust standards to allow the migration of the systems applications from one platform to another. It is the application of suitable Open Systems standards that has allowed the Digital Corporation to claim that 'open VMS is an open operating system'. The standards used, such as those from POSIX, relate to the portability of code between platforms and the interworking and interoperability of systems platform components. It is in this that Digital, more than any other vendor, has excelled.

There is one great weakness in this view of the world and that is the standards themselves. There are few jobs more cumbersome or political than being on the body of a standards committee. The time taken to define the standards is long (something that the industry does urgently need is speed in the definition of the standards) and then, just when the standard is in place, we start to find that at the edges of the standards there are extensions and differing interpretations which expose the problems in the standards' implementations themselves.

This is not to say that the approach is wrong, just one in which there are restrictions in the time and precision of the end result. The best results seen in the industry in a timely manner are generally driven not from the basis of an abstract standard but from the convergence of the industry on an agreed *de-facto* standard in a particular area. It is not likely that Digital VMS could be adopted as the basis for such a *de-facto* standard in the industry, but Digital may well see some features of VMS being incorporated into a number of other Open Systems at some point in the future.

Standards or standardization, then, is about the choice of one system or the co-existence of many. It is an issue that in the PC world Microsoft won by being the natural first choice, by being the standard operating system. However, in the multi-user market there are some big fish, they have teeth and they will not be caught easily. At present UNIX is the choice for most Open Systems engineering, and among the many versions, AT&T UNIX System V.4 is, in my opinion, one of the best. (There have been rumours that we will see System V.4 on Alpha. I think that this is very likely but the work is likely to be done not by Digital or AT&T but some other third-party hardware vendor such as Olivetti.)

In Figure 2.3 I have tried to sum up the issues. At one extreme, standardization means that only one can win and this, in the multi-user market, is an optimistic view. At the other end of the scale, standardization allows the existence of proprietary systems and is a realistic if troubled process.

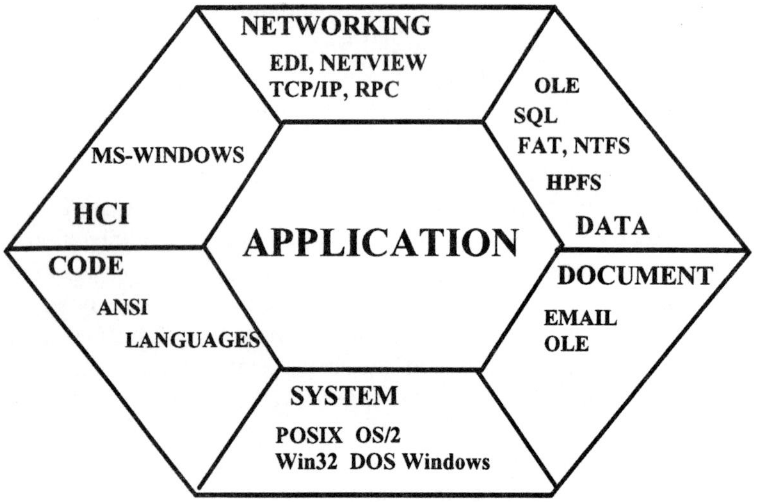

Figure 2.4

Needs of the Applications Developer The only reason that there is any sort of requirement for the systems in the first place is so that the applications can run and support some function. In Figure 2.4 I have shown the application as the centre of the view with the surrounding services on the outside. The developer or the owner of any application needs to keep this picture in mind as they think about their systems strategy.

Programming Languages These are the basis of any development work and represent one of the fundamental levels upon which portability is based. By the language I mean all the components shown in Figure 2.4, i.e. the libraries of object modules and the compiler and the linker. The main standards for programming languages are defined by ANSI at the source level, although the definition of the libraries of object modules that perform standard functions is less well carried out. In the case of Digital's Alpha programme, there are a number of languages being provided, some directly from Digital and some from third-party sources. Standards have a part to play in a number of language-related areas. For instance, POSIX 1013.3 sets some strong standards for the use of the C language and thereby tries to improve the chances of applications portability. It is clear that Digital will be supporting POSIX compliance with their full range of hardware and the Digital C code compiler. By way of *de-facto* standards, Microfocus, the largest independent vendor of COBOL compilers in the world, are to support both the NT operating system and OSF/1 with their compiler and are soon to announce a full object version of COBOL which, with the other facilities of the Alpha platform, will be a very powerful combination indeed (sadly, likely to be limited to Microfocus NT and UNIX versions but an excellent tool in downsizing). Among the languages to be made available on the Alpha VMS, UNIX or NT platforms are the following:

- C++
- COBOL (VAX and Microfocus)
- FORTRAN
- PASCAL
- ADA
- PROLOG
- BASIC
- BLISS (not on NT)
- LISP

Any developer trying to achieve the portability of the application at the data level has to consider what the mechanism for the access of that data should be. In the relational world this is ANSI SQL and on UNIX in the non-relational world it is Informix CISAM.

On the NT operating system, for instance, there is a file management system of its own called NTFS. This file system is fully compatible with the OS/2 HPFS file system but adds a transactional log that records each disk access to speed up recovery after a crash. The NT operating system can also read and write OS/2 and DOS files, thus providing the system with the ability to readily interface to a host of other systems in the market at present. The capabilities of Open VMS will allow the access of other databases by calls using ANSI standard SQL. On the VMS system, the files will be stored in RMS file format. With the other operating systems such as UNIX, local file management will be undertaken with appropriate protocols, such as C-ISAM.

At this level then, the approach of Digital with Alpha is to use *de-facto* standards and allow the interface of other people's software to provide the standards support for more general ones such as ANSI, IEEE, etc.

Communications services are required by the applications developer to interoperate with other applications on remote versions of the same system or on different systems altogether. These services may be at a number of levels and may be provided over a range of network types and standards. It is true to say that networking is the key to the market for systems now and in this respect Digital are in one of the strongest positions with a lead built up in local and wide area networking over the years.

User Interface Apple changed this forever and MS Windows took many of the same concepts into the true mass market. This can be viewed as the first-generation windowing UI; the second generation is based around a subtly different approach using Objects. However, this also requires an Object-based file system. While there have been a number of moves in the past few years to provide a more powerful graphically-based interface to systems via standard-based solutions like X Windows and Motif or via other more proprietary solutions like the interface to OS/2, none to date have provided the level of object orientation available in the Microsoft NT operating system which does include a good level of data object level functionality. On VMS I think it is highly likely that the user interface will gradually start to use Microsoft NT servers as a common method for providing a low-cost, high-functionality user interface to these systems. Support for the existing interfaces, including VT and X, will ensure that the investment in applications there today will be preserved (but should be re-examined).

Applications Programming Interface API Perhaps the two most essential components of the API on the Alpha-based system (here I restrict the view to OSF/1 and OpenVMS only) is the support of POSIX standards and of ANSI language standards. Together these set down the basis of highly portable software for the developer to exploit. However, if the platforms are used as targets for downsizing of existing legacy systems, it is likely that in most cases the original code being ported across will not conform to POSIX standards and is likely to deviate somewhat from ANSI language standards, especially for code using proprietary compilers and operating systems. Additional support for standards that impinge on all elements of an application is strong for both OpenVMS and OSF/1. This is best shown in Figure 2.4.

A Short History of UNIX

UNIX has its history back in the 1960s, a development in the world-famous Bell Laboratories in the United States of America owned and run by AT&T. UNIX and the programming language C have histories that are inextricably linked together and futures that are now beginning to separate slightly, as will be seen. UNIX, perhaps more than any other operating system in the history of computing, changed the rules of the game forever. Designed with the principles of portability in mind and first intended to be used by technologists, UNIX carried something of the Bell Laboratories ethos with it, a feeling of intellectual freedom and arrogance.

UNIX began over 20 years ago. To be precise, UNIX was conceived in its basic principles in AT&T Bell laboratories back in 1969 by three notable figures: K. Thompson, R. Canaday and D. Ritchie. During the 1960s AT&T Bell Laboratories had been developing and designing an operating system called 'Multics'. Multics was to be a multi-user, interactive operating system and work was taking place on a GE-645 computer. There were a number of problems with this system and in 1968 these became so serious that the Computer Science and Research Department of AT&T Bell Laboratories withdrew from the Multics project.

In 1969 Thompson, Canaday and Ritchie began to search for a new system as an alternative. It was this team that in 1969 designed a file structure for the new operating system, a file structure that gave birth to that found in all UNIX systems. At the same time and in true Bell Laboratories style, Thompson had developed a space simulation game called 'Space Travel' and was unhappy at the difficulties in running Space Travel caused by serious machine limitations using Multics on the GE-645 hardware.

At this point Ritchie and Thompson got hold of a DEC PDP-7 computer at Bell Laboratories and Space Travel was rewritten to run on the PDP-7. At the same time, Thompson implemented the Multics file system on the PDP-7 together with the utilities required to handle the files. UNIX had been ported to its first new home, the PDP-7.

It was not until 1970 that the name UNIX was suggested for the operating system. It is said that this was B. Kernighan's idea, naming UNIX to follow on from Multics. By 1970 Kernighan and Ritchie had developed a programming language, C, and it was this that had been used to implement most of the UNIX operating system, with the exception of the Kernel, this being written in machine-specific assembler. Much of UNIX's portability is due to the fact that Kernighan and Ritchie had developed the C programming language in which the system had been written. It should be remembered that at this time AT&T, the owners of Bell Laboratories, were a monopolistic US corporation. When the US government broke up AT&T (once the employers of over 1 million people) and Bell Laboratories were set on a more independent course, then Bell Laboratories had a vested interest in the commercial success of UNIX in the market.

UNIX had originally be viewed by its creators as an environment for program development, and in the early part of the 1970s the operating system remained largely an in-house development at Bell Laboratories. By the mid-1970s the UNIX operating system had found its way into academic circles in the USA, Europe and elsewhere. This happened following the introduction of UNIX to the Department of Computer Science at the University of California at Berkeley. UNIX had been brought to the University of California by Thompson who was acting as a visiting professor. Furthermore, this move to introduce UNIX into the academic world was fully supported by Bell Laboratories. In the latter part of the 1970s most good computer science courses around the world were using UNIX as the vehicle for teaching, especially for those components that referred to operating systems and languages.

By providing a cheap and freely available operating system to the world community of computer scientists in academia, the popularity of UNIX as an operating system was assured. As the graduates of the universities and colleges found their way into industry, government and commerce, they started asking for the operating system that they were used to, UNIX. Commercialization of UNIX followed swiftly on from this.

This rapid and widespread uptake of the UNIX operating system had some disadvantages, the main one being a proliferation of versions. The takeup was dramatic. Hardware vendors, software vendors and, of course, AT&T itself all moved off from the same original starting point in different directions. It is this problem of different versions that makes the whole object of standards at once essential and, by definition, difficult to achieve. The latest version of UNIX from UNIX Systems Laboratories (no longer wholly owned by AT&T) is UNIX System V.4. The release of System V.4 brought together three major variants of the original UNIX system, System V (the old foundation-level system), Berkeley UNIX and XENIX, the version of UNIX developed by no other than Microsoft for the low end of the market.

That brings us up to today. UNIX (System V.4) is a fast-growing system with functionality being added at a great rate. At this point in time some 500 Open Systems vendors have released System V.4 on a wide range of systems from desktop to mainframe-level computers. Around 300 source licences have been sold and over 1 million System V units were shipped in 1991 supported by some 5500 applications ported specifically to System V and a further 12,500 able to run under System V.4. UNIX is here in a big way and here to stay. Challenges from Microsoft NT, for instance, will have to do much to displace UNIX from its present market leading position.

UNIX now has a rich set of functions and features which make it a very different animal to the lean, stark original of the 1960s. Presently UNIX System V has a 79% market share of the Open Systems marketplace. Other vendors, such as IBM, DEC, HP, etc., have failed to come together on a common standard towards which their own UNIX versions will converge. The hope for this was the Open Software Foundation (OSF), now in severe disarray.

If I confine the following comments to System V.4 things will therefore be a little clearer. First, all the vendors who use System V.4 get the same base operating system from which to work. This has the advantage of allowing easy portability of code, especially between different hardware on the same microprocessor architecture, i.e. NCR Intel-based systems to ICL Intel-based systems. The software shipped with the operating system base release for UNIX System V.4 extends to much more than just the Kernel and includes; security, file system, communications, drivers, systems administration, etc. These features are those which other vendors of UNIX, DEC for example, add as specific 'proprietary' extensions to their own (in DEC's case ULTRIX) versions of the UNIX operating system (IBM's AIX variant has 2000 additional systems calls, for instance).

UNIX Systems Laboratories has a roadmap for the features and functions that it wants to include in the operating system and works collaboratively with other partners to add functions and features. In terms of the general market share for new systems over time Tables 2.1 and 2.2 are rather interesting.

Table 2.1 Percentage market shares in the mid-range for new system sales, 1990 to 1994

	1990	1992	1994
Proprietary	88	83	76
UNIX	12	17	23

Note: Proprietary includes MS-DOS, Microsoft Windows and OS/2

Table 2.2 Percentage market shares in low end for new system sales

	1990	1992	1994
Proprietary	78	68	57
UNIX	22	32	43

There is a very large and fast-growing number of UNIX systems in the market today with UNIX System V.4 being seen as the datum for the industry. But what of the future for UNIX, how is it likely to change and adapt to the challenges ahead in the IT industry?

It is certain that the future looks secure for the moment, with the prospect for collaboration between USL and its industrial partners continuing to be good, and more functionality is going to be provided in the next few years. The main points of this I have summarized as follows:

1. The evolution of the UNIX System V operating system has been the focus of activity between UNIX International and its members since December 1988. Recently the scope of this work has expanded outside the constraints of the base operating system in an attempt to encompass a complete systems software environment for Open Systems based on UNIX System V. The name of this project is UI-ATLAS.
2. UI-ATLAS was formally announced in September 1991 and is a comprehensive model defining system services interfaces relating to a distributed processing environment. The basis of the UI-ATLAS model is a set of standard Application Programming interfaces, Data formats and Protocols. These APIs, data formats and protocols are aimed at the integration of present and emergent technologies into the overall UI-ATLAS model. In 1992, UNIX International published a roadmap for UNIX System V and UI-ATLAS.The published roadmap for UI-ATLAS defines :

- A framework for systems management
- A definition for transaction processing management
- Distributed computing environment (DCE) support
- Enhanced networking functionality

- Enhanced desktop functions for UNIX System V

Functionality in detail for the UI-ATLAS model is:

- *Desktop functions for UNIX System V.* UNIX International feel that there will be a significant change in the role of the desktop computing device in the closing years of this century based on a more flexible computing approach with information as the central focus in the enterprise. The key elements of this trend are flexibility, interoperability, connectivity and distributed processing. UNIX International are of the opinion that multimedia will be an important factor in the desktop of the future and will therefore have to be based on object-oriented technologies with their associated datacentric approach to computing. Key parts of this desktop will be an object-based metaphor, independent look and feel, fault tolerance and distributed systems management.
- *Server functions for UNIX System V.* It will be essential for UNIX-based servers to interoperate with both proprietary and Open Systems. The approach taken for Open Systems is for the support of distributed object-based applications by the use of systems services without the need for the modification of the installed base. A number of other functions are also specified such as security, data integrity and distributed systems management.
- *Transaction-based functionality.* Due to the mission-critical nature of data in the corporate environment, the need to manage transactions in a fundamentally secure and efficient manner is paramount to the strategy for UNIX System V in the future. In response to this need, UNIX International's roadmap for UNIX System V includes, for a distributed heterogeneous environment; transaction management, transactional processing in symmetric multi-processing environments, fault management, security and capacity planning. While these functions address the on-line transactional style of processing, other modes of computation such as batch are also supported in the roadmap by way of the proposed APIs.

2.3.2 Commercial

The type and manner of business transaction in the industry began to change significantly over the past five to ten years. In the days since the formation of Digital, the way business is done has altered immeasurably. There are a number of reasons for this. First, the end users of systems have become much more sophisticated. This has led to a reduced imbalance in the power relationship between the vendor and the user.

Second, the technology itself is now very much cheaper than it used to be. Price performance, as I have already stated, is huge compared even with five years ago.

Third, the effect of the IBM PC on the industry and of Apple has been to force significant improvements in product interfaces, both at the systems and the applications level.

Fourth, the value of sales and the mix within a sale has changed radically. From my own experience in the mid-range market, it is clear that the average system sales value has fallen by at least 70% over the last four years. To make up for this shortfall, people in the industry have had to change the mixture in the sale. Now the emphasis is on high-value services rather than hardware, a trend Digital are heavily involved with.

Fifth comes the implications of Open Systems. In the extreme case, Open Systems would allow the running of almost any software on almost any hardware. This at least is the goal, even if it is not achievable. The result of this philosophy is to significantly reduce the scope of uniqueness. After all, that was the single issue that drove the development of proprietary systems. By reducing uniqueness, the only ways a company can compete in the market is by price, performance and loyalty (see Figure 2.5).

Now loyalty is a factor, but so long as one is dealing with a large corporation, it is a fairly small factor in the overall decision process. The significant factors are price and performance, the implication being that the market becomes a commodities game, which for many of the hardware vendors is the case. Unfortunately, the skills needed to develop applications and systems software and still in many respects to manage the overall network are scarce and expensive.

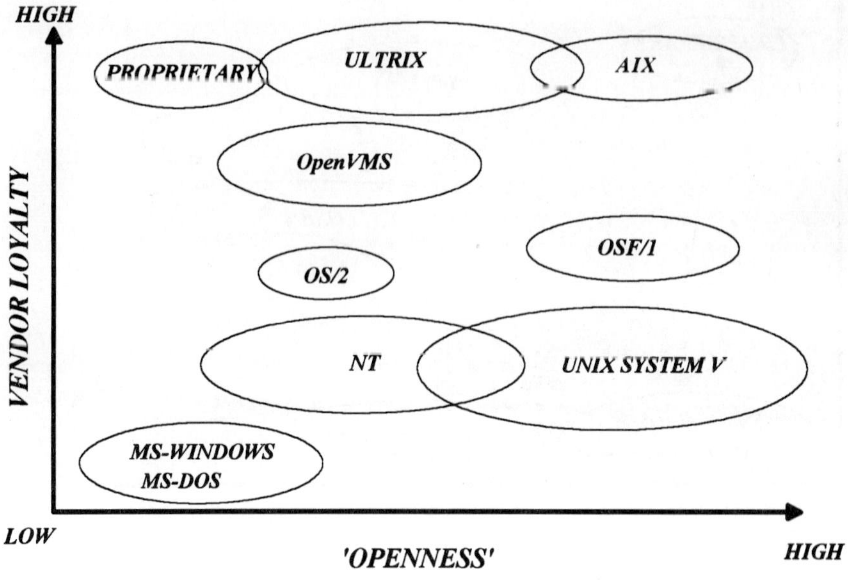

Figure 2.5

The downward pressure on hardware costs had forced many applications to be priced lower, and this in turn sets a lower expectation on the costs of services (see Figure 2.6). The end result of all of this is that the volume production of high-performance and low-price hardware is essential and that the ability to keep service costs to a minimum while retaining and, if possible, growing service value becomes the two essential criteria for winning in the present climate.

On both of these issues Digital can now be said to be in a very powerful position. It is likely that the cost base will be cut back further over the next few years and that there will now be a shift to emphasize the saleable skills in the organization. The Alpha processor is price competitive for the performance and promises to set the pace for the foreseeable future. All that now remains is sales. In order that the whole of the Digital strategy comes off, the cost of sales has to be reduced. This means that the channel strategy needs to be more closely managed and focused with clearer positioning of sales channels and tighter monitoring and control of channel performance.

The extension of the sales channels themselves is needed. To this end Digital are striking some joint deals on the hardware, software and services fronts. The key to winning in the commodities market is to have as many people as possible selling your commodity. Historically it has been in the direct sales channels that Digital has performed worse than one might have liked. Much of Digital's success can be seen to be dependent on the abilities of its third-party sales channels such as the Value Added Re-sellers (VAR) and the like.

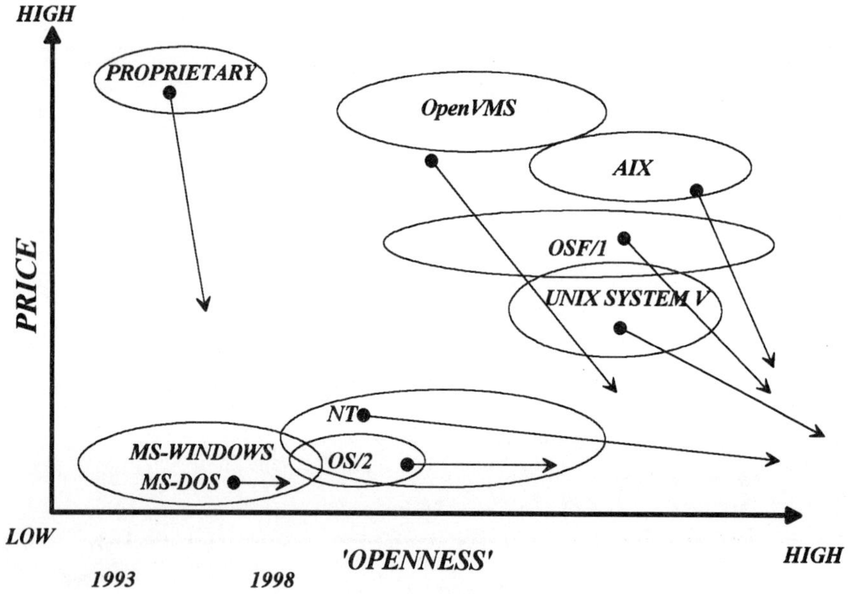

Figure 2.6

The recent acquisition of 800-SOFTWARE has shown that in the right circumstances, Digital are prepared to buy in specialized sales skills for markets in which they have performed badly. Direct selling from Digital now accounts for a growing proportion of sales in many areas, especially the UNIX/RISC MIPS market.

To achieve this Digital had to invent DECDirect, a direct telesales system. This in turn required a major streamlining of the administrative processes involved in the supply of systems.

All in all, Digital have been slower or a little less able to respond as well in the commercial sales area than they have in the technology space. Commercial changes to note lately are the move to user-based licensing. This enables either a designated user or users to operate a piece of software on a network or cluster or even just a specified number of users to do so. The result is that instead of being deterred from buying software for a large machine by the licence price if only a restricted number of users are going to access the software, the user community has responded very well, buying software now to use on larger systems that previously proved to be a financial disincentive. This move to more open licensing practices is another essential element in the Digital armoury for the future shape of the business.

2.3.3 Services

Services have been around in the computing industry for a long time and Digital have always provided high-quality services to the market. However, the realization that the services business needed to move forward and become a major contributor to the business happened in the mid-1980s, since which time Digital have put more and more emphasis on the services business. It is now interesting to note that the services side of Digital's business has, since 1989, been larger than the rest, a trend that, for the other reasons I have outlined, will continue. Digital is likely to be one of the most successful services companies in the world, one reason being its excellent record in employee relations. The other reason is Digital's proven ability to adapt to and manage the process of change successfully throughout the organization.

2.3.4 Philosophy

Digital had its philosophy made by the inspiration and ideas of one man in particular, Ken Olsen. At the time of writing, Olsen has retired from Digital and the future of the company is finally in the hands of others. I find it difficult to believe that there will be no changes to the philosophy and style at Digital. Likewise, I think the lasting philosophy of excellence, innovation and caring management will endure all that the future brings. Early in its life Digital established a reputation for being a good place to work. This clearly provided a largely stable workforce upon which to build the corporation to its present size.

The future, with its requirement for service leadership, will require this management policy to continue. Technical innovation has always been at the heart of the corporate drive and until recently most of the innovations, definitely the majors like PDP and VAX, came from within the corporation itself. When the deal was struck with MIPS, the corporation appeared to be banking on external sources for the future. Indeed in the announcement in 1992 that Intel and Digital would work together on massively parallel computing, it looked again as if the corporation's philosophy had changed to look outside for the drive rather than within. It would seem that there is a camp within Digital that starts these hares running so that an alternative strategy can be followed if the main one fails and that this camp has become a lot stronger since the late 1980s. If this is the case, I would applaud the caution but condemn the implementation. All that the announcements do is to weaken the public perception of Digital as a clear and focused organization with a strong policy as a first-class technology leader.

Certainly Digital have changed since the early 1980s. Acquisitions have taken off, with some major ones like Philips and Kienzle. I think this trend is now strong and likely to continue as a fundamental part of the overall philosophy. Digital now are often heard to describe themselves as a services company and it is true to say that many of the older managers in the corporation have moved out or over (Piere Carlo Falotti going to ASK Ingress, for instance) and with such moves there is bound to be a significant realignment of the corporation to newer directions in the industry. In fact the move to services might never have been successful if it had not been for the philosophy that made Digital great: everyone has a right to contribute and being right is not the same as being senior.

2.3.5 Summary

Digital has moved a very long way in the last 35 years. Most of its growth in the last 15 years was built on the back of the VAX and Digital today is a strong corporation with a sound financial base. Product proliferation has to be rationalized at this transition point in its history, Digital cannot carry spare baggage into the next century if its growth rate is to be maintained. Perhaps the most important thing is for Digital to keep hold of its philosophy, its style and not to sacrifice the future for the sake of changes in management style and approach today.

In Digital, being effective is a question of knowing the right person to ask for the answer you need. Knowing their boss instead does little or no good. In a corporation with such a personal style of working, I think the present size of operation is perhaps the biggest that can be maintained without inefficiencies creeping in. Growing therefore will require a splitting, probably along service, software and hardware lines to allow the corporation to function more fully. Already there are signs of this happening.

2.4 Chapter Summary

This chapter set out to answer two specific questions. First, given Digital's aims and objectives for the next 25 years, does its past performance and present behaviour lead us to believe that this is achievable? Second, what are the wider trends in industry, both specifically in the information technology industry and in the wider world?

By using the historical perspective of the operation of Digital I hope that the reader is now in a position to understand the performance of the corporation and the reasoning behind some of the arguments about the commercial and technical future based on the Alpha programme.

In the chronicle, I gave a very brief history of Digital from its earliest times up to the present so that the context of decisions about products, services, sales and marketing can be adequately appreciated. For a more detailed description of the fascinating history of the corporation I would refer the reader to the book edited by Pearson, a good reference for all the main events in Digital's history.

I hope that the reader is now in a position to move on to the other chapters of the book prepared with a full understanding of the events leading up to the Alpha programme, the Alpha technology developments and the commercial context into which this all fits.

2.4.1 Main Chapter Themes and Issues

The long and profoundly successful history of Digital underpins a base of 10 million customers using VAX hardware and running VMS. Products have driven Digital forward over the years and have proliferated to a major extent. One of the tasks of the Alpha programme will be to rationalize some of these products and lighten the cost burden on the corporation for the future. However, this has to be achieved without losing the confidence of the user base or exposing key clients to undue risk. Clearly Digital are at the mercy of market trends. RISC technology has become the key to performance and the older CISC-based VAX had to be replaced. Rightly, Digital opted to move forward to RISC but without dropping or downgrading VMS and with the minimum disruption to the end-user community. This technology move put Digital in the lead with the Alpha processor, moving to a RISC technology without the detriment of a me-too policy. Far from being back in the systems game, Digital are clearly leading the field again and by a long way (see Figure 2.7). This figure shows the point at which a major architecture change is required from the leading microprocessor vendors.

The trends in the business are to have a smaller number of major players driving the game and Digital are out in front on technology. I have raised the question of Digital and its sales and marketing capabilities (issues that I will return to later in this book) and the Alpha programme also addresses these issues. It is by the development of markets and alternative production and sales channels for Alpha that Digital will broaden the selling base and maximize the penetration rate into the market. The balance of business has changed significantly in the past ten years to a corporate financial profile that is based mainly on services.

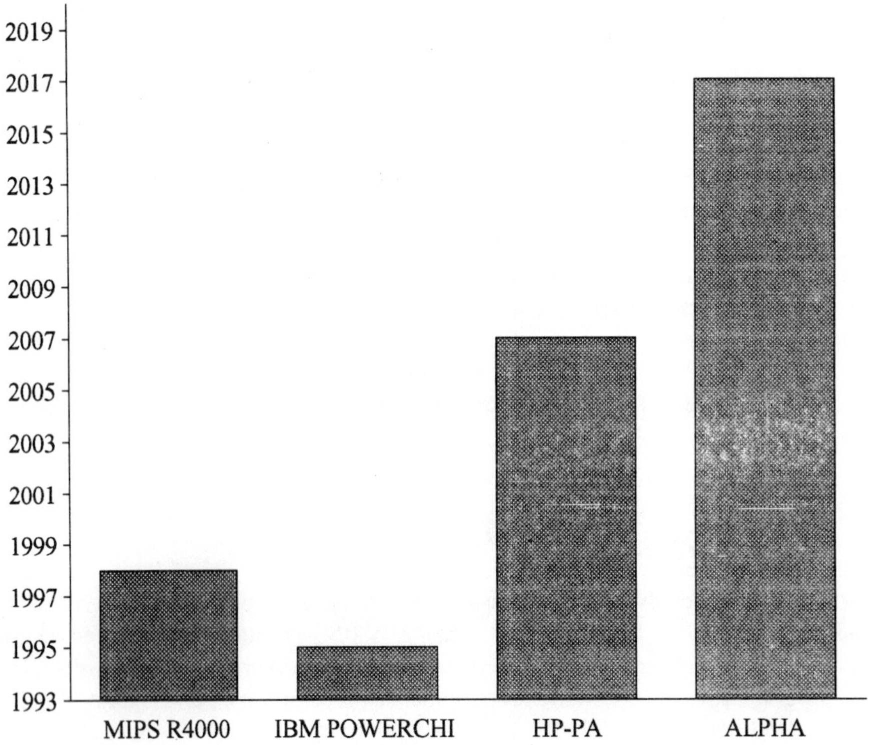

Figure 2.7

The trend became most noticeable in 1989 when service revenues exceeded others for the first time. It is important to note that approximately one half of these service revenues are from genuine value-added services in their own right while the other half comes in as a direct result of product sales. This trend to services has to continue for Digital as with all other corporations in the information technology sector. Digital's management philosophy and style together with their track record over the past 35 years are a convincing argument in favour of their likely success in the services sector.

2.4.2 Questions Raised by this Chapter

Having put Digital and its products and services into context historically, it is essential that we now look into the reasons for change. Broadly these fall into the following categories:

1. Technology changes
2. Commercial issues
3. Changed expectations and requirements
4. Competitive RISC architectures

It is important to explore these in detail and to understand the issues so that an accurate picture may be built up of the overall strategy that Digital have adopted with Alpha. It is essential to understand these issues also from the point of view of:

- End user
- Developer
- Analyst

so that the broader impact of the Alpha technology can be fully considered from the readers own point of view.

2.4.3 Conclusions

The main conclusions of this chapter are as follows:

1. Digital's historical performance. This has been excellent in all respects, financially and technologically.
2. Digital's historical weaknesses. The main problems faced by Digital in the past have been a sales and marketing operation that never seemed in the same league as the technology operation and a failure in the personal computing market given Digital's privileged position as vendors of networking systems.
3. Digital's capabilities. The big question is, can Digital change and cope with that change? I believe, based on past performance and personal experience, that the answer to this is yes.
4. Digital's organization. For a long time Digital have had a structure that has grown without much regard for effectiveness or efficiency. Although drastic manpower cuts have been made over the last year or two, the corporation has to go much further in reducing its cost base. However, manpower is not the place where such savings need to be made now.
5. Digital's corporate structure. By making the organization much leaner, a lot of the waste was cut out. One key area to target is the dispersed nature of the business. Anyone who has driven around Boston will know that Digital seem to have spread out with little regard for an efficient concentration of operations. This problem is one that has been repeated on a global scale and Digital must reduce the number of small, disparate operations.

Further Reading

C.J. Leach, *Microsoft Windows NT: A Strategic Review*, Prentice Hall International: Hemel Hempstead, 1993.

J.P. Pearson (ed.), *Digital at Work: Snapshots from the first 35 years*, Digital Press: Burlington, MA, USA 1992.

CHAPTER 3

The Reasons to Change

3.1 Introduction

Despite being a very successful corporation to date, managing to increase market share, expand from humble beginnings and end up, today, with a turnover of around $13 billion, Digital had to change and we need to look at the reasons why.

Clearly, the policy of running a corporation built on technical excellence, mainly based on a proprietary hardware and operating system strategy has been a winner, but the strategy for the future looks different in a number of fundamental respects. The world in which Digital trades and does business has and is changing dramatically, and many of the changes that are occurring have been driven from the technology level.

Many people in the industry feel that Digital has left it too late, that the policy of marginalizing UNIX-based systems in the 1980s was fundamentally damaging to the future of the corporation. I tend to agree with this only in part. True it was a foolish approach to try to ignore the fundamental trends in the market, but Digital may well pull out of the strategic dive. Quite simply, the technical advances that Digital have made with the Alpha microprocessor are so substantial that they are, for one, really leading the field. The fundamental issue in the minds of the IT community is 'will Digital manage the commercial side of the operation sufficiently well?'

Technology changes in the industry can be typified by the concepts of Open Systems, a philosophy with vendor independence as the theoretical guiding principle. I have given a brief overview of the concepts of Open Systems including a review of the main issues surrounding the definition of platforms and the arguments about standards and standardization (this concerns the issue of doing things the same on a number of platforms or just having one industry-standard platform).

Clearly the principles of Open Systems engineering have been a key to the design philosophy that Digital have adopted in relation to the Alpha programme. If all that was required was a replacement for the VAX (which, as I explain, was not the prime objective) then why not just beef up the VAX processor? In this chapter I look at the issues surrounding the decision to move away from the VAX processor as Digital's primary tool in the market and consider the reasoning behind the move to the Alpha processor family.

A few years ago, Digital got involved with the MIPS Corporation who manufacture advanced RISC microprocessors. This involvement has gone as far as Digital taking a minority stake in the MIPS Corporation and Digital have used the MIPS microprocessors to power their UNIX (ULTRIX)-based offerings in the 5000 range of systems. By doing this Digital entered the arena of the UNIX market quickly and with a very competitive range of systems. One might ask why Digital did not continue with the policy of using the MIPS offerings to drive the next generation of systems rather than go down the route of spending billions of dollars on a speculative hardware strategy. The answer is simple and twofold. First, MIPS processors could not run VMS without severely limiting VMS and Digital would be mad to abandon its 10 million VMS customers. Second, MIPS would be a me-too strategy and one not owned by Digital.

For similar reasons, the Intel offerings could not form the basis of the Digital future strategy, though in both the Intel and the MIPS cases, Digital look set to continue with some components of their more peripheral, less strategic hardware product range being based on these technologies. Technology change, then, is a significant factor in the rationale behind Digital's reasons to change its ongoing hardware strategy. However, the whole commercial picture of the industry has changed very significantly over the past five years and across the world. Primarily, the balance of the business has changed, by which I refer to the mix of typical business in terms of hardware, software and services.

We are all aware of the continuing downward trend of price coupled with the upward trend in the performance of the hardware and this has had a knock-on effect in the rest of the business, from applications and telecommunications through to services, a worrying trend in a business that is so intensely people-based.

I have explored the area of general commercial issues in this chapter to explain some of the non-technical reasoning that has underpinned Digital's decisions to produce the Alpha technology and the associated programme of services. All of this depends on the money from the end users, and this group has changed its expectations in relation to the pricing of hardware, software and services. The massive downwards movement of average hardware prices has caused a significant downwards shift in the price of applications and a perception that equivalent movements in the price of services can be expected. I have argued in the section on commercial issues that this associated reduction in software and service pricing is neither reasonable or possible. Clearly there are risks to the existing customer base for Digital in going down the route of more Open Systems and associated business practices. Digital have, with the Alpha programme, taken the course of least risk and highest possible return from their existing base of VMS customers. All this leaves Digital with a very different sort of business, one in which the importance of the services element has significantly increased and which will build its future success as much on the ability of Digital to build and manage relationships as on the technical basis of the hardware platform.

The changes in the industry are driven by technology and commercial forces. However, there are changing requirements to be met, based partly on the general trends in markets around the world towards greater verticalization and associated shorter development cycles and lower related costs. In this chapter I will show that the change in the expectations of the market and in the actual requirements for the systems are driven by the changes in the other markets in the world and in the nature and scope of the end user's desire for systems of greater sophistication. It has been the case in the past that the response of the software and systems providers to great technology innovations has been generally to produce applications of no more sophistication than the last generation but running on a cheaper hardware platform. If this is the response of the market to the Alpha innovation then the business is in a downwards spiral and in deep trouble.

Applications that are imaginative, advanced and which use techniques which until today could not realistically be provided at acceptable costs are now a possibility. Alpha makes this so. Alpha has to be seen as a liberator for the software and applications business, a tool for the support of applications that take the industry forward to match or overtake the expectations of a user community that seems always to be let down by the lack of imagination shown by most applications developers. But what of the existing systems? The mass of old software, the so-called legacy systems, are a reality that will not vanish. I have explored the needs of the legacy system user and tried to highlight the areas in which the Alpha technology can be applied both indirectly and directly. The problems of the software mountain, that pile of old code that simply cannot be thrown away, is one that faces all of industry and which we all need to look at. I have spent a considerable amount of time having to deal with systems that have to be sustained by a mixture of adaptive and corrective maintenance (see Boehm, 1981) (and generally a mixture of the two). This task is one that Alpha can help with in very real ways, either as a tool for the engineer or as a component of some downsized system.

3.1.1 Structure of the Chapter

I have split the chapter into three main sections: the first, 'Technology Changes', deals with the primary driving force in the industry, that of technical innovation. The second, 'Commercial Issues', looks at the overall change in the nature of the business that has resulted from the technology changes (and some of the factors that drive the technology). Finally, the section on 'Changing Requirements' investigates the changed needs in the market, the rapidly altering expectations about what value systems should and can bring to the end-user organization. The changes in the industry over the past few years have been complex and interrelated, but the main driving force has been in the area of hardware. Therefore the first section on technology change looks at the driving philosophy that has been at the root of the changes in design over the past few years, the philosophy of Open Systems. The section then goes on to consider the VAX, that solid base upon which Digital has grown to become the leading supplier of mid-range systems in the world today.

The VAX has its limitations and these are the fundamental reason why the Alpha project had to start and go ahead and the section explores in some detail the reasoning behind the decision to move away from the purely proprietary system to a much more open set of concepts. In the course of the investigation into the technology changes in the industry, I have included a review of the RISC technology from MIPS and of the alternative offerings from Intel with a reasoned review of why these, rather than a home-developed Alpha microprocessor, were inappropriate technologies for Digital's needs in meeting the challenges of the market. I have a personal definition of engineering. I like to think that the difference between engineering and pure science is that engineering is science for money, and the information technology business is a good example of this. In the second section of the chapter I explore the money aspects of the industry, the commercial issues that have changed so dramatically over the past few years as a direct result of the fiercely competitive changes in the hardware areas of the business. This section starts with an overview of the commercial background as it looks now and then explores how the balance of the business has changed and what the implications of this are for Digital and for the Alpha programme specifically and the information technology industry in general.

The perceptions of price and value in the market are explored next as are the risks presented to the existing base of Digital customers by the move to the Alpha technology with its highly focused Open Systems objectives. All of this results in a very different sort of business for Digital, one in which the move to services is the key and the successful management of third-party relationships will be absolutely vital. Having looked at the technology that has changed and that is forcing the pace of reshaping the industry, and then gone on to consider the alterations in the commercial environment caused by these changes, I finally explore the requirements of the customers. Never before have these changed so fast and so extensively, and in the final section on changing requirements I have taken a look at how and why this is so. The information technology industry is now going to have to keep up in a world where the pace of change in other major sectors is also increasing. This last section begins with a review of the general trends in the markets around the world, and this is most strongly typified by greater levels of specialization and a need to exploit transitory and highly vertical markets. Competition on price in the information technology business is no longer the real way to win business. The key is the level of value that the technology adds to the customers' operations.

In Section 3.4.2 I explore the issues concerning the value that technology adds and the needs for the applications developers and system integrators to increase the level of added value from their offerings. In this section it is apparent that the Alpha technology from Digital offers a significant edge over the competition as it has the true capability to allow the development of applications that stretch the user and at a realistic price. For many applications and advanced techniques, this has not been realistically the case to date, certainly not with systems that have guaranteed longevity into the next century.

At that time, however, we will still have systems that date back to the latter part of this century. These are legacy systems and will, by their nature, form part of the market potential for the Alpha systems. Downsizing, the move from older, larger, more expensive systems to smaller, faster, cheaper platforms, is a significant opportunity for Digital with Alpha. In the section on legacy systems I look briefly at the direct and indirect possible uses of the technology in the context of legacy systems. Finally, I take a view on the positive feedback loop in the industry, the way in which market expectations seem constantly to exceed the systems' abilities to perform the functions we want in the way the market desires them.

I look at the reasons why the market expectations are so high and seemingly insatiable, some of which are reasonable, some based on unfulfillable expectation. The section finishes by putting the challenge back to the system integrators and the applications developers. They are the people who now lag far behind the capabilities of the platforms, especially those of the Alpha platform. One of the assignments I was involved in recently was for an applications developer who said to me 'With all the power of the Alpha platforms, what should we do and how could we best use it?' My answer ran to many pages, but can be summarized as 'First take a complete look at the application domain and add in a lot more functionality, second, look at the technology domain, think about the addition of AI tools and of multimedia for some of the applications 'power users'. Interestingly, the client's view was that this would use up all of that nice, cheap power, forcing the system price up. I had to point out that the price was not the issue, the issue was the value the system added to a client's business compared with the price. Expectations are rising all the time, and Alpha enables the software engineer to stretch the applications in ways rarely seen in the industry to date. All that is needed is imagination and skill.

3.1.2 Issues Covered in this Chapter

The key issues covered in this chapter are those related to the changes that have caused Digital to alter the existing, VAX-oriented strategy to the present Alpha-based approach to the market. I have explained in some detail what the factors affecting Digital's business were, specifically with reference to the technology, marketing and customers.

There were a number of alternative options for Digital to follow, other than the Alpha route. In this chapter I will consider these issues and try to explain why Digital changed in the way they did. For instance, when they had a good system like the 5000 series, running on a proven processor like the MIPS RISC processor, why go out on a limb and develop one's own RISC technology, spend in excess of $2 billion and then try to storm the market? The reasons are clear and simple. I think that the reader will, by the end of the chapter, agree that Digital not only took the best and most sensible course of action in the prevailing and predicted market circumstances, but did so in a timely manner and in the right way for the best chances of success. This is not to say that the route Digital have chosen is without significant risk, especially to the present VMS customer base, and this chapter also highlights the key risks that Digital are taking, including the new areas, like third-party relationships, where they have to compete and win consistently if they are to be able to continue growing in an aggressive and sound manner.

By the end of the chapter, I hope that the reader will have gained an understanding of the basic issues in the industry that surround the policy of Digital to move to the Alpha hardware range and that fires the Alpha programme. Finally, one of the key issues raised in this chapter is that of the application of the technology to the end users' problems and the relationship of this to the commercial structure of the industry. Alpha must not be regarded as just a cheap, fast hardware platform. It is a liberating technology, one that should drive the software, especially the applications industry, forward into new realms. I have been quite scathing in my criticism of the applications industry for a lack of foresight, imagination and skill in the development of applications and the use of technology.

To balance the argument, it is true to say that prior to Alpha, the amount of real usable power was, though fast and relatively cheap, still limited for the use of really advanced techniques. Alpha changes that, the excuses are gone I argue, and now the expectations of the system users should be met and exceeded by the applications that follow in the wake of the Alpha programme.

3.1.3 Questions Raised in the Previous Chapter

The previous chapter put Digital and its technology and commercial performance and problems into an historical context. The main questions raised by the chapter were in the following four main areas:

1. Technology changes
2. Commercial issues
3. Changed expectations and requirements
4. Competitive RISC architectures.

3.1.4 An Example of Where this Chapter is Relevant

Engineering cannot be separated from the commercial world. The reasons we design and develop are closely associated with the needs of the market. Therefore, if you have a primarily technical interest in Alpha, this chapter will give you an understanding of the context and the rationale in which Alpha was conceived and in which it must operate.

By taking the time to look at the issues surrounding the commercial issues and the changes in requirements in the market, I hope that the technical reader will be prompted to think hard about the real use to which the technology could be put and the way in which it can be used to add value to end users. If you have a commercial rather than a technical interest in Alpha, I hope that the sections on the technology reasons for change and the altered requirements in the market will cause you to think about the driving factors in the industry at the moment and the reasons why Digital had to go down the Alpha route rather than choose a strategy based on, say, MIPS or Intel. In all cases I hope the reader will appreciate the risks still present in the strategy for Digital and be aware of the fundamental changes in the business that have been and are still required to make Digital successful in this area with the chosen strategy.

3.1.5 Questions to be Addressed

This is a chapter about why Digital had to change. If you are presently just interested in the reasoning behind the strategy, then I hope that this chapter will explain that reasoning to you in some measure. On the other hand, if you have a more direct interest, for instance as an end user, an application developer or systems integrator, then the reasoning that has had to go into Digital's decision process to use Alpha is worth examining from your own perspective. First, for the end user, the needs of your organization and the ability of competing technologies to provide for this are important issues for you to understand. As important is the issue of the value that the systems used in your organization add to the organization's main activity. I hope that my views on the real usefulness of applications and the potential that Alpha liberates will cause you to examine just how and where you might use such power.

For the applications developer and systems integrator the key question is 'What does Alpha mean and how does one make money from it?' I hope that the answer is becoming clear, that the route is to use technology power to justify higher added value and not just a simplistic attempt to reduce system prices further. The chapter also deals with the difficult issue of legacy systems, but this is raised only briefly. Legacy systems, those large entities that sit in the industry doing useful work and which can be huge, can, I feel, benefit from Alpha. I look at the basic direct and indirect methods with which Alpha can be used to alleviate the problems of old systems and porting to newer or very different platforms. Finally, the central question of the chapter is 'Why did Digital have to change and why choose the Alpha route?' I hope that by the end of the chapter the reader will have a much clearer idea as to the reasons why and the issues surrounding the decision process for Digital. Much of the thinking and reasoning in this section is directly relevant to the technical strategy in end-user and applications development communities.

3.2 Technology Changes

The information technology business changes faster than any other. I have heard a statistic that 30% of the information in the information technology business goes out of date in 2 years. Even if this is wrong (it would be hard to prove), it is certainly the case that the pace and scale of change in this industry are high. One attribute of this change cycle is that the change occurs very close to the experimental or academic edge of the industry. No sooner is an idea thought up than one finds it in production somewhere. Change is therefore a base component of the industry, and it is also a tool in use by all corporations in an effort to ensure some level of selling advantage in competitive situations. Indeed many of IBM's troubles can be put down to a slower rate of technology change and innovation than many of their competitors. Central in the move in the information technology industry has been the exponential growth in real computing power available per unit of spend over the past ten years.

The introduction of the first real desktop computer in volume by IBM in the early 1980s was the beginning of the revolution that has now changed the shape of the industry and its supporting technology forever. In its time, Digital has been one of the key driving forces in the industry for technology-based change, often years ahead of its competitors that were left struggling to catch up. Digital were the suppliers of the first true mini and super-mini computers in the world. I have often though how things might have turned out if the corporation had made VAX and VMS more widely available as they are doing with Alpha and as AT&T did with UNIX. It is likely that the picture would have been a lot more complicated but that the corporation would have had a much stronger industry position in the mid-range and workstation level.

One area in which Digital never really succeeded well was the desktop personal computer market. Interestingly, it is in this area that the volume growth in the industry has been and for technical reasons is likely to be for the foreseeable future. For most of the 1970s and 1980s the microprocessors were SISC-based (Sophisticated Instruction Set Chips). In these systems, one instruction on the microprocessor may actually execute a whole host of sub-instructions (such as on the VAX). There were two specific problems with this technology. The first was that there are theoretical limits to the maximum speed of such devices given the density of the microprocessor, the complexity of the instructions and the rate at which the microprocessor can run (known as the clock speed and measured in MHz). The second problem was that everyone started making their own SISC chips (like the VAX and like IBM's S36, S38 and AS400). The consequence was that software written for these platforms was difficult (if not impossible) to move across to other systems, thereby locking the users into one vendor. This was a direct result of feature-based competition between hardware vendors.

In a university in the USA the idea of the RISC chip was born (Reduced Instruction Set Chip). As the name suggests this operates by using fewer instructions. Consequently these instructions have to be built up in sequences that achieve the same logical outcome as a more sophisticated instruction. The results from each operation are stored each cycle of the clock, and the resulting smaller chip size and reduced complexity combined allow much higher clock speeds and therefore significant increases in raw performance. The whole world suddenly wanted to move over to RISC.

3.2.1 Open Systems and All That

In the days of the proprietary market in systems, competition was based on the differentiation of functionality and feature. This was generally achieved within the constraints of hardware architectures that were substantially different from one system to another. In some cases (such as IBM) this differentiation existed even between ranges of computers from the same manufacturer. The end result of this policy in the market was that software became locked into the specific systems it was originally written for. Code portability, possible in theory, was often impractical in the real world.

It is true to say, however, that the proprietary systems approach had its merits and these can be summarised as:

- Standards within the system range were rigidly set and adhered to
- Unique technology attributes could be fully exploited
- Users locked into a proprietary architecture were relatively safe from competition
- Single technology means that the support is simplified for the system vendor and manufacturer.

In some instances, the exploitation of unique attributes became self-defeating. IBM, for example, had a number of systems ranges between which porting was difficult, needing significant levels of rework to accomplish the task.

Digital were no different from the rest. The PDP and then the VAX were proprietary architectures that owed little to the high ideals of Open Systems. However, they did try to accomplish the goal of code portability within a range of systems. With the PDP and then with the VAX, Digital managed to produce systems that allowed applications to run on the smallest to the largest of the range with no change to the code and no recompilation. When the range of systems changed from the PDP to the VAX, the jump was a noticeable one. Digital had many troubles with the porting of code from one system to another, despite great efforts to provide migration tools and services. This was a lesson that they would take to heart when planning the Alpha project.

Digital had a problem when they entered the business, the issue of their size. By comparison, IBM were much larger and had a big lead in the IT market. Digital realized that to make any headway, they had to trade off innovation for market presence. By concentrating on the mid-range system, Digital were able to successfully penetrate the market at a number of levels, notably: small office, departmental and finally, small data centre. However, they were never a real hit in the large data centres of the major organizations. To achieve this innovative position, the corporation had, from the outset, to make it possible for their platforms to interoperate with other vendors' equipment. It was through this route that Digital made its name in the networked systems market around the world.

This level of interoperability started out at the data level, essentially allowing the distributed processing of information kept centrally. The strategy then moved to general levels of data distribution in which the information was held at a number of locations closer to the point at which it was used. It was the data distribution phase of the corporations success that heralded the need for portable applications. The reason for this change was simple. Digital were starting to replace a number of the old departmental mainframes with the new, powerful range of VAX/VMS systems. The clients needed to take applications off the mainframes and onto the VAXs. However, this was never simple and often impractical.

At about this time, the IBM PC was gaining ground. It must be remembered that this was the single most important move in the IT market in the late twentieth century. The advent of the PC heralded the fundamental changes in computing that have taken place in the past ten years. The PC, cheap, simple and powerful, democratized computing. No longer were computers a machine for the experts, they were tools for the everyday person. Technical innovations in the PC also brought about changes in the market. Suddenly the volumes of microprocessors needed to supply the computing industry shot up with consequent falls in unit price. The competition got in on the idea and suddenly computers started to look like a commodity.

With this move to computers for everyone came a number of challenges from the end users. I well remember sitting in the offices of a client in the 1980s when he asked 'But why can't I move software across from that Wang system to a VAX without work? I can swap software from my IBM PC to my Amstrad!' This was a typical response from the end user community, suddenly they had woken up to the commercial and technical arrogance that had underpinned the proprietary systems market for all those years. The hunt was on for Open Systems.

Open Systems were nothing new. The idea of common standards, of portable code and of the principles of the partitioning of design considerations into the logical and physical were long understood. UNIX had been around since the 1960s and we all had a good idea what it could do if it were let run riot in the market. For many reasons this took a long time to happen. One reason was the inherent self-interest of the proprietary systems vendors. Another was the inherent weakness in the earlier UNIX releases, especially at the security level. In the early 1980s, AT&T used to call me up and tell me that ' This year UNIX will *really* take off!' Year after year they got it wrong.

One thing many failed to notice was the insidious rise in the number of ex-university graduates who had lots of exposure to UNIX. AT&T had a new generation of UNIX-trained engineers available (I think by accident rather than by design) and it would be these people who would finally help UNIX out into the light of commercial systems.

The PC revolution forced hardware prices down. The technological innovations that accompanied it were to force speed and functionality up and this was a fertile environment in which to plant the seeds of UNIX, a small, self-contained, powerful operating system. UNIX became, in the minds of many, the basis for Open Systems engineering. This was a really ill-informed position and one that in some respects, slowed down the advance of real Open Systems engineering.

Let us look for a moment at Digital and consider what the move to the Open System meant to them. Because of the need to coexist in a multi-vendor environment, Digital had developed a lot of powerful interfaces to the systems at a number of levels (both physical and logical). Digital were very active supporters of international standards and in many respects were typical of the vendor community in the late 1980s (IBM being less active due to its persistent desire to remain proprietary).

All the work on standards and on interfaces was really important, however, it was an indicator of the future move to more Open Systems. One day, some time in the future, it was clear that open interfaces was not enough. People wanted common systems that software could be ported from and to with the minimum of cost. In short, people wanted competition among vendors and freedom from the constraints of proprietary architectures.

In addition to all of this, the proliferation of computing made greater and greater demands on the systems and resources available and on the technologies that underpinned them. Just as 16-bit gave way to 32-bit, it was clear that 64-bit machines would be needed some time soon. I was involved in a discussion at GEC in London early in 1982, where we looked at the needs of the systems in the period up to the year 2020. Many around the table thought that 32-bit systems would carry on providing for the needs of the market until around the year 2010. The engineers around the table were not so optimistic. We could see how fast the processors were changing and how rapidly the data manipulated was growing in real applications. We, somewhat pessimistically, viewed 64-bit systems as essential by the year 1990.

At Digital they were aware that while the systems were excellent, the best in the world in terms of interoperability with other systems, there remained the problem of portability. The software issue had to be addressed in terms of applications portability across platforms and across operating systems. All this technology change had some impact on the marketing and commercial side of the business as well. Open Systems also implied a change in business practices. No longer could one look at growth in terms of the single proprietary chip manufactured by Digital and sold in Digital hardware.

The difficult truth to face was that the new horizon was one of complex interrelationships at all levels among systems developers and vendors. Digital would have to make its technology freely available to any number of key partners if it was to succeed. This technology had to be Open inasmuch as it must allow a number of operating systems to run on it and be capable of supporting the industry needs well into the next century. Alpha had to accomplish all of this. So, it is clear that Digital had to change for a combination of technology and commercial reasons. One of its greatest assets was also its greatest problem: the users of the VAX/VMS system. This ten million-strong customer base had to be protected. As part of this, the upgrading and porting from the old to the new architecture had to be considered right from the start. Alpha could not strand the users, as this would have been suicide.

Digital's main problems which Alpha was to address can be summarized as follows:

- Need for a new, 64-bit architecture
- Support and migration of VAX/VMS base
- New business on UNIX and other operating systems
- Must support all present and forthcoming standards
- Cannot afford to be a 'me-too' solution

By the provision of an architecture as powerful and flexible as Alpha, Digital have, in one move, placed themselves in the strongest position of all manufacturers when it comes to Open Systems engineering. For reasons we will see later, the Alpha architecture is capable of supporting almost any operating system likely to lead in the open system front, be it UNIX, OSF/1, Windows NT, OpenVMS or something completely new. Alpha was a smart move.

3.2.2 What's Wrong with VAX?

In short, not a lot. But it is true to say that as a SISC architecture, the VAX has reached the end of the useful life for systems which want to be seen as state of the art. (Remember, the information technology business is like the fashion business, people are influenced by what is 'in' more than what they know they need.) There is a strong issue that makes VAX unsuitable for the role that the Alpha has now taken on and this is the issue of the ability of the VAX to support other operating systems. While this can be done, the VAX is far from ideal as a basis for an Open Systems strategy in this respect.

The Alpha microprocessor was, of course, designed to facilitate just this sort of approach to the market. The VAX is drawing to the end of its life, but this is not to say that they have no use. The VAX is a powerful system still capable of delivering the goods, but Digital need something that will carry the corporation on for the next 25 years and Alpha is it (though judging from the time it has taken to try to kill off the PDP the VAX will be with us for a very long time yet!).

3.2.3 Why Not MIPS RISC?

The reasons for this are many and various. First, there are hardware reasons for not choosing the MIPS RISC chip, and these relate to the requirements of the VMS operating system (which could not be supported), the speed and power of the chip (the present MIPS offering is only 32-bit) and a number of lesser considerations. So it is clear that the MIPS offering would not, for technical reasons alone, provide a suitable platform for VMS and to Digital this has to be a non-starter with 10 million users. Second, while Digital do have a range of systems based on the MIPS RISC offering, they were never likely to base their entire future on a hardware strategy that they did not own.

It would have been possible for Digital to buy out MIPS but the cost of doing this would have given them little competitive edge over their rivals and would still have left the VMS community isolated. In the face of such compelling technical and commercial objections, it is not surprising that Digital decided to go down the route which eventually led to the design and development of the Alpha range of hardware. One thing Digital did prove by going along with MIPS for a while was that the RISC market really was happening, the technology really was in demand and could be counted on to deliver the financial performance in the corporation's business that they so urgently required.

3.2.4 Intel

Intel was made in the 1980s when IBM took the fateful decision to adopt the i86 processor as the basis for the (then) new IBM personal computer. This decision not only changed forever the face of the computing industry and pushed forward advances in application design, it also sealed the success of the Intel Corporation for the next decade. The volumes of i86 range microprocessors produced by Intel are amazing. In 1991, they shipped over 23 million chips. The development budget for the P5 was in excess of $2 billion. However, the Intel range of microprocessors are not true RISC processors in the MIPS or Alpha sense and would have given Digital the same problems as the MIPS offerings had they used these as the basis of their hardware. Intel do drive the industry forward on the volume front, though.

The influence of Intel-based systems on the future of the industry has been profound. Most of the client/server concepts that underpin modern systems design have their roots in Intel-based systems. It was Intel that put fast, cheap processing power on the desktops of hundreds of millions of users world-wide and it was in the networking of these systems that the topologies we now consider as standard: networked, client/server, parallel array, etc. came into being. Intel's answer to the threats presented in the next decade was the Pentium microprocessor. This technology is going to be in competition with the Alpha when it is ready. At the time of writing this book, the Pentium microprocessor is later to the market than had been expected and had a number of technical problems to be resolved. Undoubtedly this will be the mainstream competitor for the Alpha market sector, especially on Microsoft Windows NT.

3.2.5 Summary

Change is an integral component of this industry, a function of the technology and its immature nature. Because of the closeness between technology research and productization, we see the rapid innovation in the academic and research worlds translated into product with only a small time delay. Turmoil and change caused by the advances in the research communities gets translated directly into change and innovation in the commercial world. Clearly in all of this the VAX processor has stood the test of time, introduced in 1977 and only now, in 1993, being superseded by the DECchip 21064, a full 16 years later, during which Digital has grown vastly in size, IBM has made the biggest loss in global corporate history and Intel has produced a full five generations of processor. Finally, however, Digital had to change its base hardware system to take account of the needs of the next decade and beyond. Digital are an interesting corporation to study. One clear pattern emerges from any consideration of them as an organization; they innovate and they are pre-emptive in their response to changing markets. Just as IBM appear to take forever to make things happen, Digital changes suddenly. They innovate, usually technically, and use this innovation to move forward in the market.

The shape of the industry has now been dramatically changed. Open Systems principles and technical innovation mean that the systems cost has dropped along with the margins. Given this, the cost structures that corporations used to carry have had to be substantially reviewed and altered. More emphasis has had to be thrown onto services, and the need to win new market sectors and bigger market share has never been so acute. Digital have responded true to form with an innovative move to get the Alpha systems out through as many channels as possible and into the market.

3.3 Commercial Issues

By the late 1980s it became apparent that the models used to predict growth in the computer industry had to be reviewed. Infinite growth was not going to happen, there were going to be rationalizations and big changes and mostly these would manifest themselves in the commercial operations of the industry. The corporations that realized this and reacted would survive, and those that did not would have a difficult time of it, if they survived at all. As we have now seen, the golden world of the information technology business has taken some ravaging in the past few years of the world recession. Some of this had to happen and was a direct consequence of the recession itself. Much, however, was the result of poor and unrealistic management of an industry without due regard to the warning signs in the technology. As the 1980s drew to a close Digital was one of the switched-on corporations that realized change was inevitable, change in technology and changes in the commercial operations that surrounded this technology.

3.3.1 The Balance of Business

The cost of hardware has fallen, not just in terms of price performance measurements but also in real terms. To put a system on-site, including software and services, gets cheaper all the time. The driving factor in this is the hardware cost. As this fell sharply, the licence prices for all the software had to come down. The users would not accept otherwise and this goes for the operating systems as well as the applications themselves. As these licences and hardware prices fell, then, in real terms the only place to make up the shortfall was in volume and services.

These factors affected the balances and style in the business. For example, if the hardware cost falls and the margin takes a hit, then companies like Digital and IBM have to try to shift the cost of sale to some third-party who in turn will need more than just the hardware to sell in order to make a decent living. Likewise, Digital have thought up ways of changing their approach to the selling of the systems, from DECdirect, the telemarketing arm of Digital selling, through to the licensing of other third parties (like Cray and Olivetti) to use their new Alpha technology. The classic approach to such issues has been for companies such as Digital to look to move more into the provision of services which, indeed, they have done with some success. The figure quoted today is that 55% of Digital's business is in services. This is a little deceptive, however, since it includes the revenues from hardware and systems maintenance and support. If we exclude these (since they are more a function of the hardware sale than of the true, independent service business itself) the real service volume is about halved to more like 25% of total turnover (but still a big business in its own right at around a $3 billion turnover).

Clearly Digital will continue to focus on the services element of the business and intend to grow this and ensure that they are further immunized against the worst ravages of the changing business. There is a need for associated cultural change though. The people one requires in an organization that has services as a focus are very different from those in a development-led organization. In order that they are able to deliver a wide range of changing services, it is the ability to work closely with clients and to pick up new skills that one requires from such individuals. Another change in the commercial fabric has been the influence of the hot-box shops. These organizations from the very small through to the medium-sized make a market in fast, Intel-based systems at basic cost plus a small mark-up. The catch comes when one looks at the level of service, support and quality that comes with such offerings. However, I do know a number of organizations that use such off-the-peg hardware to build large network systems (though the overall reliability might not be too good). The influence of such organizations has been to drive down the price of hardware further and produce unrealistic expectations in the minds of many end users as to the ultimate costs of sophisticated systems.

There is clearly going to be further change in the direction of other systems containing Alpha microprocessors. As more and more of the vendors sign up to this,

Digital will ensure for itself a large and secure revenue stream for both existing and future versions of the processor. It will be interesting to see who is first operator to start producing Alpha microprocessors under license from Digital, and this will be another quantum jump in the strategy. The nature of the business mix changing will inevitably lead to lots of changes in the structure and approach of Digital to the market. I think that the main area for review over the next few years will be the sales channel strategy, which has to be modified to reflect the variations in the relative values of the offerings to the market. Already the sales philosophy has changed significantly with sales teams now enabled far more than they were in the past and able to do deals that only five years ago would have required several levels of sign-off. This change in the way Digital approaches the selling of its products in general and its new Alpha range of products in particular will lead to Digital having to compete in market sectors (such as the power PC market) that until lately it has avoided. One probable outcome of all this is that the organization will have to be more clearly subdivided. There are already signs of this happening with more clearly defined divisionalization and responsibility beginning to appear in Digital's structure. Inevitably, this will lead in turn to changes in the culture. This in itself is a risk. For a long time Digital has been a winner on the basis of being highly influenced by its technology, and it remains to be seen if this will be the case in the future.

3.3.2 Where the Money Comes From

The changes in the mix of business caused by the emergence of Open Systems and of small, fast, cheap competitive hardware have had a profound impact on the overall funding situation for a corporation like Digital. With such severely reduced hardware prices in the market (and, due to the now common practice of discounting, lower actual margins). The heady days of growth that we witnessed in the 1970s and 1980s are unlikely to return. Growth in real terms will happen, but at a much reduced rate than previously. Furthermore, as the industry takes an upturn on the back of the gradual global easing of the recession, then we are likely to see system prices continuing to fall as the players all try to gain greater market share or enter new market sectors.

Hardware, then, is not likely to bring in the big margins of days gone by. Software prices have fallen in real terms along with those of hardware. However, this is unlikely to continue for much longer, due to the cost of development and maintenance of software. Compared to hardware, software (application or other) is still relatively expensive to produce and much more costly to maintain and support in the field. Also most of the work in the development and maintenance of software is still manual, unlike many of the functions in the hardware business. The end result is that the software side of the industry still requires a lot of bright, well-qualified people to keep it running. Unless one is in the high-volume market, the return on the labour cost employed is only a fraction of that in the hardware industry. For this reason, the expectations of the market, that software prices will continue to fall in line with the hardware, will be sadly disappointed. In many cases I come across at the present time, the price being charged for software by companies is lower than the development and maintenance cost. This results in cash flow problems for the companies concerned and, if continued, will lead to their demise.

Digital with the Alpha programme will require innovation from the applications marketplace to make appropriate use of the available power of the systems rather than just viewing the hardware as a cheaper box to run present applications on. If the Alpha programme is to be really successful, the applications developers that Digital really need to concentrate on will be those with the highest added value, innovative solutions to the industry problems that use the full power of the Digital hardware. By making these applications higher value, the return on the labour costs for the software supplier will look more realistic, and this is essential for the long-term health of the industry in general and the Alpha programme in particular. Other market sectors, for instance the high-volume consumer electronics sector, are seen by key Digital personnel as being attractive places to position the Alpha technology. Some at Digital believe that Alpha might make realistic Virtual Reality systems in the home a possibility in the near future.

Services have long been held out to be the panacea of the computer industry. Just sell a few days' services and up goes the revenue (well, almost). First, the services business is now getting a little more mature. One result of this is that there has to be more focused services offered to better-defined markets. However, the costs of developing a service product are not inconsiderable, and the cheapest would be training. For each day delivered as a course, the preparation is likely to be between 10 and 20 days. In addition, the sales and marketing programme for such a course is likely to take a further 10 days work. Therefore, in the case of a 5-day training course, the up-front investment is going to be in the order of 60 days.

Given the continued move towards more and more specialized courses, it is likely (assuming that the quality does not suffer) that the price of services will have to remain high in order that the investment be fully recouped. For more specialized services such investment can be higher and more at risk (for instance, consultants who are in constant contact with clients and who are highly paid and cost lots to train are at risk of being poached by the clients themselves). Quality of service is also essential for success in this market and the service quality is being scrutinized as never before (see Berry *et al*, 1990). There is one significant source of income to the Digital corporate business: that of the maintenance revenues for the existing customers. It is estimated that this is in the region of $3 billion per year, a sizeable revenue that Digital are unlikely to put at risk. One consequence of this is that there is likely to be a significant cut-over period from VAX to Alpha in this market area as it will take time for all of the base to upgrade applications to Alpha platforms as and when required. The picture I have painted, then, is one in which the traditional source of high-value, high-margin revenues is in fast decline. Software and services have bottomed out in price but attract subsequently lower margins than for the hardware. One response to this from Digital has been to increase its activities in the financial services area.

By aggressively launching into the leasing and finance world, Digital are hoping to regain some of the lost revenues that result from the other changes in the industry. Ultimately, of course, the money comes from the customers and while inevitably Digital will benefit from the move to downsizing by many mainframe users going to Alpha-based solutions, there is a trend for clients to measure the effective value of systems in their organizations. This further strengthens my argument for more powerful, value-added applications.

3.3.3 Risks to the Existing Base

As I said earlier, about 25% of Digital's annual turnover comes from the maintenance and support revenues from its massive installed base of customers. I have summarized the primary risks to this customer base in Figure 3.1. Furthermore, a significant amount of repeat business is done with this base by way of other hardware, software and services. Such a significant base is indeed a valued asset. However, those clients who have already decided or who will in the future decide to move to UNIX are in a different class.

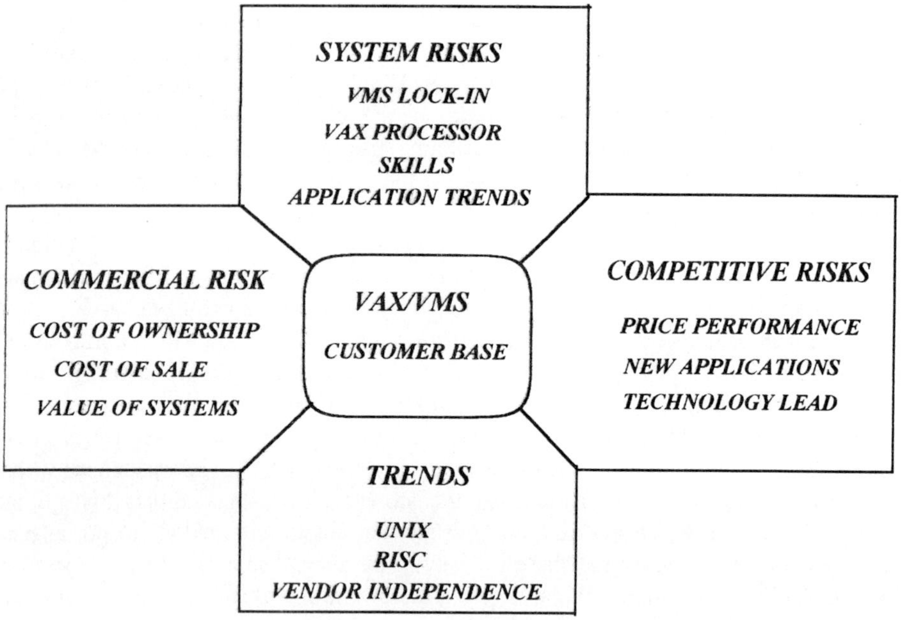

Figure 3.1

In the UNIX world there is less strong vendor loyalty (an inevitable result of the overall philosophy of Open Systems). In fact changing to another vendor and using any significantly different version of UNIX is rather difficult, but it is still possible. For these customers then, there is the possibility of moving to other platforms. Now some of these clients might be tempted by ultra-low-price hardware, or by corporate decision to switch vendor, for instance. However, for the great majority of the base, the change-over from systems based on VMS to others based, say, on UNIX is likely to be very slow indeed. This is the core that Digital will concentrate on protecting by getting them across onto Alpha-based systems and then continuing to encourage them to stay on VMS as an operating system choice.

By developing a systems architecture based on the Alpha technology, Digital have taken the policy decision to make the attractions of staying with VMS (albeit OpenVMS) based solutions infinitely more attractive than the alternative of moving to another operating system or hardware platform for the following reasons:

- Disruption
- Cost
- Quality
- Reliability
- Training
- Alpha performance
- Alpha facilities
- High value to vendors

The subtle move has been in changing the direction of the business by allowing other system vendors to develop hardware based on the Alpha technology. By doing this Digital are increasing their ultimate customer base size, even if this is by indirect means rather than their previously direct methods. Of all the risks to Digital's existing customer base, the biggest comes in the form of their relationship with Microsoft.

Microsoft NT is a new and powerful operating system designed under the guidance of the person who was largely responsible for the design of VMS and before he left Digital he also worked on RISC. The powerful, graphic nature of this multitasking, fully pre-emptive, object capable, operating system (capable of a multi-user server role) coupled with the low cost and high functionality will make Microsoft NT an attractive front-end service to the VMS community. However, if and when it is installed in such server situations, then the gradual erosion of other parts of VMS-based systems will be possible and indeed likely.

Clearly there is not going to be a wholesale switch from VMS to UNIX or Microsoft NT overnight, but a gradual erosion of the shores of the VMS continent by the relentless power of Microsoft seems inevitable. I think that Digital's response to this is likely to be the addition of more graphical facilities within later versions of the OpenVMS operating system together with a level of Object manipulation at the basic level to provide functionality which would compete with Microsoft NT.

3.3.4 A Different Sort of Business

For a long time, Digital have been riding on the high-volume, high-value, high-margin business. Now Alpha will continue to ensure that the volumes remain high, but it is not likely that the margins of the 1970s and 1980s will ever be seen again. This all leaves Digital as a newer and very different sort of business to the old corporation. So what has their response been? First, Digital has taken the initiative and is making its technology more publicly available through a whole host of different routes. The end result of this has been the dispersal of the technology and the increasing public awareness and dependence on the Alpha offerings from Digital. Second, there will be an increase in the volumes of Alpha-based systems shipped due to the inclusion of the third-party relationships for Alpha-based systems into the market. Third, Digital will continue to move into the services sector. Finally costs will continue to be reduced. I estimate a 23% improvement in the earnings per head ratio for Digital by the end of 1996.

3.3.5 Summary

The commercial climate in the information technology industry has changed significantly over the last five years. Many corporations have failed to tackle the issues that this raises for them in terms of management, sales and technology, but Digital have not been among them.

The Alpha programme, not just the technology but the whole range of responses being made by Digital to the prevailing conditions in the industry, clearly sets Digital on track to continue as an industry leader. This is not to say that the future will be free of troubles or risks. Digital has to consolidate the technical lead that it has gained with the introduction of the Alpha technology by the careful management of the third-party relationships it has forged to date and by continuing to move aggressively forward on the same front. In addition, it is clear that the developers of key applications in the industry sectors which Digital see as vital (like banking, finance, engineering, aerospace, etc.) have to continue to be won over to the Alpha platforms. Third, the existing customer base needs to be encouraged to move over to the new Alpha range of systems with as many as possible staying on the OpenVMS version. Last of all, Digital needs to continue the restructuring that it started some time ago in order to further reduce its cost base which still looks rather high to me. These things all have to be achieved while continuing to grow the services side of Digital's business and in the face of significant changes in the mix of business and the changed values of the components.

The technology that drives the information technology industry is, once again, in the process of fundamental change, and one aspect of this is the Alpha technology from Digital. However, there are other fundamental issues related to this change, one of which is the available power for applications and the need for these applications to exploit this power in a meaningful and valuable way. It is certainly the case that applications are continuing to become more specialized, more vertical and more accurately targeted to narrower and more focused areas of the available market. In addition, the entry cost to the market for the would-be developer of applications is low and falling in real terms (for hardware, software and tools). When this is coupled with the productivity gains that are now realistically achievable using very fast, powerful systems (such as those based on Alpha microprocessors) then the applications world looks set to become much more competitive and specialized. Digital will, if they get the commercial relationship right, be able to benefit from this trend in the market, a trend that will be encouraged by end users who continue to seek applications that are more and more closely aligned to their requirements (which themselves are changing at an increasing pace).

This trend will lead to the increased specialization of systems in general and not just the applications (since some applications will have very different system requirements, for instance CAD-based systems, multimedia systems and shop-floor data collection and analysis). Such system, or system component, specialization will require different levels of system build. Today this can be achieved using disparate hardware and operating systems, but the end result is seldom elegant and the design and development generally troublesome. By developing the Alpha technology, Digital are able to offer appropriate 'flavours' of the microprocessor and its Privilege Access Libraries (PALs) to cope with all the needs of the applications world. Therefore the design and implementation of systems with highly different requirements for the individual components and applications that run on them is made significantly simpler than is presently the case with other hardware-based systems. It would therefore appear that the job of the systems integrator is going to become more important over the next few years than at any time in the past.

To date, Digital have had experience of this side of the business. Now I would argue that it needs to become a more mainstream activity in their services sector, one that apart from generating significant revenues will be of strategic importance to their relationship with the end user. It is possible, given the new business practices adopted by Digital in the Alpha programme, that one might see Digital eventually integrating systems made not by them, running operating systems that are not from Digital and using third-party applications, so long as the base technology is Alpha. Clearly, the balance of business being taken into Digital has changed fundamentally over the past three years and is still in the process of realignment to the new conditions in the market. Digital has had to change its own structure in response to this and has, furthermore, had to change its mixture of product offerings and create a more service-based bias in the business. Digital will be significantly assisted in this by the Alpha programme. First, because of all the services that they can potentially sell to the users who want to migrate from VAX/VMS to Alpha/OpenVMS and second, because, due to Digital's new open business practices, there are a broader range of other service opportunities to be realized by the Digital salesforce. For instance, in the case of Microsoft NT, Digital may very well end up selling services to its existing VMS users who want to incorporate Alpha systems running Microsoft NT into their overall systems design. One can easily think of many more examples of additional services that the Alpha technology will enable Digital to realize.

Digital have changed in response to changing business conditions, without doubt. How they will perform over the next few years is more dependent on the effectivity with which they manage their own service business than on any other factor. The Alpha technology helps Digital in this area while also giving the corporation yet another world lead in a technology-based area.

The market has changed its expectations about what it wants from suppliers. No longer is it happy to accept an arrogant view that some of the larger computing suppliers have expressed in the past. The watchword of the market today is responsiveness. This in turn implies the ability to be flexible and to respond very rapidly to the changing requirements of the market. By developing the Alpha technology and supporting programme, Digital have put themselves in poll position to take the lead in this new climate. The end user, however, has some difficult lessons to learn, the hardest of which is likely to be that while the hardware costs have fallen and will continue to fall, the cost of software and services simply cannot continue the same trend. Software engineers and service providers do not come off production lines and in the last analysis the shortages of technical skills that the industry predicted five years ago is now with us. From the last demographic analysis that I saw, this situation is, even at the present levels of consumption, likely to remain acute for the next decade at least. It is therefore inevitable that Digital will continue to grow its services section and to become more involved (by acquisition or licensing rather than in-house development) of a number of applications for the key market segments.

3.4 Changing Requirements

Once upon a time, it was pretty unusual to meet people who used computers, let alone people who made or understood them, but these days they are (literally) child's play. Computers are all around us and not only do we all take them for granted, we have expectations that generally exceed the performance of all the systems that we use every day of our lives (the lift is always too slow, the video recorder difficult to use and why, oh, why did I forget to save that document before I went to lunch!...). Other areas in the world are changing too. Markets in general for all products are on the move and a general trend is emerging relating to value and specialization. Some of what we all want is related to how much value the systems we all use and need add to our lives and our businesses, which, despite our grumbles, still depend on an awful lot of very old software to keep going.

These legacy systems are an inherited problem for the world we live in and are, at the same time, a great but hidden resource for the future. All in all, then, our expectations greatly exceed what we have today. The rate of expectation growth has considerably increased recently as the first of the truly computer-literate generation starts to come through into the mainstream decision-making class of user. These and many more factors are driving the requirements of the market for information technology, and it is this fast growth in end-user expectation that has fuelled the move by Digital to increase its processor power so significantly and in such a flexible manner. In this section I want to explore some of the issues that have shaped the vision of the market for information technology in the future and which have to be matched by the capabilities of the Alpha microprocessor systems.

In addition to a view on the requirements newly generated by the incessantly rising expectation of the market, I will consider the issue of legacy systems. Legacy systems are those systems that are with us today, that support users at some level and which we have to go forward with in the future (this constitutes in excess of 80% of all software in use today). However, for technical and structural reasons this area is one that is fraught with problems, as we shall see later. Digital's Alpha systems do have something to offer in the legacy debate, both directly and indirectly and in a manner that is fairly unique in the market today. In many ways, the market for information technology is a positive feedback system. The greater the need for change, the greater the change, resulting in an even greater need for change and so on.

One reason that has been put forward for this phenomenon is that the industry itself sets the expectations of the end users far above what is realistically achievable. Another explanation is that the more one gives an end user by the way of computing power, the more they realize what they can do and want more. Personally I think that the positive feedback phenomenon is a combination of both factors. As an engineer I have often had to try to 'develop up to the sales presentation' as opposed to the specification. However, I have spent a lot of time with users who, no sooner have they installed a system, are realizing just what they could achieve 'if only we had a ...!' This section explores some of these issues in relation to Digital's Alpha technology.

3.4.1 General Trends in Markets

In the past, the volume markets in the world have mainly been for general products that meet the needs of general expectations. In recent times, however, there has been a growing desire for uniqueness and specialisation, for the product to be in some way different from all of the rest. A good example of this is the BMW automobile where, once one has chosen the basic model, the extras are all variable. The days of general products will always be with us (after all, gasoline is gasoline whatever colour the pump) but for the non-commodity items specialization, personalization and focused marketing have all become important and the trend looks set to stay for the foreseeable future. Furthermore, the identification of markets with such specialized features has become time dependent and therefore the reaction to the market opportunity has to be fast. In general, this trend towards more specialization and personalization, the move to increasingly higher degrees of focus in the definition of market sectors, has led to a concentration on the higher-value end of markets. In addition, the end result of more specialization is that the price for functionally equivalent things in the market is different, with a premium being paid by the end consumer for the more specialized item. Again I will use the BMW automobile as an example. A functionally equivalent Ford is available but people will pay up to 100% more for the 'special' characteristics of the BMW.

To realize these market opportunities, the response to the markets has to be fast, partly because the opportunity itself may be short-lived, partly because there are a whole bunch of other people out there trawling around in the same space for the same kind of opportunities. There are many example of companies that exploit such rapid and highly focused areas in the market, one example (to continue the automobile analogy) being the Japanese automobile industry. The Toyota team spent 6 months in the USA living a lifestyle that might be classed in marketspeak as 'A1, B1' (i.e. wealthy professionals) and then designed a 'classic' convertible roadster to suit a need the market did not even know it had!

The outcome of such fast-changing and highly focused markets is that they result in changes to the systems requirements of the end-user organizations to keep pace with the needs of the market, to the manufacturing methods required to fulfil these needs and to the efficiency that has to underpin such operations in order to generate the levels of return on capital that are desired by the investors.

It is likely that one aspect of the systems requirements is therefore some level of consistency through periods of great change, possibly upwards or downwards in scale but still giving the same functional base. In addition, there is an implied need for the systems that have to support our fast-changing industrial base to be able to cope with wider and more disparate forms of data. The systems in the market today are simply not able to offer the level of flexibility, longevity and sheer power to cope with the needs of industry in such a market of change and competition. Even if, using a reasonably 'Open' system like UNIX, one has the basis of an overall architecture, the underlying hardware is unlikely to cope with the long-term needs of the market for greater power and flexibility without significant disruption or expense.

Perhaps one of the most interesting trends in industry in general (and in the sector that is focusing on the more specialized markets in particular) is that there is a fast-growing need to cope with data of very differing types and from differing sources and in much larger volumes. Information about design, finish, colour, markets and almost anything one can consider is now becoming fair game for the product industries (in which I include service as well as traditional products) around the world.

Clearly the ability to manipulate such large amounts of complex information is going to be one of the fundamental requirements of systems today and in years to come, a need that will have to be catered for in a manner that allows the systems of today to grow into the systems of tomorrow and keep pace with the appetites of the end-user community in a highly competitive global market. Alpha can offer a lot in response to this need for systems. First, the power of the Alpha 64-bit architecture is more than sufficient in either the single- or multiple-processor family to enable the systems of today to grow with the data requirements of industry into the solutions of tomorrow. Second, the architecture of Digital's Alpha microprocessor is such that the changes in the operating systems that will come along in the next few years to support more of the needs of the industry (like Objects) will be simple to cope with. Third and finally, the Alpha hardware range is owned by one supplier but is available from an ever-growing range of the industry's top vendors. This makes the ultimate end user's interests better protected than in the case of a solution based on a technology that is only in the hands of one manufacturer like IBM with the RS hardware and AIX.

3.4.2 Technology Adding Value

Before we can think about adding value at any point in a business we have to look at understanding the needs of the business. While this sounds a little trite, it is important to remember that an awful lot of businesses run without anyone properly understanding where the present value sits or how the value of the business should be improved. I have spent a lot of my life, often sitting into the long reaches of the night, in the board-rooms of corporations trying to understand where a business's real value sits and how to improve upon it, and the problem is common across all businesses. The implication is clear. Until a company really understands what they want to achieve, it is impossible to see how any change should be made for the better, let alone a technology change with all its secondary implications. All that we can say with certainty is that cheaper technology is a generally good thing. This, however, ignores the real value in the power, the liberating and empowering function of modern systems whose value can and should far outweigh their cost.

It is in the area of requirements definition and planning that the systems integrator makes the plan by which they and their project will finally be judged. It is this area that Digital needs to get into in a big way and fast in order to drive the game. One major implication of the need to understand the value in a business is that it requires a significant understanding of the business itself so that there can be a real impact of value on the problems. This is experience that will not normally be possessed by the average software engineer but rather by those in the particular business application area. The translation of this knowledge into a usable specification is very time-consuming at present. However, I think that there will soon be an explosion in the number and type of tools offered on the market to assist in the definition of the requirements for a system by the end users. The output from these systems will initially be crude but specific and of a form that engineers can then work from with a lower level of direct interaction with the user than is presently the case. All this gives us is a specification of the problem that is faced by the business today. True, solving this will in itself add value, but the solutions of the next decade of systems are likely to look on these individual solution elements as components of a larger whole.

By the use of techniques such as object orientation, the solution elements themselves can be crafted into more valuable superstructures directly by the end user in many cases (and so long as the systems have the horsepower to keep up!). One excellent example of this is in Microsoft Windows NT, where the operating system allows the simple manipulation of Objects in documents across networks in a manner that is compatible with the average end user. For instance, an Object can be embedded into a document to run an application and use the end results of the application to input new data to update the spreadsheets and graphs in the same document.

By allowing the interaction of the business expertise so closely with the applications domain, to really add value and not just change the present methods of working, a system has to be able to grow with the newly found needs of the business and also to identify the areas of the business that could further benefit from changes in the system itself. To do this requires that the system be expandable, flexible and capable of generating a very wide range of 'what if?' scenarios in an acceptable timeframe for the business. Until the advent of Alpha, these were functions that were, for any substantial business, only possible with very expensive hardware. Adding real value implies that the business itself is given a capability that it did not previously have. The direct technical implication of this is that it is likely to involve the generation of substantially more data and the use of significantly more processing power than present systems. How often have you met someone, who used to have a real job for a company and now they have become the company's 'expert' on the new system and no longer have time for their other job (the one that relates to the company business)?

Systems can be complex and require armies of people to manage them. However, the power of systems should enable management functions to become far more automatic and user friendly, requiring less time and effort from people than in the past. The systems must not become ends in themselves if value is truly to be added to the organizations that purchase them. So that this may be accomplished, the systems have to have sufficient power and sophistication to be able to liberate many of the lower-order functions in the system to automatic control and management. Microsoft NT is an example of way forward and of the level of system requirement to truly exhibit the power and sophistication of the operating system.

The highly sophisticated graphical front end of Microsoft NT and the power of the underlying object technology in the operating environment mean that systems using this as a front end to the overall mass of (probably) disparate systems of today will be bringing these together as the solution of tomorrow. This in itself is only part of the solution. Without doubt, the next revolution in the computing world will be the availability of a wide range of AI and Neural Networking tools, first as decision support systems and then as more fundamental tools and components of the overall application design. All of this eats power, memory and disk, making the Alpha-based processors from Digital the only available choice in the market that can, in the spirit of true Open Systems engineering, deliver the level of power required to the end user.

3.4.3 Legacy Systems

One statistic that I read recently stated that about 87% of the software in the world was written in Cobol. Now I doubt the ability of the publication to prove this, but even if the number is wrong, the order of magnitude is likely to be correct. What we can say is that there is a lot of old software around and much of it is written in Cobol. The important issue is that most of this software is not written in C, C++, Ada or any of the other languages that have, in the past few years, been hailed as the saviours of the industry. This is not because the new languages were in any way poor, it is just that most software was being written for industry and in the Common Business Oriented Language (Cobol). This software will not be going away now or in the near future. In this section I want to look at the implications of such 'legacy' systems. I have a very enthusiastic colleague, who regards all the old and difficult to maintain software in the world as the sub-standard output of a misguided generation. His solution to the problem of legacy systems is simple, just scrap them and start over. Now like a lot of people in the software industry I understand his frustration and his desire for a better world (at least at the level of the software). It is very frustrating and difficult to try to fix someone else's old code or to try to keep it going or port it to a new system. However, the simple fact is that these legacy systems are often mission-critical to many organizations, and unless we suddenly come up with unimaginable amounts of money and time (to say nothing of the need to start clone farms for software engineers) then the legacy systems simply cannot be scrapped or rewritten from scratch. Typically, however, the end user of a legacy system wants to reduce the system hardware costs, take advantage of new technology and performance and not impinge on the smooth running of the organization. This is a potential market opportunity for Digital's new Alpha-based systems so I want to look now at the areas where Alpha systems might be of benefit in the overall area of legacy systems.

The use of Alpha in the re-engineering and maintenance of legacy systems falls into two categories:

1. The primary use of Alpha-based systems to replace present hardware
2. The secondary use of Alpha systems as a tool to help with the process of re-engineering and support.

I want first to deal with the secondary use of Alpha in the context of legacy systems. Whatever the target system one is aiming for, when an existing piece of software is to be ported across to a new base system, the engineering effort required is normally quite considerable. Whole books have been written on the subject of porting and re-engineering, but basically, if the software is written in a conventional third-generation language, then powerful tools are going to be needed to do the job of porting efficiently and effectively. Modern software tools can significantly reduce the time taken to do the work and provide much higher-quality results than the manual approach. (There are, however, no fully automated methods, nor are there likely to be.)

To do the job effectively, most approaches to re-engineering start with the source code and then generate some form of meta-level code, often one that is a higher-order representation of the design. This has several advantages. First, it is smaller than the original source code, second, it is often in a graphical form, allowing human interaction and reasoning about the design aspects of the system (these are often closely coupled to the actual implementation). Lastly, the higher-order meta-design language allows a simpler transition into the same or another source language, often with the introduction of better or more appropriate structure. A good example of such a tool is REVENGE from LBMS in London. Alpha workstations and systems are ideal platforms for the manipulation of large source code-based systems with tools like REVENGE. What is needed is lots of memory and processor power, something that the Alpha systems offer at a very low cost.

However, there are two other advantages to Alpha. First, OpenVMS has a very wide range of powerful software engineering tools available which are first-class for the engineer wishing to port or maintain legacy systems. These include source code analysers, performance analysis and tuning tools, design and code management systems and much more besides. For the user who opts for a UNIX platform as the engineering tool, then the OSF/1 version of the Alpha platform will allow the use of most of the very wide range of software tools available on UNIX. The primary use of Digital Alpha as replacement systems for existing hardware is a more complex subject. Clearly, for the user of VMS and VAX today, a move to Alpha looks to be the most sensible route forward. Users of UNIX-based systems should also look at the power of Alpha/OSF/1 systems as a replacement for their existing system strategy, though going from one UNIX to another can be quite as interesting as from a proprietary system to a UNIX system.

One way in which Alpha-based systems (running whatever operating system) can be used in conjunction with existing systems is to alleviate the strain on a present day legacy system. I have a client who is moving his database onto Alpha but leaving the application on his existing system (an IBM), thus allowing the fast, powerful and cheap Alpha machine to do a big chunk of the work rather than relying on having to try to port a complex and very proprietary application across. I have another client who is looking to use Alpha and Microsoft NT to add a lot of value to his existing HP-based systems, again without trying to port the existing application yet. The second of my examples starts to fall into the category of adding functional blocks without touching the core application itself, and this is, in my experience, the most likely method for Alpha to initially gain a foothold in the legacy domain. Like it or not, legacy systems are here to stay. Alpha is a good tool for the support and re-engineering of such old and difficult software and in many circumstances, Alpha is a good alternative, for functional block addition, removing strain or as a full replacement to existing systems. Clearly, if one has an RPG-based system running on an IBM S38, then going to Alpha and, say, UNIX is more complex (in this case it could be achieved using Software Ireland's

Unibol product). However, Alpha is going to offer a lot in the re-engineering world for many of the existing systems and it is an excellent platform for the engineer to use.

One important thing to remember is that Alpha was designed to be independent of operating system and it is true to say that environments can be generated for the Alpha platform other than VMS, OSF/1 and Microsoft Windows NT. Who knows what operating systems might find their way onto Alpha in the future?

3.4.4 The Cascade of Expectations

When computerization started to enter the workplace, people had no idea of what to expect. It is unfashionable but true to say that there are still an awful lot of places in industry that have no computerization, or so little that many of the employees never see it. So there is still a class of people who do not know what to expect. However, the information technology market is driven by those in the know (or at least with some awareness) and it is this class of user that starts to see what computers might have to offer if only they were cheaper/faster/smarter ... etc. Many people I talk to are very disillusioned with their computer systems. This implies that at some point they had their expectations and they were not met. Commonly I find that even the most mundane user has expectations or desires for the system that far outstrip what it is, or in many cases ever could be, capable of. Partly this is a problem of ignorance, partly misinformation from the media and the salespeople, but it adds up to a desire for systems that are beyond the abilities of those installed today, a sort of expected built-in obsolescence. One example of the kind of phenomenon I am referring to is the computerization of an operation that was previously mainly manual.

I once worked with a large organization that had to computerize its distribution system. Until then the system had been a purely manual exercise. After much work, consulting and development a system was developed, installed and went live. Once this had happened it caused the company concerned to review its operations and evaluate the system that had now been running for just a few months. The outcome was that they now understood so much more about their business and the stock movements, that the company needed to be restructured, the working practices thoroughly overhauled and the computer system significantly changed to take account of all of this. In my experience, this effect of positive feedback is common. Expectations, even where they do not exist in the first place, seem able to climb to altitude pretty fast. Social changes will do much to further increase the desire for more complex, faster and more functional systems. We are now seeing a generation coming up that have a much greater acceptance of the computer as a tool in society. The expectations of these young people have been set by the Apple and Nintendo, and they expect fast, graphical systems with few faults and an imaginative response to the problem of communicating with the system (including documentation). I talked to a young person recently who had just started work in an office and was using an application to look up parts in a catalogue on a PC. He said to me 'This system is junk, why are there no pictures of the parts? My game system at home is better than this!' Now we all know the technical answers to his view, but his expectation is reasonable and should be serviced. I argue that the Alpha system is the only cost-effective way to do such things, the only truly sensible route for an organization to take if it wants power, flexibility and investment protection. As the young people like the one in my example come into the decision-making roles, they will be the ones demanding so much more of systems than those in service today.

Today it is no longer the hardware that is lacking. The capabilities of Digital's Alpha range of systems is more than adequate to meet the needs of the market. It is the applications that lack the edge. The argument used to be that the power for advanced facilities was simply too expensive, but this is no longer true. I look at lots of applications in a whole host of areas, and I have to say that the lack of imagination in their design and in the use of any really advanced computing concepts is a real disgrace to the industry. (I know this is a generalization, so apologies in advance to those few who do not fit this picture.) The winners cannot be those who keep selling the same tired old applications on cheaper and cheaper hardware for lower and lower licence prices.

The winners will be the ones with the highest added value, the ones that have the best applications functions and the best use of advanced facilities including graphics, multimedia and AI. The trend of expectations is likely to increase over time and will continue to drive the industry on. Already the areas of the world that are starting to look like being in the lead with application design are the Far East, followed by Europe. These are the places where the power applications of the future will be fashioned. I use that word with care. Fashion is likely to have an influence on the design of applications just as it does on the design of automobiles, consumer electronics and office furniture.

3.4.5 Summary

This section is entitled 'Changing Requirements' because it seems to me that the market and the technology that services the needs of the market are inextricably linked in a positive feedback system. Not only is the technology changing but so is the expectation and needs of the market it serves. As I work in the industry, one of the concerns that I have is for the application developers and system integrators who view faster, more powerful technologies simply in terms of competition on the basis of price alone. When I look at the Alpha system, work on them and understand the real power and speed of these platforms, be they running OpenVMS, OSF/1 or Microsoft NT, I am inspired that finally, solutions can be engineered that can make proper use of advances like AI, Multimedia, etc. at a cost that is affordable by the great majority of companies and with adequate performance.

Digital have looked into the future, they have thought with care and inspiration about the requirements that should exist over the next 25 years and have designed Alpha as a response. It is possible that the Alpha systems that we see in 10 years' time will be running a completely new operating system, with access to mass storage devices that have capacity measured in terabytes and an interface to the end user that is written not typed and spoken as an option. These systems may have little to do with VMS or UNIX or even Microsoft Windows NT, but underpinning them will be the Alpha technology, running faster then than we can conceive now, still as adaptable, still challenging the designers of systems and software to stretch their creativity. Around the world and in all markets there are changes afoot.

The trend to more focus in the search to exploit ever-narrowing markets is driving organizations to consider the way in which they compete. Individuals want style and specialization of product or service, and the providers of these to the markets have some difficult problems to solve. So that the market for specialized, personalized or just highly focused products may be exploited, organizations need to be highly reactive. In terms of the systems that support the trend in industry for higher levels of specialization, shorter product design and development cycles, the requirement can only effectively be serviced with systems that are capable of very large levels of growth in power and performance while maintaining the underlying investment in the data, applications and skills to use them.

Too often we have seen new, faster and more powerful technologies in the market simply looked upon as a method of selling the functionally equivalent systems of yesterday at a lower price. In these situations the value added by the technology innovation is marginal. The Digital Alpha programme really brings to the market systems of a power and sophistication that are unheard of. The real added value of Digital's Alpha technology is in the area of potential. The technology is so powerful, so sophisticated and capable of such a long life, that the potential liberated by the technology is truly massive. Application developers and systems integrators really have to start looking at the ways in which the power can meaningfully be used to add real value to the organizations that buy it. In the history of the information technology business, the software sector has always lagged behind the hardware. Often the excuse was the availability of affordable power and sophistication. This is no longer an acceptable stance, and the organization that really picks up this message will be the one that starts to drive the software market out of the last age of computing and into the next. This in itself will liberate the great potential of information from the industry's largely untouched mountains of data. Part of the picture of changing requirements is the huge issue of legacy systems.

The last three decades have seen an explosion in the availability of computers in almost every area imaginable. The software written for many of the systems still perform functions that are essential to the long-term wellbeing of the organizations that use them. Clearly there is not the time, money or human resource to write replacement systems from scratch and organizations have to find ways of living with the issue of legacy systems. Digital's Alpha technology has several things to offer. At the very least,

Alpha provides an unbeatable platform for the engineering work required to maintain and port applications in the legacy category. It is reasonable now also to look at Alpha as a replacement for individual components of a system or as the seat of new functional modules in an existing system.

Clearly the position of those using VAX and VMS has to be to move over to the Alpha platform as soon as possible and then to look at their applications with the developers and try to see where Alpha can add real value by liberating the applications from the constraints of the older systems. Finally, Digital Alpha, either running OpenVMS or OSF/1, is a first-class target in any downsizing exercise. For all the reasons I explore in the chapter on the Alpha technology itself, Digital have an unbeatable platform from whichever way one looks at the issue. The expectations of the new generation of users will eventually force the applications developers to really use their creativity. Already there are operations out in the field looking to the Alpha platform as the basis of applications in a number of new arenas and with levels of sophistication that are unmatched by any of the competitors.

3.5 Competitive RISC Platforms

There are a number of competitive RISC technology platforms on the market at present. Without doubt, all of them will have to go through a significant architectural change a long time before this is necessary for the Alpha microprocessor-based systems. In this section I am going to give a brief overview of the competition for reference.

3.5.1 IBM

IBM have had a long and uneasy relationship with the UNIX operating system, and, like Digital, they were very late to the fold. In the market today, IBM have hung their hat on the RS6000 range of systems running AIX, the IBM implementation of UNIX. The AIX system is powered by IBM's RISC processor and comes in a range of server and workstation configurations. From the marketing point of view, IBM made a big mistake with the RS systems, and this was the conflict between the proprietary systems groups and the UNIX systems groups within the corporation. Finally, it seems that IBM is waking up to UNIX, but unfortunately this is too late. The RS series of systems is no longer the technically advanced hardware it was when first launched. IBM have waited too long and committed too half-heartedly to make the move into Open Systems. By comparison with the Alpha range of systems, IBM have no technical edge with the RS series systems. In just a few years from now, the RS will require a major architecture change, cutting off the old applications and requiring a huge investment by the corporation.

3.5.2 HP

Hewlett Packard were one of the first of the major corporations to make the transition to the UNIX operating system, their implementation being called HPUX. While the cut from the old proprietary operating system was significant, the corporation made this as a real change and early on. The results of this move have been great. HP now have a real market, leading the commercial sector of the UNIX market. Like IBM, and Digital, HP have a RISC processor, but unfortunately they will, like IBM soon need an architecture change.

3.5.3 Other

Of all the many manufacturers of systems, perhaps the most interesting has been DG. This company managed to provide a route for their applications to move from DGAOS (the proprietary operating system) to UNIX at the object code level. Couple this with the great performance of their hardware and one sees a corporation that (at least at one level) has done the right thing. Like all the other manufacturers, the technical edge of the Alpha microprocessor is very significant indeed by comparison with the DG hardware strategy.

3.5.4 Summary

By comparison, Digital has a significant technology lead with the Alpha chip against the opposition. It is clear that for once they have the chance to escape a position that seemed, in the early 1990s, to be set on a fast spiral downwards. Unfortunately, the decision to move over to UNIX as a strategic operating system and to adopt more aggressive marketing and sales tactics has been very late in the day. The truth is that the corporation has had to achieve and exhibit a significant philosophical change at the senior management level. Changes of technology are relatively simple to achieve and bring to the market by comparison with changes of the hearts and minds of senior management. We wait with bated breath to see if the corporation and management at Digital have what Tom Wolfe called ' The Right Stuff'.

3.6 Chapter Summary

This is a chapter on the issues that surround Digital's decision to go with the Alpha strategy. It is easy to wax lyrical about 200 MIP systems and microprocessor features. It is all too simple to look at the amazing semiconductor fabrication technology that results in 1,700,000 transistors on a little piece of silicon, but at the end of the day, this technology is a response, not to the theoretical challenges of pure science but to the real and far less esoteric issues of commerce and industry.

I have tried to give an overall view of the issues that surround the need for Digital to change not just in terms of the technology advantage but from the commercial and customer requirement perspectives as well. It should be remembered that this change did not take five minutes. The Alpha programme has been ongoing since 1988 in some form and Digital have had to look with care and precision at a fast-changing commercial marketplace in order to make the right decision in difficult circumstances. Alpha is Digital's mainstream strategic initiative, but it is not Digital's only technology initiative. As we have seen, Digital have made an excellent business in the UNIX world on a hardware platform (the 5000 series)-based on the third-party MIPS RISC offering. Likewise, Digital have a sound Intel strategy that now goes up to the massively parallel systems.

The end result of these moves is to cover the eventualities of systems markets which predicate either MIPS or Intel as the processor base. In addition, the MIPS systems bought time while the Alpha systems were in the development phase. The business climate of today is significantly different to that of five or so years ago. The changed climate has been fired up now by the very significant moves to the Open Systems by the market. Unfortunately, this has generally manifested itself in terms of plunging systems prices rather than of higher functionality or utility in the applications products themselves. This provides a challenge for the applications vendors, the challenge of utilization and value. This I have argued is the true power of the Alpha technology. The issues raised in this chapter, those of technical, commercial and end user factors, affect not just system developers like Digital but the applications developers, system integrators and end users themselves.

I hope that having read this chapter, the main issues in the business will be a little clearer and the nature of Alpha together with its place in the overall information technology business will be apparent. The proof of success will be the uptake of Alpha in the market and the retention of the VAX and VMS userbase by Digital. To date, we are in the very early days of the systems, but it is interesting to see that Digital are doing very well and that Alpha is indeed taking off fast and to great acclaim.

3.6.1 Main Chapter Themes and Issues

The chapter's three main themes have been:

- Technology
- Commercial issues
- End-user requirements

These are the central issues facing the information technology business today. The central theme, that of a response to the changes in the industry, is at the heart of the whole Alpha programme. Alpha is not simply a technology jump, it is an overall programme that addresses the issues central to the industry and which will be a move for radical change within the entire Digital organization, from the business practices to the pricing strategy. Alpha raises a central question, that of the potential value that offerings add to the end users. Finally, the potential to use the real power of software technology in its advanced form with such technologies as neural networks, AI and multimedia is provided by Alpha.

These technologies can and now should be used as fundamental components of application software and Alpha is in the winning position. Digital's biggest challenge is their ability to form and manage appropriate third-party relationships so that the Alpha technology really achieves the market penetration for which it has been designed.

3.6.2 Questions Raised by this Chapter

The most fundamental questions raised in this chapter are 'Have Digital done the right, thing, is Alpha the optimum response?' The final answers to these questions will be the performance of the Alpha programme in the market over the next few years. I hope, however, that having now gained an understanding of the reasons Digital had to change their ongoing technical strategy, readers will be in a better position to judge for themselves the accuracy of Digital's response to the three key areas of challenge, namely: technology, commercial and user requirements.

I think that it is fair to say that, given the constraints of having an extant user base of some 10 million and the goal of wanting both to own a technology and to have it accepted as the leader in the field, then Digital have a winner in the Alpha programme. One very significant factor for Digital is their ability to get the third-party relationships off the ground and make them successful. This is a very different form of business for them and one that while potentially lucrative also exposes them to a certain degree of risk. To date, the roll call of signed-up partners makes impressive reading: Cray Research, Kubota Pacific and Olivetti, for starters.

The next big deals will most likely be in the desktop arena and third-party semiconductor manufacturers. Mitsubishi are already signed up to manufacture the Alpha technology microprocessors, this is just the first of a number. Another question raised in this chapter is that of the protection of the VMS userbase. I feel that this is assured because of the nature of Alpha, thought there are cases of VMS users who will not be able to upgrade to Alpha in native mode since their layered products may not be moved over to the Alpha platform by Digital. Like IBM, Digital's large base of proprietary users is a very valuable asset. Like the IBM proprietary users, most of the Digital VMS users would find it difficult or uneconomic to move their software over to other systems. However, Digital have been very clever. By developing Alpha, they have not only been able to offer most of their users a way forward into the future with their existing VMS-based systems, they have also done this using a common platform for all the operating systems that they (or, for that matter, their partners) may wish to support. IBM, on the other hand, are in the position of having a number of proprietary systems, with users locked in but with no route forward on more general hardware.

The inevitable outcome of this is the gradual move away by the IBM base to other, more open solutions, but this may well be a move away from IBM in the long run. It is interesting to see that IBM's move into the UNIX arena with the RS6000 series machines running AIX seemed to be one of constant internal conflict with the proprietary systems areas of the IBM empire. The end result of all this is that instead of the mainframe and proprietary mid-range market for IBM systems being under threat from its own offerings, the threat now comes from outside. All this goes to illustrate just how smart the commercial judgement at Digital was in conceiving the Alpha programme. Ironically, Alpha will be one of the systems that will threaten the IBM mainframe and proprietary mid-range systems markets. The question that remains is whether IBM will take on Alpha-based technologies themselves. Personally, I doubt it, but given the massive corporate losses suffered by IBM in 1992-1993, then anything , at least in theory, is possible!

3.6.3 Conclusions of this Chapter

The world of information technology is a fast-changing one, though recently the changes have been particularly significant. The three driving factors in the recent changes to the scope, nature and content of the information technology business have been: technology, commercial factors and end user requirements.

In all these areas the changes have been enormous, interrelated and far-reaching. The whole industry has been thrown into turmoil because of these changes and each player has had to formulate their own response to the threats and opportunities that the changes have created. Digital have, in the light of the arguments put forward in this chapter, made the right technical choice to meet the turbulent changes of the next few years by opting to go with the Alpha programme, a well-focused technical response to the full range of issues that we can see as vital to the information technology industry at present and for the foreseeable future. Briefly these technical issues can be summarized in the following table:

Table 3.1 Technical issues in the market to which Digital had to respond.

ISSUE	IMPACT	DOES ALPHA RESPOND?
Market move to RISC	Vax is SISC-based	Yes, Alpha is RISC-based
Market move Open Systems	VAX is not an Open Architecture	Alpha is a really Open Architecture
Need much higher performance	VAX is close to its limits	Alpha starts at the top of market and has 1000-fold potential growth
Need long life span for systems	VAX is near the end of its life	Alpha was designed with longevity in mind
Legacy systems are a problem	VAX is not Open and is too slow	Alpha has the power and is very Open

From the commercial angle, there are also some very significant changes taking place, these are causing fundamental restructuring at all levels, in all countries and in all areas of the information technology business.

To respond to this set of problems, Digital have had to define and construct the Alpha programme, the whole set of sales, marketing and service functions that will support the changed business Digital now find themselves in and which will support the Alpha technology as it comes on line into the market.

The approach to the main commercial issues I have briefly summarized in the following table:

Table 3.2 Commercial issues in the market to which Digital have had to respond

ISSUE	IMPACT	DOES ALPHA RESPOND?
Falling hardware prices	Reduced revenues for DEC	Yes, by higher valued systems and increased market share
Services is the growth area	DEC must sell more of these	Yes, more services of higher value with Alpha to userbase and new customers
Userbase is under threat	10 million VMS users at risk	Yes, offers the best technical and commercial option
Systems value is falling with hardware	Reduced revenues for DEC and partners	Yes, Alpha allows higher value systems and services
Competition is now very fierce	VAX is being hit by fast RISC	Yes, joint ventures with Olivetti and the like is an aggressive response
Markets becoming specialized	Technology has to be more flexible	Alpha is the most flexible of all RISC systems

One might reasonably expand the list of commercial problems facing the information technology business to a long and complex list but these main issues are the major driving factors that have led to the huge changes taking place at the moment. The Alpha programme from Digital does address these issues, and does so well. The risks come from the need for Digital to successfully form and manage more third-party relationships, and from the ongoing competition for the Open Systems area of the market. Competition is stiff from the lighter-weight competitors whose only weapon in the market battle is price. In the commercial market, the way Digital does business, and the partners it does business with, will change and continue to strengthen its overall business. In itself this will move Digital towards a higher focus on services. Finally, the big changes in the market are also being driven by the altered requirements and expectations of the end-user communities. They are the people who ultimately have to justify the need for new technologies and the associated spend that goes with them. The expectation cycle is one of positive feedback as a mechanism. One in which essentially the more the end user gets, the more they want. In addition to this, the systems in the market today need to have much more functional value to the end-user organizations that use them. One aspect of this is the use of technologies in the software, hardware and communications areas, that provide very advanced facilities to the end user. In the following table I have set out the main issues related to the altered expectations and requirements of the market and the Alpha response to them as I see them.

Table 3.3 Changed requirements of the market to which Digital must respond.

ISSUE	IMPACT	DOES ALPHA RESPOND?
Expectations rising fast	VAX technology outlived	Capabilities provide power at a price better than competition
Need for higher added value	Limited by VAX technology	Alpha technology solves this
Broader data and application integration	Limited by VAX technology/price	Alpha technology solves this at a realistic price

The constantly rising expectations of the market are a real problem and also an opportunity to the industry. Digital's challenge now is to drive the applications developers and the systems integrators to produce solutions of higher value instead of just continuing to sell the same, tired old software on cheaper systems. This is not what the end users want. They clearly want higher value to be added to their applications and systems to get more for their own businesses.

Finally, one last point about Digital and the challenge of the changing times we live in. Digital has cut its cost base significantly in the past few years. I am of the opinion that the cost cutting has not yet gone far enough. Digital has to look closely at what its strengths are and cut out some of the costs in non-productive areas. I know that if they increase margin and turnover the ratio will improve in any case. I think, however, that the leaner, meaner philosophy is a sound lesson that Digital had to learn and one which still needs to be advocated at the most senior levels in a public but balanced way. As part of this, I think that Digital ought to look closely at the way they employ people, reward them and what the value systems are of their people in key areas of the business. This might (in my opinion, would) lead to some interesting and very different structures and systems in the business, ones that share the risks more evenly and link reward to success more closely. Digital have embarked on the Alpha road. I hope that this chapter has shown just what the reasons are for having to change. IBM seem to have taken a long time and have not done a very successful job to date. Compared to

Digital they are in a much weaker situation. Digital's Alpha programme will continue to match the capabilities of the organization to the opportunities in the market. In all senses of the phrase, Alpha is, was and will be the right choice for Digital.

3.6.4 Reader Checklist

The following simple checklist is intended to help the reader to think about the main issues in the chapter and how they affect them.

1 End Users' Technology Checklist

First, *existing VAX users*. You should look carefully at exactly what you are using on the system and specifically at the third-party and Digital layered products being used. With Digital you then need to find out what the replacement systems options are (for some VAX systems, a board swap gives you the Alpha system!). With the applications suppliers you need to look at the timescales involved in the provision of native Alpha applications. It is very likely that the move will be highly cost-effective. In the next phase you need to look at what Alpha can then do for you (see later). Alpha is a real protection for your systems for the long term.

Second, *5000 series MIPS-based users*. Again, the move to Alpha depends on the applications you are using, but the move would be a smart one in performance terms alone. The future potential of the systems is the real reason to move (see later).

Third, *those with an Open Systems strategy*. I will assume that these are non-Digital users at present, looking at Alpha as a potential component of their systems overall. To this group I must say, move to Alpha now. I cannot stress too strongly that this technology is simply the fastest, most open technology around with the highest potential for the future. However, the move to the hardware will depend very much on the operating system that you are using. If this is UNIX System V.4MK, the move will have to wait for the port. I have strong reasons to believe that this is not far away, being done by a third party for release in late 1994. I would strongly recommend a long look at OpenVMS, this really is Open. I know that in a mixed environment there would be issues about operating system skills, but nevertheless, the power of VMS, coupled with the very wide range of supported standards, make it a serious contender for any heavyweight systems design exercise in my experience.

Commercial checklist First, if you are looking at systems as commodity items, think on a little. Alpha is power, future security and standardization. Furthermore, it is worth looking at the ever-growing number of third parties signing up to use the technology as their system base. Alpha could now be a good move, but it will depend on applications and operating systems.

Second, if you are in an industry that is fast changing, one in which you need to respond very fast to exploit short-lived and highly specialized markets, then I think

Alpha may have a lot to offer now and certainly in the long term. For the CAD-based systems in the market, for the design and analysis phase of product development, then Alpha potentially could do a very great deal to add power to your organization, even without the higher-value applications I am keen to promote. In the long run, however, the potential for data manipulation and integration across a wide range of systems and networks will allow you to play in a more global market and in a more professional and effective manner.

Third, expect a new approach from Digital. If you do not see it, then start shouting. It is clear from this chapter that you should expect to see a wider range of services from Digital and also a change in their style and approach to the end user. In terms of assisting you to move to Alpha, in selling in a more inventive and entrepreneurial way to you and in being more open to the need of the customers. In their defence, it is impossible to achieve this unless they receive customer feedback. Set your expectations high and keep putting them up is my advice.

Fourth, do not be unrealistic about prices. This is really important especially in relation to the cost of services and software. The fact of the matter is that these two items cannot be treated in the same way as hardware, the economics do not match up. The important thing to do is to look at the real added value that comes from a system and think about the price accordingly. Cheapest does not mean best value. This is obvious but is often forgotten by buyers in the information technology market.

Requirements Checklist First, look closely at your business and at your systems and get a clear picture of the real requirements you have. This is especially important if you are in the process of formulating a new technical strategy for the company, for instance when downsizing or moving from a proprietary system to Open systems. In coming to the decision about the future, make certain that you understand the real growth requirements of the system that you will be using and also of the potential that the applications and software you use could ultimately offer. I think that in the light of the potential and of the probable growth, then Alpha might look a good option for all the reasons I have given earlier.

Second, talk to Digital and to your systems integrators and the application developers about what might ultimately be achieved with the systems in use by your organization, given the use of Alpha levels of power, performance, openness and sophistication.

Third, if you use VMS or Ultrix at present take a look at Microsoft NT and think carefully about adding an Alpha-based server running Microsoft NT to add a higher level of usable front-end functionality to your systems. The costs would not be high in most cases and the real improvement in usability of many systems by such a move is more than justified.

2 Application Developers' Technology Checklist

First of all, if you are a developer of applications with a focus on VMS today, then it will be relatively straightforward for you to go to the Alpha platform in most cases (see later in the book on porting). However, you need to look at the additional functionality and power that you could support and the ways this could be supported on Alpha systems, for instance the use of other front ends to applications.

Second, if you develop for general Open systems platforms at the moment, then I think it would be wise to move fast and get your applications over onto the Digital Alpha platform. Already the sales of this system are increasing fast and the third-party licensing agreements mean that the range of systems will increase over time. In addition, remember that Digital are aiming for a large slice of the microprocessor market. If they only get 20% of what they aim for, this would be a massive market and they are playing in it with the best technology.

Third, get the jump on your rivals by using the Alpha power to add functions, features and other components to provide much higher levels of added value from the systems, for instance by the addition of other media types such as document image processing in office automation systems, AI in systems that offer decision support or the integration of highly interactive front ends (such as pen-based input) for systems. Remember, Alpha makes possible at a PC price today what would have required a mid-range system yesterday, so use the power, not the price, to win.

Commercial Checklist In the section on the commercial aspects of the reasons to change in this chapter, I looked at the general trends for industry to exploit narrowly defined market sectors and how this had to be achieved rapidly and innovatively. This is a real opportunity for the applications of tomorrow, the ability to assist the end user in the exploitation of such markets and the opportunity to do this by allowing the broadest integration of data and application components in a highly interactive way. You may find that certain clients even want the opportunity to rent applications with great degrees of specialization while they exploit certain features for short-lived market opportunities. Think about this and how Alpha's power, flexibility and openness make this achievable.

Second, like Digital, you will have found that the margins on hardware have had a real effect on your business, and expectations of applications prices and service costs have tended to follow the move down in the hardware price. You have to compete on value and not on price to make a good business from your skills. That means the addition of good functionality and features. However, you will also be moving, as most of the industry is, towards the provision of services as a larger component of your business portfolio. In order to achieve reasonable returns quickly in this area there is a real opportunity for you, if you are working with Digital VAX VMS or 5000 and ULTRIX today, for the assistance in the upgrade of clients to the Alpha platforms themselves. In many cases there will be some technology changes, and there may well be a chance to look at putting the new Alpha platforms to more valued use. In all of these areas the service opportunities are large.

Last, getting the best return on your development investment is what Open Systems has meant to most application developers, Alpha is a good choice of platform for one big reason, that today it is more open than any other hardware platform around and is likely to stay that way for a long time.

Requirements Checklist Expectations, as I have said often in this chapter, continually exceed the abilities of the systems. Now is the chance to do something about this. It is worth addressing since to exceed the expectations of the users for once would significantly improve the chances of retaining that customer in the long term.

Legacy systems are ripe for attack, either indirectly using Alpha-based platforms as tools to do the re-engineering or directly by using these platforms to replace large, outdated systems.

Finally, your own development requirements are worth a look. If today you are developing on a VAX platform or even a 5000 system, then consider a move to Alpha, probably in terms of workstations and servers. The productivity gains from this level of power, especially when used in conjunction with the VAXset tools, make a great deal of sense both technically and economically.

Further Reading

L. Berry, V. Zeithaml and A. Parasuraman, 'Five imperatives for improving service quality', *Sloan Management Review*, 1990.

B. Boehm, *Software Engineering Economics,* Prentice Hall: Englewood Cliffs, NJ, 1981.

I can recommend the following document to those planning an architecture who want to see a major corporation's view of how to keep control in these changing times:

Technical Requirements of Multi-vendor Integration Architecture, TR55001, Technology Research Department, NTT, Tokyo.

CHAPTER 4

What is Alpha?

4.1 Introduction

What is Alpha? As this chapter will show, Digital's Alpha programme is far more than just a remarkably fast microprocessor, it is a complete programme of technology, sales, marketing and service designed to carry Digital through well into the next century. The barriers to entry into the market for any organization wishing to produce a new range of computer system are high and getting higher if they wish, as part of this process to produce a competitive microprocessor. Budget spend in this arena is measured in billions of dollars and the scale of facility required to produce such hardware is grand. However, innovation in the hardware arena is not enough by itself, there has to be a fully supporting programme of sales, marketing and services to make the technology happen in the real world. As this chapter will show, the commitment Digital has put into all areas of the Alpha project to date is paying off to the benefit of the customers and of Digital itself.

The dangers of failing in the goal to move forward with the Alpha programme are significant. If Digital do not succeed in making Alpha as competitive as the VAX has been, then I fear that Digital will be in serious commercial trouble and open to any bidder that has the funds. On the other hand, I think Digital will succeed with Alpha, the signs are already good and the positioning of Alpha as a best of breed technology is certain. I hope that this chapter will explain the scope, nature and power that is Alpha.

4.1.1 Structure of the Chapter

This chapter begins with an overview of the Alpha technology programme including a section on the Alpha 21064 microprocessor's main functions and features. 'Making the Machine' covers the area of the actual development and production of the Alpha microprocessor and the next section considers the comparative price performance issues of Alpha and its rivals. Clearly Digital are in the game for the long term, and as a consequence Digital have had to build in longevity as a fundamental component of the design project.

As I have already mentioned, the Alpha programme is a complete project in the Digital organization which is very much more than just a world-beating technology. Section 4.3 covers the other main aspects of Digital's Alpha programme. OpenVMS, Digital's response to the basic propositions of the Open Systems engineering school, is just one of the three initial operating systems that will be provided on the early Digital Alpha platforms. The other two, OSF/1 and Microsoft NT, are likely to be significant in the longer term for Digital. The issue of operating systems is one component of the advanced Alpha microprocessor architecture which has been developed to allow the introduction of almost any operating system onto the chip by the use of Privileged Access Library (PAL) software, among other features.

By escaping the tie to any particular operating system, Digital have been able both to ensure the longevity of the hardware in an uncertain market and to maximize the potential market for the system. No system can be thought of as complete without the availability of layered products, and in this Digital have a long list of such products upon which the overall design and implementation of actual systems depends. Section 4.3.2 looks at the list of main layered products from Digital and takes a view on the availability (or not) of these products on the new Alpha platform (either OpenVMS or OSF/1). Naturally, no overall programme for the introduction of such a major new product range coming to market can be achieved without a sufficiently focused and appropriately managed sales and marketing campaign. I have said elsewhere in this book that the weakest component of the Digital organization has been seen in the past as sales and marketing. In the Alpha release Digital have, as you will see, taken this to heart and got things right. Like all other corporations in the market, Digital have had to ensure that there are sufficiently good, broad and competitive services to support the product and sales operations in the marketplace.

Section 4.3.4 gives an overview of the service philosophy behind the Alpha programme and draws attention to the area of possible risk in its early days. Alpha, like VAX before it, is the basis of a large and fast-growing range of systems, and these are systems that will stretch from the palm-top to the mainframe class system using from one to thousands of Alpha microprocessors as raw power.

I have included an illustrative section on the introductory range of systems from Digital, which covers the range from the PC level through the workgroup servers to the datacentre. I have also included a section, illustratively entitled '???', on possible future developments for Alpha systems. Digital are, however, not the sole users of the Alpha systems and in Section 4.5 I have taken a look at the offerings from some of the major third-party users of this incredible 64-bit microprocessor technology. I have included sections on Cray Research, the manufacturers of the world's most powerful supercomputers, on Kubota Pacific, who make some of the most powerful workstations in the world, on Olivetti and on the other users of the Alpha chip.

4.1.2 Issues Covered in this Chapter

In this chapter I have described the Alpha project itself in some detail for the reader to view. Clearly the central issue is that of the power and flexibility of the technology itself. Digital had as its central themes for the project the following issues:

- Longevity
- Extensibility
- Operating system independence
- Performance
- Openness

In one way or another these are also the main themes of this chapter. In a book like this, one that sets out to put the technology into the context of the wider commercial environment, it is important to try to interweave the threads of the technology and commercial arguments in such a way as to allow the easy translation of the terms and the concerns of both of the camps. This is the skill I attempt to bring to bear on the topic. I hope that by the end of the chapter the reader will be better able to understand the technology that is intended to drive the Digital Equipment Corporation forward and to have a clear understanding of the commercial factors, functions and processors that are required to support this technology and which help or threaten the future of the Alpha programme.

4.1.3 Questions Raised in the Previous Chapter

In the previous chapter the key questions that were raised were concerned with the reasons for Digital changing over from its present product range to the new, expensive and, to some extent, risky Alpha programme. In essence, one of these questions was 'How do you follow an act like VAX?' This is the key question that I hope I have addressed in this chapter, I have endeavoured to allow the reader of this book to understand just how, at all levels, Digital are going to top the VAX act and indeed how, in many ways, Alpha, far from threatening the VAX community, is designed, from the outset, to provide a secure and fundamentally advanced future. Another key question raised in the previous chapter was 'How could Digital counter the threats to its base from the hot-box UNIX market?' This question, while not explicitly addressed in this chapter, is investigated in terms of the technology options available for the user of Alpha-based systems either from Digital or from one of its licensed technology users. Perhaps the answer implied in this chapter to that particular question is, at least in part Napoleon's adage 'The best defence is attack'. Alpha is Digital's attack on the threats of the hot-box vendors. Either Alpha will win in competition with these systems or it will be the basis of the systems themselves (the win/win philosophy!).

4.1.4 Where this Chapter is Relevant

Whoever you are and whatever your interest in the Alpha programme, this chapter is central to your understanding of the Alpha project. If you have any technical interest, then the section on the Alpha technology goes into reasonable depth. If you have just a passing interest in the technology, there may be places where you may get a little lost. This chapter also contains sections on the overall programme of sales, marketing and services that will be supporting the technology in the commercial arena. Perhaps to the person who wants to get some more general idea of whether Alpha is of interest to them or not, then this is the section that will most likely answer that question in part by giving a basic overview of the technology and supporting functions and also by raising a number of other issues in relation to overall technical and commercial strategy. It should also be noted that Section 4.2, an overview of the Alpha technology itself, is rather technical. This is unavoidable but should be skipped by the non-technical reader.

4.1.5 Questions to be Answered

What is Alpha? This is the central theme of the chapter, and some other key questions that are addressed are:

- What is the Alpha technology, what does it consist of and how does it work?
- How will the technology be delivered and bundled by Digital and others?
- What are the products themselves?
- How many applications are being provided for the Alpha systems?
- What types of applications are going to be available on the Alpha platforms?

4.2 Alpha Technology Overview

In this section I will be dealing with the Alpha hardware technology itself, the basis for the whole of the Alpha programme and the future of the Digital Equipment Corporation.

4.2.1 The Alpha Processor

The Alpha processor range is based on RISC technology (see earlier) and as such is a general-purpose engine which Digital have been keen to exploit widely. It is considered by Digital, and by many others, to be a response to the challenges in computing that will last into the next century and is capable, over its planned 25-year life, of giving a massive thousandfold increase in performance. The architecture of the VAX microprocessor and the Alpha microprocessor are significantly different in two major respects. First, Alpha microprocessor is a RISC processor (see earlier) as opposed to the VAX microprocessor, which is a CISC architecture. The VAX supports a virtual address size of 32-bits, a physical address size of up to 32-bits, a memory page size of 512 bytes, instruction lengths from 1 to 51 bytes, general registers are 16x32-bit, it has 21 addressing modes, uses a general instruction set and supports integer, floating, bit field, queue, character string and decimal string data types.

The Alpha microprocessor, on the other hand, supports a virtual address size of 64-bits, a physical address size of up to 48-bits, a memory page size of between 8 and 64 KByte, general registers are 64x64-bit, instruction lengths 4 bytes, it has three addressing modes, uses a load-store instruction set and supports integer and floating data types only.

Second, the VAX has a 32-bit architecture, but the Alpha processor uses a true 64-bit architecture. The implication of this is that the virtual memory addressable directly on an Alpha system is massively increased to a 64-bit range of bytes in the system virtual memory. In addition, the physical memory address range supported is 48-bits. The need for such large amounts of directly addressable memory exists in advanced applications in such fields as mechanical and electronic design, biomedical applications and very large databases.

The Alpha is a true 64-bit, load/store RISC architecture microprocessor that has been designed to have excellent performance over a long service life, be extendable and operating system independent and capable of allowing the existing VAX and MIPS customers in the Digital base to upgrade with ease to the new systems.

The three most important things in the design of the microprocessor that affect the end performance are the clock rate, multiple instruction capability and the need for architecting the microprocessor into multiple processor systems. This has been achieved without any bias towards a particular operating system (not even VMS) and without any dependence or bias towards particular programming languages. The true 64-bit nature of the Alpha microprocessor means that all registers are 64-bits in length and all operations are performed between registers, unlike some 32-bit architectures on the market later upgrading to 64-bit implementations. Alpha can address approximately 4 billion times as much addressable memory space as existing microprocessors. The Alpha architecture will, during its lifespan, be implemented in different forms and for different purposes, all targeted towards very high performance.

The simple instruction set in which all instructions are 32-bit and in which all operations are loads or stores relies on registers for all data manipulation, hence great speed. With the first implementation of the Alpha architecture, there is the facility to issue two instructions per CPU cycle. This is achieved partly by pipelining multiple instances of the same operation, and mainly by the way instructions interact, by one writing a register or to a memory address and another reading from the same location. In principle, future implementations may issue more than two instructions per cycle with further performance benefits. The method of byte manipulation used in the Alpha architecture has several advantages.

First, single byte store instructions are not supported, making it simpler to pipeline multiple byte operations, byte shift-and-mask logic does not have to be incorporated into cache and memory implementations, sequencer logic does not have to do read-modify-write on memory locations, there is often a requirement to build high performance error correcting write-back cache when implementing high-speed RISC systems and the Alpha method of byte manipulation optimizes this. These benefits are achieved entirely by byte shifting and masking using the microprocessor's normal 64-bit registers and register-to-register instructions. Furthermore, Alpha uses an innovative method of approach to arithmetic traps (like underflow and overflow) by allowing the software developer to specify the precision of these arithmetic traps by making the Alpha architecture for arithmetic traps imprecise. For instance, an arithmetic trap can be triggered and the result delivered some number of instructions later. In addition, the facility exists for the results of traps from many different instructions to be reported simultaneously.

Since the Alpha microprocessor, or more correctly the 21064 microprocessor (I was told that the 21 stands for 21st century and the 64 for 64-bit), is designed to be operating system independent, there have to be features which allow the different implementations of the architecture to support a wide range of present and future operating systems. One of these features is the Privileged Access Library. The Privilege Access Library is a collection of software subroutines which are defined for a particular instance of an operating system on a defined Alpha implementation.

The issues of memory management, exceptions, interrupts and context switching are all handled by these subroutines at a primitive level for the particular operating system and Alpha implementation set. For instance, in the case of OSF/1, Digital's chosen variant of UNIX for the Alpha AXP systems, the Privilege Access Library code emulates many of the RISC/MIPS/ULTRIX features. In the case of OpenVMS, the particular Privileged Access Library code libraries used mirror many of the features one would find on a VAX. This is achieved with only slightly more hardware than a conventional RISC processor, just enough to support the PAL mode bit and 4 extra protection bits in each translation buffer entry.

Clearly, the task of providing a VMS version and of porting applications across to the Alpha AXP range will be generally simple. The implication of the PAL approach is that there can be a large number of different libraries developed for a range of different purposes, for instance real-time systems for process control. I said earlier that there had to be support in the Alpha architecture for multiple processors, and this is clearly a requirement of a number of application domains. The Alpha architecture supports multiprocessor shared memory by letting an implementation re-order any sequence of reads and writes from another processor. This therefore facilitates such features as pipelined writes, multibank caches, write merging, etc. In addition, memory barrier instructions can be included in a program where the integrity of explicit access ordering must not be breached.

The interlocking defined in the Alpha architecture has to be able to scale up to very highly parallel systems. This is achieved by using a standard RISC *load_locked*, *modify*, *store_conditional* method. As long as this sequence runs without interruption the conditional store will succeed. However, if this sequence is interrupted the store will fail but the program will have to backwards branch and retry the same sequence at some point. Of course, the Alpha architecture has to consider the developer and in this respect it succeeds, being a very nice system for the compilation of a wide range of programming languages. Two examples of this are that Alpha contains no global integer overflow enable bit, and as this would have to be changed at the subroutine call from, say, a FORTRAN program to a C program, compilation of large heterogeneous programs is made simple. Furthermore, there is no subroutine call instruction to move a register window by a set amount, making Alpha a suitable platform for the implementation of compilers for languages with few or many parameters.

4.2.2 Making the Machine

Like its predecessor the VAX, the DECchip 21064 Alpha microprocessor is manufactured in-house by Digital using methods that in themselves push back the boundaries of semiconductor design and manufacture. It has taken several years for the development programme to come to fruition and now, in 1993, real volume shipments of the DECchip 21064 Alpha microprocessors are a proven fact of life for Digital. Simple facts about the Alpha microprocessor make great reading. I think as I write this book that there is probably a whole book called *Interesting and Amazing Facts about Alpha to Stun Your Friends with,* that could be written. First, the Alpha microprocessor is only a quarter of an inch square (7 mm in metric) and contains almost 2 million transistors. The present Alpha chips run at an astounding 400 million instructions per second, and in the time it takes light to cross a room, the Alpha chip can launch two instructions. The Alpha chip has a peak performance equivalent to that of a Cray-1 supercomputer. By the year 2000 Digital are predicting that 80% of the businesses in Europe will be using technology-based on Alpha. The Alpha multiple instruction, pipelined 64-bit microprocessor is manufactured using CMOS (Complementary Metal Oxide Semiconductor) technology and contains around 1.7 million transistors. The minimum feature size is 0.75 microns, the transistor channel length is just 0.5 microns and the microprocessor is powered at 3.3 volts and consumes 30 watts of power. The clock rate for the present implementations can go up to 200 MHz delivering 400 MIPs. The Alpha chip includes the complete CPU, full integer and floating point units. The chip includes two high-speed memory caches: an 8 KByte instruction cache providing two full 32-bit instructions per clock cycle to the instruction despatch unit and an 8 KByte data cache that can provide a 64-bit data access during each cycle. This gives an astounding cache bandwidth of 3.2 gigabytes per second. Digital's CMOS technology seems to run faster than that of any other manufacturer, including Intel, Motorola, IBM, TI, Cypress, NEC and Toshiba. CMOS-4 is Digital's fourth generation of CMOS technology microprocessor. Earlier generations of CMOS microprocessor from Digital have delivered the world's fastest CISC performance (for example, the VAX 6500 with

CMOS-3 microprocessors running at 62.5 MHz in 1990). CMOS-4 technology is used in the VAX 6600 running at 83 MHz, the same technology used to build the Alpha 21064 microprocessor.

Following many years of research, the Alpha processor architecture from Digital has been the result of a great team effort. Now being produced both in the United States of America and in South Queensferry, Scotland, the microprocessor has pushed back the boundaries of semiconductor production technology all over the world. Digital are reputed to have spent well over $2 billion in the development to date and one sees little sign of any abate in the development spend. A truly international effort, the production of the Alpha 21064 microprocessor within Digital marks some of the cultural changes that I spoke of earlier. The Alpha microprocessor technology will, however, also be used in other vendors' hardware systems and there is likely to be an announcement soon on the licensing of Alpha technology to other manufacturers of microprocessors.

4.2.3 Price and Performance

Price performance is a real, key issue for the developers of the Alpha systems. It is in the field of advanced applications that the Alpha systems will initially win. It is too early to report on real installations using Alpha technology, but Table 4.1 shows some interesting figures.

Table 4.1 Comparative performance and competitive positioning of the Digital Alpha 21064A microprocessor.

Vendor	Device	Clock (MHz)	Number of chips	Peak (MIPS)	Peak (MFLOPS)	Base Design Architecture (bits)
DEC	21064A	200	1	400	200	64
MIPS	R4000	100	1	100	50	64
Sun/TI	Viking	50	1	150	50	32
IBM	RIOS	50	7 to 9	200	100	32
HP	PA-4	66	2	132	132	32
Intel	i860XP	50	1	150	100	32
Motorola	88110	50	1	150	100	32

In Figures 4.1 and 4.2, the positioning of the VAX and the Alpha architectures relative to the industry competitive microprocessors can be clearly seen.

In Figure, 4.1 it is clear that since 1988, the Digital VAX processors have established a growing lead against the industry standard CISC microprocessors such as Motorola and Intel. Turning now to Figure 4.2, the positioning of the Alpha RISC microprocessor versus the industry best-performing competitors can be seen clearly. The Digital Alpha microprocessor, even at prototype stage, was ahead of the game. At the release point its lead, in pure performance terms, is both impressive and likely to grow considerably over the next few years. Alpha is likely to be the fastest microprocessor around for a very long time to come.

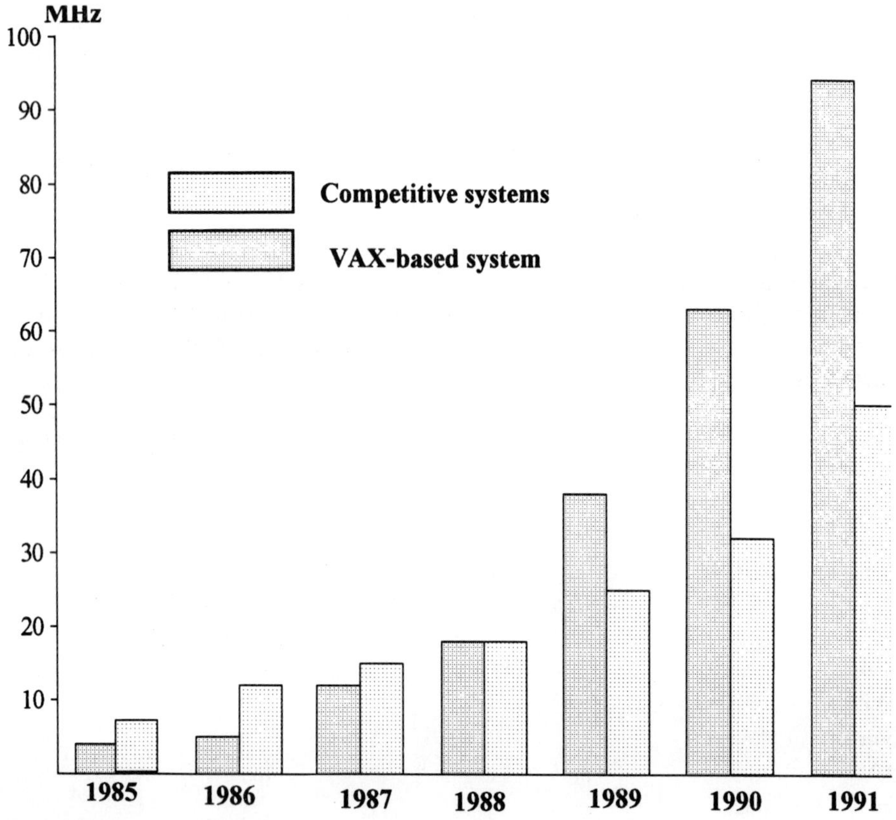

Figure 4.1

4.2.4 Lifespan

The Alpha microprocessor had longevity as one of its earliest design goals. From a technical point of view this amounts to the architecture being able to cope with the changes to the operating systems and architectures of systems developed in the next 25 years. From another technical point of view, the system has to be able to cope with the performance requirements of applications that will be making increasing use of a wider range of more detailed and disparate information such as those required by multimedia applications over this period.

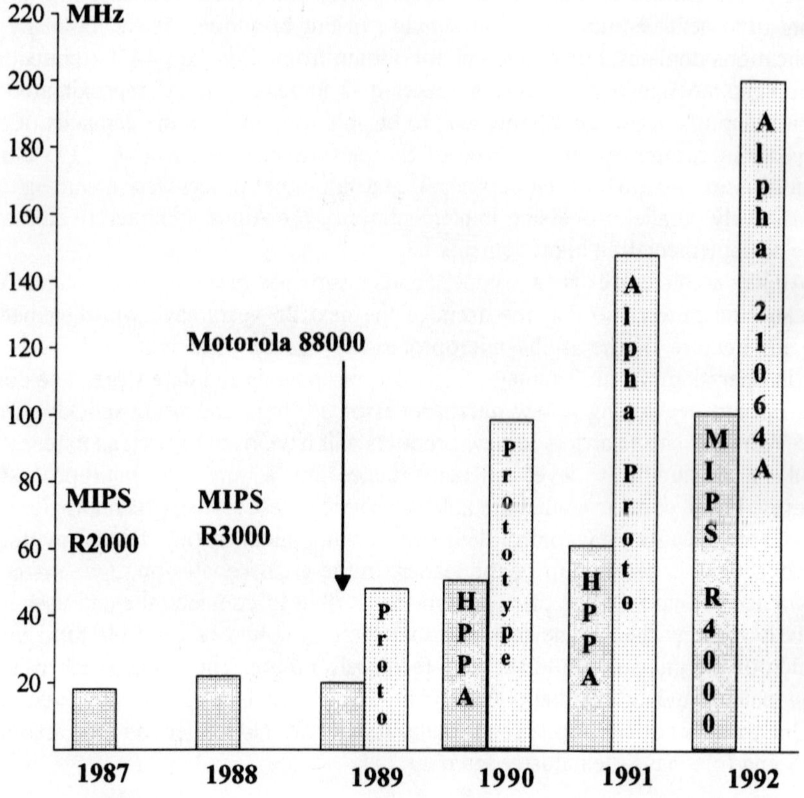

Figure 4.2

The extensibility of the Alpha architecture, its capacity to improve on already leading performance by a thousandfold, means that the architecture can rightly be seen as one offering the power for the next 25 years. In addition, the Alpha architecture is crafted in a manner that will allow compatibility between hardware platforms using the Alpha microprocessor to be achieved simply and easily. On systems with the same operating system, the Alpha-based code will upgrade without compilation. On systems that use different operating systems, binary compatibility will be ensured with the running portability of the code dependent only on the PAL code levels of the host and target platforms. The ability to scale computing solutions is paramount in the criteria for a long-lived computing systems architecture. Clearly the architectures that will succeed in the next century will be able to implement on a single microprocessor at the low end and as arrays of thousands of microprocessors at the top end of the range. Alpha makes this simple and effective, as we have seen.

The most important driving factors for the future are memory technology, advances in which will be required to meet the needs of visualization, large databases, imaging, multimedia, simulation and modelling. While CISC and RISC systems will drive forward into the next century, they will simply run out of address space for many of these applications domains, but Alpha will not. Going from 32-bit to 64-bit architecture is not doubling the size of the address space, it is increasing it by approximately 4 billion times, enough, most consultants feel, to be able to cope with the demands of the next 50 years in computing. In all three of the performance dimensions: CPU clock speed, multi-issue instruction (superscalar) and multiple processors including, of course, massively parallel processing implementations, the Alpha architecture can take advantage of implementation improvements.

The Alpha architecture is a simultaneous leap forward in size, standards, compatibility and power. So that the users of the next 25 years have will their needs met, the architecture of the Alpha microprocessors has to cope with real levels of openness in operating system, language, compiler, peripherals and data store. The costs of setting up and developing a new microprocessor are high and rising quickly. Over the next 5 years the entry barriers to new products will have risen to such an extent that there will be a significant level of convergence on a few key microprocessor architectures. Those companies that are able to produce these few key technologies will be the survivors because they control their own technological destiny. Digital, with the Alpha architecture, is destined to be the leader. In the great debates on Open systems, the real winner will now be the organization that is able to convince the end user that they really have done their homework and that there is now a realistic platform upon which much of the industry could (at least technically) unite. The commercial realities of this happening and of this being-based on Alpha from Digital are, however, less certain. One thing *is* certain. Alpha changes the status quo. No longer can it be assumed that MIPS and Intel have the industry sewn up.

4.2.5 Summary

In this section I have given a very brief overview of the Digital Alpha technology. Clearly this book's scope falls far short of a full and in-depth text on the technology itself but I hope that the reader will now understand the fundamentals of the microprocessor architecture, the production and performance issues and can see that Digital's Alpha architecture is one that has a long lifespan. In the next section I will consider Digital's Alpha programme, including a review of the operating systems issues, layered product availability on the first-generation systems, the sales and marketing programme that is bringing the technology to the market and the services that are such a key component in the development of any new computing system. Before I close this section it is interesting to remember one thing. Ten years ago, to get the same power one has on an Alpha AXP chip today would have been state of the art, filled a complete room and cost over $1 million. Today it fits on a finger and is yours (at the processor level) for less than $2,000.

4.3 Digital's Alpha Programme

So we see that there is this really hot technology called Alpha, 64-bit, CMOS-4, 200 MHz, 400 MIPs, 200 MFLOPS. In short the technology sounds great, but? I just finished speaking on the phone to a major financial institution, and they are interested in Alpha, but they are not in the business of buying it just because it has 64-bit, CMOS-4, 200 MHz, 400 MIPs, 200 MFLOPS or any other wiz-bang feature. They may just buy it because it runs OSF/1 or because they like DECtp or because they believe the marketing message about securing the future with Alpha. In this section I want to take a quick look at the processes that support the technology, the other aspects in the Alpha programme that are just as important to the market as the technology itself.

4.3.1 Operating Systems

There are a lot of people using Digital's VMS operating system. The best estimate is over 10 million and Digital are not about to give these up. In line with the good engineering practices of Open Systems, Digital have now produced OpenVMS. Released in 1992, OpenVMS is a move by Digital to align the operating system with the goals of the industry with respect to software portability, common standards and a common look and feel. The Alpha AXP range of processors support OpenVMS today with incredible performance. Digital have further moved to make this change apparent by officially changing the brand name of VMS to OpenVMS and to reflect its X/Open branding by the independent Open Systems body. Digital VMS is the first commercial top-division operating system to achieve this level of systems conformance.

Peter Smith, Digital's European Vice President of Sales and Marketing, said recently 'Today OpenVMS meets every definition and provides all the benefits of a true open system, from X/Open branding through leadership price performance to unprecedented investment protection.' This commitment to Open Systems on the part of Digital is very significant indeed and represents a confident move that VMS can compete with systems like UNIX on merit alone. OpenVMS is just like ordinary VMS. If your application runs on VMS today, it will run on OpenVMS. Furthermore, OpenVMS systems are Alpha-ready. By this I mean that systems can be quickly and simply upgraded from VAX-based to Alpha-based solutions given the standards common to both platforms, the powerful Alpha architecture and the nature of OpenVMS itself.

Digital are also announcing a version of the UNIX operating system and their choice is OSF/1 from the Open Systems Foundation. This offers a full upgrade path for the users who have developed on ULTRIX and the RISC MIPS processor systems like the DECsystem 5000 range. There is talk of a port of the full AT&T UNIX System V.4 operating system from a third party, but there is no official word at the time of writing this book. One thing is for certain: the performance of OSF/1 on the Alpha hardware is astounding indeed. Porting code to the platform (see later) is not difficult, hence protecting the customers' investments to date. NT is a new, advanced version of the Microsoft Windows OS designed for higher-end multi-user machines including support for multi-processing and providing full Windows systems functions in a robust operating environment.

Windows NT offers features such as security, very high-capacity and high-performance I/O. as well as fault tolerance, a high-performance file system, integrated network support and full support for both 16-bit and 32-bit Windows applications. Microsoft NT combines the strengths of multi-user, multi-processing technology with a history of applications developed on Windowing environments. It is highly scalable and is sophisticated and powerful. This enables end users to move more mission-critical applications from mainframes, the mid-range and PCs to client server environments. Given the goals of any twenty-first-century operating system networking is a key factor in its survival and success. Perhaps the most difficult obstacle to this for Microsoft will be Novell's NetWare and in the initial market period this will be very difficult for Microsoft NT to attack. Another issue relevant to the success is Microsoft's support for provide windowing on character cell devices.

This is an important factor, since even at the corporate level, more copies of character-based DOS are sold than Windows. At the departmental level the brand leader in the networked PC market is NetWare from Novell. IBM, 3Com and Microsoft have all spent millions of US dollars trying to break this stranglehold and all have failed. At the enterprise level Microsoft is much stronger than its competitors and it is at this level that I feel NT will make the most impact against its competitors, Novell and Banyan. Initially they will face problems from competitive functionality, most notably the lack of a global directory service on the network as provided by NetWare 4.0. Recent developments have made a big change to the balance of probabilities as Novell bought UNIX Systems Laboratories (USL) from AT&T and now are in effective control of UNIX System V and the direction of Open Systems. However, I feel that this is a timing issue.

Most significantly, Microsoft NT will pose a threat to the client end of the UNIX market with the larger corporate user being unwilling to continue with the often terse and cryptic nature of the UNIX interface. Not surprisingly, there have been initial problems with the first releases of the software and the Developers Tool Kit. It is essential that all MS Windows applications written today can easily be made to run equally well on Microsoft NT. Availability is also very important and so one may expect the initial take-off in the market to be rather slow as the many hardware vendors get to grips with the operating system.

There is some confusion on the level of rearwards compatibility that will actually be available from NT with Windows applications. It now appears that Microsoft will be offering DOS and Windows 3.1 applications compatibility in the NT release but the situation for earlier software is not so clear yet. For these older applications there will need to be some level of rewrite.

The avowed Microsoft intention is to focus on the key Windows 3.1 and DOS 3.1 applications. This means that certain types of applications will require new device drivers, including any that require 3270 emulation and Windows or DOS applications that use direct disk access. The Microsoft focus is on the top hundred applications first. However, later in the book I will touch on the issue of porting to Alpha and NT. These are the releases of operating system that Digital are bringing to market with the Alpha systems first of all. It is apparent that over time this list will change to include new versions and new operating systems. The richness of function together with the variation of operating system, from the power and flexibility of OpenVMS, through UNIX to the excellent front-end functionality of Microsoft NT, means that there are a full set of systems building blocks at Digital's disposal as the Alpha hardware range is launched.

4.3.2 Layered Products

An operating system alone is not enough. Digital have to choose which key layered products will be made available on the Alpha platform both with OpenVMS and with OSF/1. Not surprisingly, the list does not include all the VAX-based layered products, TDMS, for instance, will not be made available on the Alpha/OpenVMS platform. Digital are clearly going to use this opportunity to rationalize the portfolio of layered products and weed out underperforming and redundant applications or old applications with portability problems. The definitive list changes all of the time and for this reason I have not included a reference in this book.

The important issue to grasp is that of dependence. If you have layered products that are an integral part of your system or applications, then the move to Alpha will take some careful planning. By no means all of the layered products will be available. For this reason, there will be a number of applications users that cannot move to the new Alpha-based systems.

4.3.3 Sales and Marketing

Earlier in this book I indicated that Digital had, to some extent, succeeded despite itself in the sales and marketing arena in the past. This is certainly no longer true. In line with the precision management of the rest of the Alpha programme, Digital are launching into a sales and marketing strategy that is clearly aimed at getting the maximum advantage from this technology revolution in the shortest possible time. To achieve this there have been a number of distinct things that required to be done: First, third-party systems suppliers are being worked on to utilize this powerful technology in their systems development and design. Clearly the big names like Kubota Pacific, Cray Research and Olivetti have seen the potential in the technology and Digital are only too happy to allow the big salesforces of these prestige companies to go out and sell lots of 21064 processors. Remember, Digital's goal is 80% of European industry using Alpha by the end of the century. Second, Digital have been in negotiation with a number of other semiconductor and microprocessor manufacturers with a view to licensing the Alpha technology to them. This is an interesting move on Digital's part. It is feasible that there could be systems running OpenVMS in the future with microprocessors using Alpha technology made not by Digital but by a third-party and running in a different third-party's hardware! This has to be a good move if you want to become a dominant player in the market though. Again this is the volumes game, the art of getting the most people you can to include your technology in their strategy. Remember, if you own the technology, you control the game.

It is ironic when I think back to discussions with fellow engineers in Digital. We often used to theorize on the merits of making VAX more public domain than it was, and finally it seems someone took the ideas seriously! Another element in the programme to bring the Alpha technology to market is the need for open licensing practices to support the move into Open Systems at the technology level. I well remember the issues that used to fly around in the Digital world regarding the licensing of VMS and also of the layered products. For a long time, the problems caused by a coarse-grained licensing philosophy were not too severe, especially given the (then) buoyant market conditions. The present gives rise to other considerations and when coupled with the general technological implications for Open Systems a change in licensing practice within Digital was essential if they were to produce a consistent market-support programme. It is now possible to buy a licence for, say, a layered product that runs on a large machine and licence just one specific user to use it anywhere on the network or a limited number of unspecified concurrent users.

Such a move to open licensing has made it possible for Digital to farm the existing base of VMS users with the wide range of layered products and gain sales which would otherwise not have occurred. It is also true that the configuration of new systems, and especially of Alpha-based systems, can now be more precisely tailored to fit the needs of the individual users of a particular system rather than a roughly aggregated representation of the individual requirements. By adopting such a stance Digital have acted intelligently both to ensure a philosophical consistency across the entire Alpha programme and to maximize the potential market for their products in the existing and potential customer base. The marketing programme for Alpha has be remarkable. All too often in the past Digital have failed to fully maximize the impact of their innovations by less than perfect marketing, but with the Alpha marketing campaign they have done an excellent job. I still meet people who have not heard of the Alpha systems and who do not understand what the implications of the technology are for their business. However, they seem to be making a concerted effort to ignore the press and mail.

I get bombarded with information on Alpha, both directly in the mail and through the press. To illustrate the success of the marketing campaign, I went to the official launch of the AXP systems in London, and Digital had invited about 200 people from the press, but by the time the event opened more than twice that number had turned up! (no, the event was not being held in a brewery). One essential element in the campaign to bring Alpha to market is the assistance one receives in porting applications to the new platforms, and this is where the ARCs come in. ARCs (Alpha Resource Centres) are designated offices around the Digital empire which specialize in the porting of software to the new Alpha systems. Each of the ARCs has a number of technicians who are expert in the technology and the problems of porting to the new platforms. As one would expect, the centres also have a number of systems in-house and access via the Digital world-wide network to all manner of other resources, both people and systems. My personal experience of working with the ARCs has been first-class. The staff are dedicated, no-nonsense people who work hard to make the job of porting as simple as possible. If they do not know the answer they say so and find someone who can help. The style and extent of approach is almost unique in the mainstream of the computing industry and a very clever strategic move by Digital.

The ethos is one of making it irresistibly easy to get onto the Alpha platform. One almost has to find reasons not to move, the incentive is so great. The Alpha Resource Centres are not just places for software developers to visit, they are useful institutions for the users of systems as well. I have found that those contemplating a move to an Alpha-based platform strategy can gain a lot of good advice and help, to say little of good demonstrations of capability at the ARCs. Clearly the Alpha Resource Centres are not unbiased in their assessment of the systems capabilities, but they will work with independent consultants (like me) to come together with a customer and answer all the questions put to them, even if these are awkward and difficult at times. In short, the ARCs were a very good idea, a sound investment and are a very useful place to visit whatever your interest in Alpha.

It will be interesting to see if the Digital ARC system is extended over time to include the offerings from other vendors-based on the Alpha chip such as those from Olivetti and Cray Research. Digital's salesforce is being very proactive in the promotion of Alpha technology to the existing and prospective user base of the products. Clearly the move to make the processors available from other institutions will increase the number of people on the street selling Alpha-based solutions and this is, from Digital's point of view, no bad thing. However, the sale of Digital-sourced hardware containing Alpha microprocessors does require support from technical specialists, and this is perhaps the area of greatest weakness in the whole of the campaign. It is obvious that there will be more prospects to deal with than final buyers. Clearly this will therefore lead to a great upsurge in demand for technical pre-sales support from specialists on the Alpha systems, and these are not common animals in Digital at present.

I think the next 12 months will be the time of maximum risk as the interest in the new Alpha systems is likely to outstrip the availability of technical pre- and post-sales support staff at various times. If you are a prospective user, do not be too surprised if you have to join a queue to see a specialist on certain technical queries! The Alpha marketing programme, the services, the sales and all other aspects of the launch of this new technology have now started to pay off. The skill and smoothness with which Digital have handled this exercise, one of great complexity and risk at all levels, prove that they are still a major player in the market and are likely to remain so for the foreseeable future.

4.3.4 Services

Open services to match open software and systems has to be a basic part of the overall Alpha programme. So that they can achieve this Digital has looked closely at the future mix of business that it is likely to do. It is clear that there is a need for the corporation to continue to expand its services activities. However, it is also apparent that there are special services or market sectors that Digital cannot presently address. To attack these areas it is certain that Digital will get into joint licensing arrangements on a number of services with other vendors. One such agreement rumoured at present is with Microsoft, and others are bound to follow. Some of the service opportunities created by Digital are in the area of moving from VAX to Alpha. This is reasonably simple in most circumstances but for vendors with low-level changes to drivers, for instance, the move is more complex. To make the most of the introduction of the Alpha technology Digital are in the process of making the porting services very low price or free altogether, and this practice will get the bulk of the applications vendors on the side of Alpha. However, I think we can expect Digital to increase their prices over time. The free lunch cannot go on forever.

The general trend in the industry to a higher proportion of services in the overall business mix for all suppliers implies that Digital must have the right services available at the right time and at the right cost. I have found at times that the provision of some of the more technical courses, for instance, have been too few and too far between for the needs of a software developer. It is a difficult balance to strike. I do not think Digital should underestimate the need for more frequent access to the more technically detailed courses. It is clear that in the next five years the majority of the income to Digital Equipment will be from its services business rather than from the supply of hardware and software. New service products will be essential, as will be new methods of delivering these services to the customer. I think the market will see a rapid increase in the availability of training using multimedia and distance teaching, areas where the Alpha technology itself can make a real contribution.

The whole area of services needs the kind of revolutionary approach that Alpha brought to the hardware platform market, a quantum leap in potential with the ability to provide capacity for the next 25 years at least. The implications of this for the Digital organization are that they need people who can deliver service and who can be trained, retrained and retrained again to meet the changing demands of the market without having to constantly find new and specialized staff. Digital, like so many other employers, needs people with unlimited potential and enthusiasm as much as, if not more than, the traditional technologist with an individual specialization that is useful today, next month and next year but which will eventually erode in value. The key skill for the service provider is flexibility.

4.3.5 Summary

In this section I have given a brief overview of the supporting components of the Alpha programme. Clearly there are many aspects I have not covered such as the support operation for the hardware and software. This is because they are not yet running in any significant manner with a large customer base, and while the potential is good, it is impossible to comment at this stage on the actual performance of these elements of the programme.

To anyone contemplating Alpha, be they software developer, end user or analyst trying to see how well the Alpha technology fits into the overall market, I would say that this time Digital seem to have got the whole act right. It is not just a good technology but a fully integrated programme across the whole corporation, a single unified theme that has been thoroughly and well managed to provide a consistent message for a consistent technology in a sound and professional manner and covering all parts of the value chain from technology through marketing and sales to service.

Digital seem to have made Alpha happen in all senses of the word. Technically they have put in vast investment and continue to heavily finance the forward movement of the technology. Proper supporting programmes are designed to maximize the penetration of the technology throughout the market through both direct sales and indirect channels. Key to getting the acceptance of the technology is the availability of applications on the platforms and I have been very impressed by Digital's response to this challenge. IBM never gained the acceptance for OS/2 that the operating system rightly deserved, mainly because not enough applications were or are available to run on the system in native mode, Digital have avoided this problem by going out of their way to make the task of porting to the Alpha platform as simple, cheap and easy as possible, and this is possibly their greatest master stroke. Not only have Digital succeeded in getting the giant applications snowball rolling, they have done this in a considerate and professional manner.

4.4 The Alpha_APX Products from Digital

Digital's range of products has always been broad and fast changing. Therefore it is not possible to keep a section on specific systems fully up to date. However, I think that this section will illustrate the point that Digital are well capable of providing the broadest range of systems on the market, literally from desktop to datacentre today and soon to include a palmtop and a true supercomputer as well. I split the levels of system into four: Workstation; Deskside to Datacentre; PC Level Offerings and ??? under which I have included a prospective view of the palmtop and supercomputer offerings as I think they will look.

4.4.1 Workstations

Of all the initial systems, the workstation is perhaps the level at which the Alpha AXP processor catches the attention first. Because of the power, speed and huge data handling capabilities the workstation systems equipped with Alpha microprocessors give outstandingly impressive exhibitions of very visible computer power. In the demonstrations I have seen and when using Alpha processor-based workstations, I never fail to be impressed by the smooth, fast response, especially given the low price tag!

Digital's entry systems into the workstation arena is the DEC 3000 Model 400 AXP. This is a single-processor system running a DECchip 21064 at 133 MHz.

- The system has an 8 KB Instruction cache, an 8 KB Data cache on the Alpha_AXP.
- This system runs at 111.0 SPECfp92. Comparatively this is 65.3 SPECint92 and rates as 107.5 SPECmark89/SPECthruput89.
- The LINPACK 100 x 100 (Mflops) rating for the system is 26.4 and the Dhrystone V1.1 (MIPS) rating for the system gives 129.9.
- In terms of capacity the DEC 3000 workstation model 400 AXP initially supports 128 MB but this is upgradable to 512 MB with a forthcoming operating system release.
- Clearly systems of such power need significant amounts of disk. The workstation takes 2.1 GB in the cabinet and a total disk capacity of 9.5 GB.
- The maximum I/O rate for the system is 90 MB/sec.
- The I/O supported is 2-off SCSI-2, 3-slot TURBOchannel, Ethernet, FDDI and DECram.
- Both ISDN and Prestoserve will be available in the forthcoming operating system release.
- In addition, the workstation also supports voice quality audio.
- In the forthcoming operating system release there will also be support for OpenVMS Cluster via Ethernet and FDDI.
- Initially the graphics support on the workstation is with HX but the next operating system release will include support for TX, PXG+ and PXGT+.
- The quoted price for the entry level system at the time of going to press was $14,995.

Clearly this is a high quality, high-power workstation entering the market at a very competitive price.

The desktop version of the system is the Alpha-based DEC 3000 Model 400S AXP Desktop system. This is very similar to the DEC 3400 AXP workstation but is different in some special areas.

- Like the workstation, this is a single-processor system running a DECchip 21064 at 133 MHz. The system has an 8 KB Instruction cache, an 8 KB Data cache on the processor with a further 512 KB on the board.
- This system runs at 111.0 SPECfp92. Comparatively this is 65.3 SPECint92 and rates as 107.5 SPECmark89/SPECthruput89.
- The LINPACK 100 x 100 (Mflops) rating for the system is 26.4 and the Dhrystone V1.1 (MIPS) rating for the system gives 129.9.
- The capacity of the DEC 3000 Desktop model 400S AXP initially supports 128 MB but like the workstation this is upgradable to 512 MB with a forthcoming operating system release.
- In terms of disk, the Desktop takes 2.1 GB in the cabinet and a total disk capacity of 9.5 GB. The maximum I/O rate for the system is 90 MB/sec.
- The I/O supported is 2-off SCSI-2, 3-slot TURBOchannel, Ethernet, FDDI and DECram.
- ISDN and Prestoserve will both be available in the forthcoming operating system release.
- In the forthcoming operating system release there will also be support for OpenVMS Cluster via Ethernet and FDDI.
- The quoted price for the entry level system at the time of going to press was $18,995 for the server system and $20,720 for the ADVANTAGE SERVER system.

At the higher end of the workstation range we come to the more powerful DEC 3000 Model 500 AXP Workstation. This is a deskside system unit and high-resolution monitor. Again this system is a single CPU system running a DECchip 21064 Alpha microprocessor at 150 MHz.

- The system has an 8 KB Instruction Cache and an 8 KB Data cache on the chip with a further 512 KB on the board.
- Performance for this larger system is significantly higher than for the entry level system with an impressive 125.1 SPECfp92 score. SPECint92 rate is 74.3, the SPECmark89/SPECthruput89 score is 121.5, and the LINPACK 100 x 100 (Mflops) rating for this system is 30.1 and the good old Dhrystone V1.1 MIPS rating is 146.7.
- The maximum memory for this powerful workstation is 256 MB initially. However, the forthcoming operating system release will allow memory to be increased by up to 1 GB.
- In-cabinet disk capacity is 4.2 GB and this can be increased to a total of 11.6 GB maximum disk capacity.

- In line with the increased needs of such a system the I/O rate has been increased to 100 MB/sec. The I/O support is for 2-off SCSI-2, 6 slot TURBOchannel, Ethernet, FDDI, DECram and voice quality audio.
- OpenVMS clustering will be supported on Ethernet and FDDI in the forthcoming operating system release. In a later release of the operating system ISDN and Prestoserve will be supported as well.
- The workstation graphics supported are HX initially. However, in the forthcoming operating system release there will be support for both PXG+ and PXGT+.
- All this can be yours at the entry level for just $38,995. Clearly a power system for heavyweight graphical applications.

In terms of initial offerings on the desktop and at the workstation level, DEC 3000 and 5000 level systems are clearly going to make a big impact on the market. Not for the first time will I raise the question 'What applications are going to make sensible and effective use of such power?'

4.4.2 Deskside to Datacentre

At the lower end of the server and system range we come to the more powerful DEC 3000 Model 500S AXP Deskside system.

Like the DEC 3500 AXP workstation, this is a Deskside system unit and the Deskside unit is also a single CPU system running a DECchip 21064 Alpha microprocessor at 150 MHz.

- The system has an 8 KB Instruction Cache and an 8 KB Data cache on the chip with a further 512 KB on the board.
- Performance for this low-end system is significantly higher than for the entry level (DEC 3400S AXP system) with an increased 125.1 SPECfp92 rating. SPECint92 rate is 74.3, the SPECmark89/SPECthruput89 score is 121.5, and the LINPACK 100 x 100 (Mflops) score for this system is 30.1 and the Dhrystone V1.1 MIPS rating comes out to be 146.7.
- The maximum memory for this low-end system is 256 MB initially, but the forthcoming operating system release will provide support for this to be increased up to 1 GB.
- The in-cabinet disk capacity is 4.2 GB and this is upgradable to a total of 11.6 GB maximum disk capacity.
- With this system the I/O rate has been increased to 100 MB/sec. as compared with 90 MB/sec for the Desktop 3400S AXP.
- The I/O support is for 2-off SCSI-2, 6 slot TURBOchannel, Ethernet, FDDI, DECram. In a later release of the operating system ISDN and Prestoserve will be supported as well.

- OpenVMS clustering will be supported on Ethernet and FDDI in the forthcoming operating system release.
- The price for the system at the entry level is $41,195 for the server and $44,395 for the ADVANTAGE SERVER.

The first of the really big systems on the market is aimed at the departmental level computer needs. There are two models to choose from: the DEC 4000 Distributed/Departmental Server models 610 and 620.

The model 610 uses a single DECchip 21064 Alpha microprocessor and the model 620 is the first of the multiprocessor units with 2 DECchip 21064 Alpha microprocessors. In both cases the microprocessors run at 160 MHz.

- The normal 8 KB Instruction and Data caches are available to each of the microprocessors but in addition each processor has access to 1 MB on the board (i.e. a maximum of 2 MB for the 6220).
- As one would expect, the performance of these systems is very significant. In both cases the SPECfp92 score is 140.9, the SPECrate_fp92 rating for the 610 model is 3317.0 and for the model 620 it is 6214.5.
- The SPECint92 rating comes out at 83.5 for both of the systems and SPECrate_int92 values for the systems are 1985.8 for the model 610 and 3816.1 for the twin-processor model 620.SPECmark89 and SPECthruput89 scores for these two systems were 135.5 for the single-processor model 610 and 247.0 for the model 620. The LINPACK 100 x 100 (Mflops) comes out at 36.3 and on the Dhrystone index the systems score 158.8.
- The memory requirements for this level system are considerable and Digital have facilitated the systems with capacity for the most voracious departmental systems, the capacity being between 512 MB initially expandable to 2 GB with the forthcoming operating system release.
- The in-cabinet (personally I would prefer the term en-suite!) disk capacity of the DEC 4000 level systems is 16 GB rising to 56 GB maximum disk capacity.
- To cope with the needs of such a system the I/O rate is rated at 160 MB/ sec. I/O is supported by 4 SCSI-2, 4 DSSI, 6 Slot FUTUREBUS+, Ethernet, IPI and DECram. In the forthcoming release of the operating system additional support for FAST SCSI-2, FDDI, Prestoserve, HiPPI and VME is provided.
- The entry level price for these systems is $77,000 and the ADVANTAGE SERVER price comes in at just $102,500.

The next of the range in the Alpha-based Digital products is the datacentre class of system. These take us to the limits of the Digital market with the VAX-scale processors of the past and they move a long way further on. Known as the DEC 7000, the AXP Data Centre System has six alternative models: the 610, 620, 630, 640, 650 and 660.

These different models cope with the full range of most needs for the market for such datacentre systems. The models have different numbers of processors, the 610 being the single processor variant, the 620 has two processors, the 630 has three, the 640 has four, somewhat uniquely the 650 has five processors and the top of the range, the 660, has 6. These then are the really high power systems utilizing the full DECchip 21064A multiprocessor capabilities.

- In these systems the Alpha processor operates at 182 MHz and has its normal 8 KB Instruction cache, 8 KB Data cache on each of the chips and a full 4 MB per processor on the board giving a massive 24 MB on the 660 model system.
- Performance in these systems is really significant: the SPECfp92 score is 178.1 and the SPECrate_fp92 gives (as an indication I have only included the 610 and 640 models) ratings of: 610= 4126.0 and 640= 15739.4. In comparison, the SPECint92 rating comes out to 96.6 as opposed to 83.5 for the 4000 range systems. SPECrate_int92 scores for the 610 and 640 models are 2188.6 and 8366.8 respectively. The 7000 AXP class systems score well on the SPECmark89 and SPECthruput89 ratings giving (again as an indication) 167.4 on the 610 model and 604.4 on the 640 model. The LINPACK 100 x 100 (Mflops) rating for the system is 38.6 and finally the Dhrystone V1.1 (MIPS) score for the 7000 series system is 177.3.
- The considerable memory requirements of the applications one might reasonably suppose to be a component of such a system are catered for by having an initial memory capacity of 2 GB which on the release of the operating system at a later level will increase to 14 GB.
- Disk capacity in-cabinet is 28 GB rising to a maximum of 284 GB maximum. However, there is a new operating system release soon that will extend this to 10 Terabytes.
- Not surprisingly, the I/O transfer speed for such a system is considerable, in fact it is an astounding 400 MB/ sec. The I/O supported is 4 x 12 slot XMI, 16 Ethernet, 8 FDDI, SDI, and DECram. This, in the forthcoming operating system release, will be increased to include 3 x 9 slot Futurebus+, 10 CI, 24 DSSI, 24 SCSI-2, Prestoserve, HiPPI, IPI and VME.
- Again the OpenVMS cluster will be supported using FDDI, Ethernet, DSSI and CI when the latest release of the operating system is available.
- No million dollar price tag for this though. The entry level system comes in at just $168,000, the ADVANTAGE SERVER entering at around $187,000.

At the very top end we come to the DEC 1000 AXP Mainframe Class systems. These take Digital into a realm that has hitherto been denied to them in any real sense. This range of systems includes 6 models: the 610, 620, 630, 640, 650 and 660 each having 1,2,3,4,5 and 6 processors respectively.

- As with all this range, the microprocessor used is the DECchip 21064. However, at this end of the range the processor is running at a remarkable 200 MHz.
- The standard 8 KB on chip Instruction and Data caches are available but the Data cache area is supplemented on the board by (as with the 7000 range) a further 4 MB per processor giving a 24 MB Data cache at the top end 10660 model. Performance of this system is, as one would expect, rather amazing with a SPECfp92 rating of 196.5. At the time of writing I could not get any firm figures for the SPECrate_fp92 or SPECrate_int92 tests for these series of systems. However, the SPECint92 rating comes out at 106.9 and the SPECmark89/SPECthruput89 scores are 184.1 and 654.6 for models 610 and 640 respectively. In the LINPACK 100 x 100 (Mflops) rating the system comes up at 42.5. Finally the Dhrystone V1.1 (MIPS) rating for this series of systems is 194.5. Clearly a powerful system capable of true mainframe class performance.
- The impressive performance is backed up by equally impressive I/O and memory. The maximum (as with all of the APX systems using 4/16-Mbit chips) memory is 2 GB rising to 14 GB with the new operating system release.
- Maximum 'en-suite' disk for this monster is 56 GB with a total initial maximum of 200 GB initially (interestingly, this is less in total than for the 7000 series initially). On the new operating system release this will be extended to in excess of 10 Terabytes.
- Getting the data around the system is really fast with the 400 MB/sec maximum I/O rate. The I/O supported is the same as for the 7000 series and, like that range of systems, some features depend on the next operating system release. However, in summary, the 10000 class systems will support 4 x 12 slot XMI, 16 Ethernet, 8 FDDI, SDI, and DECram. This, as I mentioned, will be augmented in the next operating system release to include 3 x 9 slot FUTUREBUS+, 10 CI, 24 DSSI, 24 SCSI-2, Prestoserve, HiPPI, IPI and VME.
- Again the OpenVMS cluster will be supported using FDDI, Ethernet, DSSI and CI with this latest release of the operating system.
- The 10000 series costs $316,000 or $344,000 when sold as an ADVANTAGE SERVER system. The price for a system of this power is as amazing as the performance of the processor bank!

Plainly then, from the desktop to the datacentre, Digital have a full range of upgradable systems. Some of the features mentioned in my summary above may well vary from the OpenVMS release and the OSF/1 AXP systems. Conside, however, the power of being able to produce an application on a relatively cheap but immensely powerful desktop system and to transfer it to a 10000 class mainframe system and have it up and running with no modifications at all. This is the true power of the Alpha concept (as indeed it was in the VAX architecture before it).

4.4.3 PC Level Offering

Digital have never done well at the PC level. Finally, it seems that they have started to work on the sales and marketing issues that have for so long surrounded this and have, by one means or another, acquired the skills to address the market (this does not include the joint relationships with companies such as Olivetti). In addition, Digital have now formed a relationship with Microsoft to provide NT on Alpha systems. It is now likely that Digital, far from being the underdog, are in a good position to provide the high-performance end of the personal computing market with its Rolls-Royce level system, one by which the performance for all systems will be judged.

4.4.4 ???

There are two noticeable gaps in the range from Digital. First, at the very low end, the use of a DECchip 21064 in a lap- and palmtop system. If it comes, or rather when it comes (my guess is the third quarter 1994) then this is likely to sink all other PCs on the market in one go.

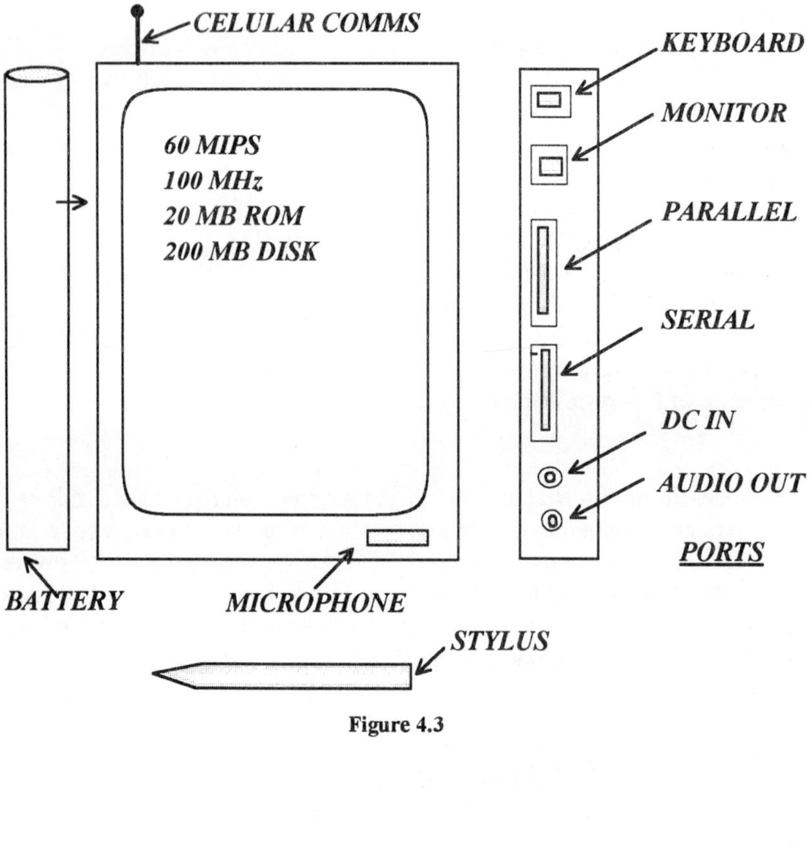

Figure 4.3

I would estimate that the performance of such a system is likely to be in the 60 MIPS range with an Alpha 21064 processor running at just below 100 MHz. Figure 4.3 is my guess at some likely features for these level systems.

Such a system is likely to go to market with, say, 10 MB of RAM and 200 MB of disk and be really fast. It is probably going to be running Microsoft Windows, possibly (in fact probably) including either Workgroups or NT connectivity for integration to 'home base'. Such a system would be aimed at the personal assistant market for the executive and is likely to come with optional cellular communications, on-board fax and email facilities and may well be bundled with licences to use a network for communications as an option. In addition, all standard user functions will be by pen input.

This really would be a system to set the world alight and one which, if I were Intel, I would be very worried by! Probably the other small-system side of the range will be using the immense power and speed of the Alpha 21064 processor to manipulate either written information in the form of pen input or to interpret and use spoken system dialogue as a primary form of communication. The implication of the voice quality audio on the low-end systems today implies that this is being considered as a real possibility in the near term. It is well known that Digital have, for a long time now, been heavily into the whole area of synthetic speech and voice recognition.

What of the top-end systems? Digital have a close working relationship with the manufacturers of the world's fastest and most powerful supercomputers: Cray Research. Cray are likely to be close to the joint development with Digital of very high-end systems, systems that even by the present complexity, power and performance of the world's supercomputers, will be judged to be significantly more awesome than anything seen to date. It is likely that the release of such a very high-end system will not come prior to the middle of 1994, most probably for operating system development timescales rather than hardware reasons.

4.4.5 Summary

Digital have produced, in the first full release of systems to use their revolutionary Alpha AXP processor, the DECchip 21064, a range of systems unparalleled in the world of computing. Never before has such a scalable system with such complete openness and-based on such advanced technology been available. When one considers the price and performance of these systems, it seems that it is more difficult to justify not having an AXP processor than to justify having one as a component of a system.

Digital have to keep the product line rolling. I think that the initial move will be to extend the range into the low and high ends and to augment them with software, services and peripherals. It is my guess that the 3000 and 4000 range will see some more systems added to them, possibly with a three-processor version in the 4000 range over the period 1993 to 1994. In addition, I think that there will be more movement in the very top end of the systems family, probably around the turn of 1994 with the addition of a system that is two to five times the size and power of the present offerings and aimed firmly at the largest data processing operations.

It will not be long before we start to see Alpha processors of some description in some of the most powerful peripherals like routers, printers and storage devices. This will hail even higher overall system performance for the Alpha-based hardware.

4.5 Non-Digital Alpha-Based Products

The move to use Alpha in several suppliers' hardware ranges has only just started. In this section I give a brief overview of the suppliers themselves and the offerings that are going to be using Digital Alpha-based systems.

4.5.1 Cray Research

Cray are the watchword for the supercomputer and were one of the very first to realize the tremendous potential of the Alpha 21064 microprocessor. They have chosen the Alpha 21064 microprocessor as the engine for its new range of massively parallel processing systems. John Rollwagen, the Chairman and CEO of Cray Research, has been supportive of the move in the press and the organization sees the single chip, leading edge functionality and performance of the Alpha microprocessor as key to the next generation of systems from Cray.

The relationship between Cray Research and Digital has strengthened over time to the point where Cray were able to exert their experience and influence on the final design of the Alpha microprocessor. The Alpha architecture is similar to Cray's own since it supports 64-bit integer, logical and floating point operations which, together with the very high clock rates of the microprocessor, make interconnection with the wider Cray architecture a sound proposition.

The Cray proposal is to couple Alpha microprocessors closely with their own general-purpose parallel vector architecture. This is a project with impressive goals, the first of which is the delivery of a system with greater than 100 gigaflops (100 billion floating point operations per second) by some time in 1994. These first-phase systems will include shared memory, Multiple Instruction Multiple Data architecture together with a system network. These first-phase systems are going to be entering the market with performance an order of magnitude higher than other massively parallel processing architectures.

4.5.2 Kubota Pacific

Kubota Pacific are in the high-performance graphics, 3D graphics and image-processing business, and are also partners with Digital and users of Alpha technology. They are a subsidiary of Kubota Corporation (based in Osaka, Japan). Kubota Corporation was founded in 1888 and has a turnover of around $7 billion. They are in the industrial and farm equipment business but have a very long history of successful diversification.

Kubota Pacific produce high-performance 3D graphics and image systems for engineering and science markets. Presently the products are in the Titan range of graphics supercomputer-based on the MIPS microprocessor which has been added to a custom-integrated vector unit and custom graphics. The systems run in a multiprocessing UNIX environment and sell for around $65,000 to $300,000. Typical applications of the Titan systems are medical imaging, remote sensing image analysis, molecular simulation, mechanical design, analysis and visualization and computational fluid dynamics.

Kubota will be using Alpha and OSF/1 to provide the power in their next generation of workstations giving world-beating 3D graphics and simulation. These systems will begin to ship to the market by mid-1993. The systems will have the option of factory integrated or field add-on Turbo-channel. The graphics software supported will be X11R5, PEX, XIE, Dore', GL and AVS.

4.5.3 Olivetti

Olivetti are one of the biggest producers of office automation systems in Europe today, and they have chosen Alpha as the basis of their next-generation systems running Microsoft NT. Olivetti plans a range of systems, first replacing its LSX and M700 systems. This will be done in a manner that provides a smooth evolutionary route for these system users thus protecting their investment.

The link between Olivetti and Digital started back in the 1980s and has been the source of a bi-directional product exchange ever since. Olivetti has been supplying Digital with PCs, ATMs and printers while Digital have sent terminals, mass storage devices and minicomputers for embedded applications to Olivetti. This alliance has been expanded to include Digital taking an equity stake in Olivetti, and this will grow to a total of 10.3% of total equity in time. Olivetti will be launching their offerings on the market in mid-1993. The tie-up with Digital also extends to a joint research project into multimedia and it is my view that we will see some Alpha-based outcome to this early in 1994.

4.5.4 Neither Last or Least

Raytheon, the military systems manufacturer, have adopted Alpha microprocessor systems. Already Raytheon are responsible for the militarization of VAX systems for the US DOD and these activities are being extended to include Alpha. This is just the first of many military uses of Alpha in both the offensive and defensive systems and in active and passive roles.

4.5.5 Summary

A diversity of partners then, from the military through the supercomputing to the office: just one more example of the very great power and flexibility of this architecture. However, we have still not seen a major semiconductor manufacturer sign up (like Motorola, Intel, Hitachi, etc.). Until we do, the ultimate goals of the Alpha programme will not be realized.

4.6 Chapter Summary

The title of this chapter invited several possible explanations. As others have done, I could have restricted my text to a detailed explanation of the particular and specific functions and features of the Digital 21064 series microprocessor. However, since this book is an overall strategic review of the positioning of the Alpha processor and therefore, by implication, its supporting programme, I have included a brief review of the extended features of the overall programme by way of a more rounded answer to the question 'What is Alpha?'

4.6.1 Main Chapter Themes and Issues

I hope that I have, in Section 4.2, the Alpha Technology Overview, given the reader a reasonable overview of the key components of the technology. Alpha is simply the fastest and most presently and potentially powerful microprocessor on the market. Alpha's true 64-bit RISC technology makes it the most suitable technical choice for any systems developer from a purely technical point of view.

The software applications developer will find the power and flexibility to drive all applications, from the simple to the most complex and demanding. Digital's CMOS-4 technology, used to build the microprocessors, is in itself the most advanced semiconductor technology on the market, and represents the technical end of a truly massive programme of research and development backed by an equally large multi-billion dollar budget today and for the foreseeable future.

The price performance of the Digital Alpha 21064A microprocessor today far outstrips its nearest rival and leaves all other competitors way behind on raw performance alone, to say nothing of the immense power of its overall architecture and huge superscalar and parallel potential. In Open Systems terms the Alpha microprocessor has been fundamentally defined to cope with all the concepts required for the support of the operating environments of today and the next 25 years. Alpha is a whole genus of systems, not just a single generation of microprocessor.

I started out by saying that Alpha was a programme covering all the levels of the value chain and not just a technology to be taken in isolation. Digital have got a really good and comprehensive programme covering all the major areas, including operating systems, layered products, sales, marketing and services. In VMS Digital have an excellent operating system with around 10 million users world-wide. It is clear, however, that UNIX (of many flavours) is in fashion at present and Digital have currently announced support for OSF/1 as their chosen variant in this market, although I think it is only a matter of time before the more widely accepted AT&T UNIX System V.4 is ported across to the platform by some organization or other.

One thing to be remembered is that some of the older and less general layered products from Digital, like TDMS, will not be made available on the Alpha platform. Users of these or people contemplating the acquisition of applications dependent on these layered products should think carefully about their future strategy in the light of Digital's decision not to go forward with them onto Alpha. It is refreshing to see Digital get the sales and marketing right on this programme.

In Alpha, Digital have proved that they have a really world-class team managing the introduction of the new product line to the marketplace, a clear sign that the corporation has come of age and has finally addressed one of the areas which was so long the subject of criticism from the outside. All this is further enhanced by the move to make the Alpha technology available through a wide and growing range of third-party channels, yet more people on the streets selling the technology. All this is fully backed up by a capability, one which is fast growing, to provide a wide range of supporting services to the market and which are able to fulfil the needs of any computing corporation of today, namely to make big and fast-growing revenues in the face of fast-declining hardware and software prices.

The range of Alpha-based products from Digital is considerable. On the day of the launch they stretched from the desktop to the datacentre, falling short of the massively parallel systems as yet. Within the first 12 months Alpha-based systems will be available from the palmtop to the massively parallel processing monsters, a range of systems capable of running the same operating systems and applications and unrivalled in the world of information technology. Digital's relationships with the likes of Kubota Pacific, Cray Research and Olivetti will see the dissemination of Alpha-based technology into a very wide range of industry sectors, from the highly powered graphics workstations, through supercomputing to the traditional office environment and small-enterprise systems and in true global markets.

Digital are doing with the 21064 microprocessor what Intel did with the i86 series in the 1980s. They are changing the face of computing.

4.6.2 Questions Raised by this Chapter

The reader will by now have realized that I think the Alpha technology is pretty hot stuff and that Digital seem to have turned a corner in the management of complex programmes to the market. Is it all really that good, can it all work, is it of use to me? I hear you thinking. There are some very specific questions that have to be answered when one looked at the longer view for Alpha. Some of these I will try to address in this book, others will have to wait for answers (and possibly a sequel?).

Three main questions raised in the chapter relate to uptake, investment and customers. First, let us consider the issue of uptake. Will enough people in enough places in enough industry sectors take up the systems-based on the Alpha 21064 processor? Will the key industry applications developers adopt the platforms and see the benefits of such power to their business? I hope to deal with these issues later in this book. We will not see the final answer for a year or so but I am impressed by the level of commitment in and around the industry in the United Kingdom, Europe and America so far.

Second is the issue of investment. Digital have spent a great deal of money on the development of the Alpha microprocessor architecture, the production facilities, the porting of the layered products, the sales marketing and services and all the million and one other things needed to take such a major new technology to market. Can they keep spending enough for long enough to win? Have they spent enough to start well? I believe the answer to the first question is and can only be yes. For reasons explored later you will see that this move to Alpha is what is known in rock climbing as a 'fully committed move'. There is and cannot be any turning back without fatal consequences. The answer to the second part of the question is more difficult. One can always spend more and, as I hinted earlier, Digital may have under-cooked the area of pre-sales support initially but the test of this comes in the next 12 months as the technology takes off in the marketplace.

Finally the customers, ten million VMS users cannot be ignored. The big question is will they buy Alpha systems and, if so, will they stay VMS or go to UNIX? In discussion with Digital I have found no clear answer to this question (either they actually do not know or they do but will not say: my guess is the former). My best guess is that about 60% of the VAX/VMS base will go up to Alpha with about 40% staying on VMS and 20% going to OSF/1 and/or Microsoft Windows NT in the next 5 years. This would suggest that Alpha systems will ship at the rate (direct from Digital) shown in Table 4.2.

Table 4.2 Likely sales (millions) by operating system type for the period 1993-1997

Year	1993	1994	1995	1996	1997
Systems	0.5	0.9	1.1	1.5	2
VMS	0.4	0.5	0.7	0.9	1.3
UNIX	0.1	0.4	0.4	0.6	0.7

4.6.3 Conclusions of this Chapter

As with so many other important events in the history of the Digital Equipment Corporation, Alpha is primarily a technology event. Technology as a driver in a market can be a weak position, and if one corporation can do it then so can another. On the other hand, technology can be a strong driver in a market if the barriers to entry are high and if the innovation itself is sufficiently unique or combined with other factors to lock out many opponents. This is the case with Digital's Alpha architecture.

The Alpha architecture is state of the art, being true 64-bit RISC-based, and therefore capable of manipulating the very large data objects that are a feature of many future applications domains such as multimedia. The processing performance of the first generation of microprocessors is already ahead of the field and is certainly capable of considerable growth.

The processor architecture for the 21064 microprocessor supports multiprocessing and multiprocessor architectures up to and including massively parallel systems. Operating system independence makes the Alpha architecture a safe bet for many wanting to decide on a hardware strategy. Support for VMS, UNIX and Microsoft NT covers all the options one might reasonably assume that the bulk of the Open Systems market might like to consider.

The performance of the Alpha architecture is not just a point solution to the needs of the market today but a mark of the massive capability of this remarkable system, a capability that can be extended to a thousandfold performance increase in the next 25 years, at which point conventional microprocessor technology may be on the way out and true optical processor technology should be making the running in the industry. Open Systems are all about futures, the whole rationale of the Open System is the protection of investment into the future, an investment in data and in applications for the end user. The Alpha programme from Digital has shown that there is now a hardware platform that really does take the protection of the end-user investment seriously. Certainly this is the case for the majority of the 10 million VMS users today, and it is also true for the multitude of potential customers looking for a good hardware platform for building the next generation of Open Systems.

The needs of the marketplace are growing fast. The weakest component in the systems engineering picture is the generally lacklustre state of many applications on the market today. These will need a considerable review to keep pace with the desires of the market for larger volumes of complex, disparate data to be quickly integrated and manipulated. The capability of the Alpha microprocessor architecture to keep pace with the needs of the market is clear, making Alpha a natural first choice for the discerning user if all else is equal.

The sales channels for the Alpha microprocessor are now extended well beyond the boundaries of the Digital organization. Direct channel selling is more commercially aware than I have ever seen and there is a new sense of purpose in the salesforce, possibly more visible to those of us outside the organization than to those within it. Certainly the Digital salesforce are now properly familiar with the UNIX sale, having cut their teeth on the MIPS-based 5000 series hardware. It remains to be seen what they will make of Microsoft NT (and indeed of Microsoft Corporation, who have a very different culture). Indirect channel selling is now starting to take off. Possibly one of the most aggressive volume channels is likely to be Olivetti,who will be taking the Alpha-based systems running Microsoft NT into the small to mid-end server market around the world.

Anyone who has dealt with Olivetti in the past will know how experienced they are in this market and, coupled with such a powerful technology, how likely they are to make a success. Care must be taken by Digital to ensure that they are not in danger of confusing the market with many suppliers of systems-based on Alpha chasing the same client. The marketing of Alpha has been refreshingly well managed and almost a victim of its own success. The releases of information to the press and public are of Digital's usually high standard but the content and targeting is better than anything I have seen.

The clear conclusion to be drawn from this is that Digital are serious about getting the market to sit up and take notice of what is happening and that, given the impact of their work to date, they are very likely to succeed and to go on succeeding. In terms of presence and awareness Digital are doing things not just well but excellently. Those developing software and designing systems-based on Alpha will doubtless be quick to spot the significant advantages to be gained by leveraging additional publicity value on the back of the Digital marketing campaign for the Alpha programme.

Services are a key component in the arsenal of any major computer corporation in the 1990s. Digital have risen to the challenge by providing the Alpha programme with a range of well-designed service offerings both for those concerned with the porting of existing software from VMS to the Alpha platform and for those developing for Alpha from scratch. Clearly Digital will be dependent for the lion's share of their revenues on their service business over the next few years and getting the services right is every-bit as important as making sure the technology platform is sound. If there is one risk in all of this it is in the area of provisioning the pre-sales technical support to a sufficient level as the Alpha programme takes off and before the majority of those in the corporation are fully experienced on the new hardware.

The implications of the new platform for services also have a bearing on the style of management adopted in the corporation and the kind of people that are of value in the future, key attributes being flexibility and a willingness to learn new skills.

Finally, Alpha is excellent. After many years in an exciting industry I am not easily impressed but Alpha does impress me in the same way that UNIX did when I first came across it in 1981. Alpha is not without risk (no pun intended). Digital could still fail, or at the very least not succeed well enough to justify the huge investments in the market.

The consequence of this would be a dramatic fall in share price followed by a takeover bid from either a competitor or one of the large Japanese electronics companies (AT&T should have bought Digital instead of NCR, it would have made a whole lot more sense in the longer term). If the reader is using an IBM 3090 or AS400 then there is still a lot that the Alpha systems could do for you. These issues I will touch on later.

4.6.4 Reader Checklist

In this section I want to go through some simple questions designed to help the reader evaluate the applicability of Digital's Alpha technology to their own situation and to see where the technology does and does not offer value.

For those who have a system preference that does not include VMS, UNIX (OSF/1) or Microsoft NT the Digital Alpha architecture and systems offerings may still have a role to play. First, as power PCs the Alpha systems are the fastest things around. You need to check that the applications you want to use can run on either the NT or UNIX versions though. Second, Alpha-based systems could form an excellent choice of front-end processor to take the primary load off a mainframe. The rapid clock speed and efficiency of execution of Alpha code mean that high interrupt loading in transaction processing environments would be handled well in either single or multiprocessor configurations. Key here is the connection to the appropriate TP monitor. Third, those considering downsizing from a proprietary mainframe to a hot box type of installation ought to consider Alpha. For my part, I would generally look at the VMS version first in a mission-critical system as VMS is better suited to this than UNIX or Microsoft NT. However, whatever the operating system, the power of the Alpha hardware makes it a much more appropriate choice than any of the competitive offerings, from either the RISC or CISC camps.

Perhaps you use VAX and VMS today. The first questions to ask are: what version of VMS are you using, what layered products are used by you and any applications on the system and what language is the application written in? Next you have to understand if any special drivers and hardware form part of your system. If special hardware and drivers are used, then you need to take advice on the porting of these to an Alpha system. Layered products and languages will determine the timeframe at which your system can then be upgraded to Alpha. From a cost point of view it is almost always going to be cheaper to get an Alpha system in than to stay on an old VAX at an out-of-date version of VMS. For many users the computer room may well be strangely empty when the Alpha system is installed. Once you have a clear and precise picture of the system and the software dependencies you can contact Digital and arrange to visit an Alpha Resource Centre. This is the point when you can get to grips with the nuts and bolts of the porting issues and the time and costs involved.

What about the UNIX user? If the UNIX you are working with is Digital ULTRIX, especially if it is ULTRIX 4.0 or later on the MIPS-based 5000 series hardware, then porting to the Alpha OSF/1 platform will be straightforward unless your software is dependent on a third-party product or a language that is not yet available on the Alpha platform (at this point in time Microfocus Cobol would cause one to have to wait). If you are on a different UNIX things depend on how different your UNIX is. AT&T System 5.4 to OSF/1 can be a little tricky, IBM AIX to OSF/1 needs care, especially if one has availed oneself of many of the 2000 AIX specific items mentioned earlier. In general, though, so long as no third-party products are involved the route is similar to the VMS/VAX to VMS/Alpha route detailed earlier. ULTRIX users on VAX hardware need to take a lot of care and advice in going down this route since ULTRIX on the VAX was rather quirky compared to Version 4.0. Certainly the performance increase you are likely to see, whatever you are running your UNIX on today, by going to Alpha is going to be very significant indeed.

You are not likely to be using Windows NT, but may be using Microsoft Windows on an Intel box. Alpha and NT will represent a real shock to you. First, be prepared for a fierce jump in performance. I have seen people physically taken aback when they see Microsoft Windows NT running on an Alpha machine: the performance is that fast. You have to consider where and how you are going to use the system. Most probably this will be in the role of server to some slower Intel-based end-user systems. However, you may be looking at Alpha-based desktop systems. Certainly you should consider this if you are a heavy user of graphical applications or multimedia. Moving to the Alpha system will require you to understand what applications end up on what systems, how and when. This needs some detailed negotiation with all your applications providers and then a trip to an Alpha Resource Centre to finalise the nuts and bolts of the systems architecture you are proposing.

In the case of a software developer or systems integrator then you need to look at your markets. First, if you are working with VAX/VMS or ULTRIX/5000 clients then it is essential that you make provision to get onto Alpha as fast as possible, and I cover details of porting elsewhere in this book. Second, if you are developing for either the UNIX market or the Microsoft Windows arena then have a look at the relevant sections above. I would argue strongly that you need to be putting effort now into getting Alpha ready from a UNIX point of view because it offers a unique platform power against your rivals and from the NT standpoint because Alpha provides an engine that can fully utilize the real potential of the Microsoft NT operating system.

As an end user Alpha may seem like an interesting esoteric issue today. However, you should conduct a little experiment. Look at the way you use your computer systems today and ask yourself, 'If price performance was not an issue, if power was so cheap I could increase what I have tenfold for almost no cost, then how would this impact on me and the role I perform?' If the answer to this question is that performance is not an issue for you, that the power offered by Alpha will do little to assist you, then Alpha has nothing of value to offer. If, on the other, hand such an increase in power would make your tasks more effective, efficient and allow you to use facilities and functions you find well out of reach at the moment, the Alpha most probably will be the best move you could make, that performance at that low cost is available today from Alpha systems.

The key question is 'So what?'. Any analyst worth their salt does not give a hoot about all this power, functionality and feature benefit (except possibly as an end user). What counts is the bottom line. Is Digital going to do well or badly out of the Alpha programme? Was it a strategic investment or an expensive mistake? Ask yourself the question 'When I look at the growth in Digital, at the real strength, what was it built on?' The simple answer for most of us is technical innovation coupled with the unique ability to be first and best in the world. Alpha is another in the long line of first and best. If you do not agree it has either to be because you know something I do not, or that you doubt Digital's abilities to make Alpha happen. If it is the second, then take a trip to an ARC. Better still, call the Digital Alpha product manager in your country. You will be pleasantly surprised by the conviction they express.

4.6.5 Summary of the Systems and Components

Alpha AXP third-party applications are being launched daily, so a list is never definitive. At the time of going to press the following list illustrates who, what, the platform variant and the estimated release date of many of the major applications in a range of industries. To date, over 1000 vendors have publicly endorsed the Alpha AXP architecture and are intending to migrate their suites of application software to the platform (either VMS or OSF/1). Clearly the outstanding quality and breadth of this portfolio are proof positive of the growing view in the industry that Alpha is a major force to be reckoned with.

SYSTEM DEC 3000 /400 AXP

- Number of processors 1
- CPU speed 133 MHz
- Cache size on chip 8 KB I, 8 KB D, on board 512 KB
- SPECfp92 111.0, SPECrate_FP92 n/a, SPECRint92 65.3, SPECrate_int92 n/a, SPECmark89 / SPECthruput89 107.5 and LINPACK 100 x 100 (Mflops) 26.4 Dhrystone V1.1 (MIPS) 129.9
- Maximum memory 128 to 512 MB
- Disk cabinet 2.1 GB
- Total 9.5 GB
- Maximum I/O rate 90 MB/ sec

- I/O support SCSI-2 Yes, FAST SCSI-2 No, 3-Slot TURBOchannel Yes, 6-Slot TURBOchannel No, 6-Slot FUTUREBUS+ No, 9-Slot FUTUREBUS+ No, Ethernet Yes, XMI No, HiPPI No, IPI No, VME No, CI No, SDI No, FDDI Yes, ISDN Yes, Prestoserve Yes, DECram Yes, Audio Yes.
- OpenVMS Clusters Ethernet Yes, FDDI Yes, DSSI No, CI No.
- Workstation graphics HX Yes, TX Yes, PXG+ Yes, PXGT+ Yes.
- Entry system price $14,995
- ADVANTAGE SERVER price n/a

SYSTEM DEC 3000 /400S AXP

- Number of processors 1
- CPU speed 133 MHz
- Cache size on chip 8 KB I, 8 KB D on board 512 KB
- SPECfp92, 111.0, SPECrate_FP92 n/a, SPECRint92 65.3, SPECrate_int92 n/a, SPECmark89 / SPECthruput89 107.5, LINPACK 100 x 100 (Mflops) 26.4 Dhrystone V1.1 (MIPS) 129.9.
- Maximum memory 128 to 512 MB
- Disk cabinet 2.1 GB Total 9.5 GB
- Maximum I/O rate 90 MB/ sec
- I/O support SCSI-2 Yes, FAST SCSI-2 No, 3-Slot TURBOchannel Yes, 6-Slot TURBOchannel No, 6-Slot FUTUREBUS+ No, 9-Slot FUTUREBUS+ No, Ethernet Yes, XMI No, HiPPI No, IPI No, VME No, CI No, SDI No, FDDI Yes, ISDN Yes, Prestoserve Yes, DECram Yes, Audio Yes.
- OpenVMS Clusters Ethernet Yes, FDDI Yes, DSSI No, CI No.
- Workstation graphics HX No, TX No, PXG+ No, PXGT+ No.
- Entry system price $18,995
- ADVANTAGE SERVER price $20,720

SYSTEM DEC 3000 /500 AXP

- Number of processors 1
- CPU speed 150 MHz
- Cache size on chip 8 KB I, 8 KB D on board 512 KB
- SPECfp92 125.1, SPECrate_FP92 n/a, SPECRint92 74.3, SPECrate_int92 n/a, SPECmark89 / SPECthruput89 121.5, LINPACK 100 x 100 (Mflops) 30.1 Dhrystone V1.1 (MIPS) 146.7,
- Maximum memory 256 MB to 1 GB
- Disk cabinet 4.2 GB Total 11.6 GB
- Maximum I/O rate 100 MB/ sec
- I/O support SCSI-2 Yes, FAST SCSI-2 No, 3-Slot TURBOchannel No, 6-Slot TURBOchannel Yes, 6-Slot FUTUREBUS+ No, 9-Slot FUTUREBUS+ No,

Ethernet Yes, XMI No, HiPPI No, IPI No, VME No, CI No, SDI No, FDDI Yes, ISDN Yes, Prestoserve Yes, DECram Yes, Audio Yes.

- OpenVMS Clusters Ethernet Yes, FDDI Yes, DSSI No, CI No.
- Workstation graphics HX Yes, TX No, PXG+ Yes, PXGT+ Yes.
- Entry system price $38,995
- ADVANTAGE SERVER price n/a

SYSTEM DEC 3000/500S AXP

- Number of processors 1
- CPU speed 150 MHz
- Cache size on chip 8 KB I, 8 KB D on board 512 KB
- SPECfp92 125.1, SPECrate_FP92 n/a, SPECRint92 74.3, SPECrate_int92 n/a, SPECmark89/ SPECthruput89 121.5, LINPACK 100 x 100 (Mflops) 30.1, Dhrystone V1.1 (MIPS) 146.7
- Maximum memory 256 MB to 1 GB
- Disk cabinet 4.2 GB Total 11.6 GB
- Maximum I/O rate 100 MB/ sec
- I/O support SCSI-2 Yes, FAST SCSI-2 No, 3-Slot TURBOchannel No, 6-Slot TURBOchannel Yes, 6-Slot FUTUREBUS+ No, 9-Slot FUTUREBUS+ No, Ethernet Yes, XMI No, HiPPI No, IPI No, VME No, CI No, SDI No, FDDI Yes, ISDN Yes, Prestoserve Yes, DECram Yes, Audio Yes.
- OpenVMS Clusters Ethernet Yes, FDDI Yes, DSSI No, CI No,
- Workstation graphics HX No, TX No, PXG+ No, PXGT+ No.
- Entry system price $41,195
- ADVANTAGE SERVER price $44,395

SYSTEM DEC 4000/610 and 620 AXP

- Number of processors 1-2
- CPU speed 160 MHz
- Cache size on chip 8 KB I, 8 KB D on board 1 MB per Processor
- SPECfp92 140.9 SPECrate_FP92 610: 3317.0, 620 6214.5 SPECint92 83.5 SPECrate_int92 610: 1985.8, 620: 3816.1 SPECmark89/SPECthruput89 610: 135.5, 620: 247.0 LINPACK 100 x 100 (Mflops) 36.3 Dhrystone V1.1 (MIPS) 158.8
- Maximum memory 512 MB to 2 GB
- Disk cabinet 16 GB Total 56 GB
- Maximum I/O rate 160 MB/ sec
- I/O support SCSI-2 Yes, FAST SCSI-2 Yes, 3-Slot TURBOchannel No, 6-Slot TURBOchannel No, 6-Slot FUTUREBUS+ Yes, 9-Slot FUTUREBUS+ No,

Ethernet Yes, XMI No, HiPPI Yes, IPI Yes, VME Yes, CI No, SDI No, FDDI Yes, ISDN No, Prestoserve Yes, DECram Yes, Audio No.
- OpenVMS Clusters Ethernet Yes, FDDI Yes, DSSI Yes, CI No.
- Workstation graphics HX No, TX No, PXG+ No, PXGT+ No.
- Entry system price $77,000
- ADVANTAGE SERVER price $102,500

SYSTEM DEC 7000 MODELS 610,20,30,40,50,60_AXP

- Number of processors 1 2 3 4 5 6
- CPU speed 182 MHz Cache size on chip 8 KB I, 8 KB D on board, 4 MB per Processor
- SPECfp92 178.1 SPECrate_FP92 610: 4126.0, 640: 15739.4 SPECint92 96.6 SPECrate_int92 610: 2188.6, 640: 8366.8 SPECmark89/SPECthruput89 610: 167.4, 640: 604.4 LINPACK 100 x 100 (Mflops) 38.6 Dhrystone V1.1 (MIPS) 177.3
- Maximum memory 2 GB to 14 GB Disk cabinet 28 GB Total 284 GB
- Maximum I/O rate 400 MB/ sec
- I/O support SCSI-2 No, FAST SCSI-2 No, 3-Slot TURBOchannel No, 6-Slot TURBOchannel No, 6-Slot FUTUREBUS+ No, 9-Slot FUTUREBUS+ Yes, Ethernet Yes, XMI Yes, HiPPI Yes, IPI Yes, VME Yes, CI Yes, SDI No, FDDI Yes, ISDN No, Prestoserve Yes, DECram Yes, Audio No.
- OpenVMS Clusters Ethernet Yes, FDDI Yes, DSSI Yes, CI Yes.
- Workstation graphics HX No, TX No, PXG+ No, PXGT+ No.
- Entry system price $168,000
- ADVANTAGE SERVER price $187,000

SYSTEM DEC 10000 MODELS 610, 620, 630, 640, 650, 660_AXP

- Number of processors 1 to 6 CPU speed 200 MHz, cache size on chip 8KB instruction, 8 KB data.
- SPECfp92 196.5 SPECrate_FP92 in progress, SPECint92 106.9 SPECrate_int92 in progress SPECmark89/SPECthruput89 610: 184.1, 640: 654.6 LINPACK 100 x 100 (Mflops) 42.5 Dhrystone V1.1 (MIPS) 194.5
- Maximum memory 2 GB to 14 GB
- Disk cabinet 56 GB Total 200 GB
- Maximum I/O rate 400 MB/ sec
- I/O support SCSI-2 No, FAST SCSI-2 No, 3-Slot TURBOchannel No, 6-Slot TURBOchannel No, 6-Slot FUTUREBUS+ No, 9-Slot FUTUREBUS+ Yes, Ethernet Yes, XMI Yes, HiPPI Yes, IPI Yes,

VME Yes, CI Yes, SDI No, FDDI Yes, ISDN No, Prestoserve Yes, DECram Yes, Audio No.
- OpenVMS Clusters Ethernet Yes, FDDI Yes, DSSI Yes, CI Yes.
- Workstation graphics HX No, TX No, PXG+ No, PXGT+ No.
- Entry system price $316,000
- ADVANTAGE SERVER price $344,000

Notes on OpenVMS

1. X/OPEN BASE SYSTEM BRANDING (XPG3) All OpenVMS systems are X/Open branded. This incorporates a very important industry standard into the VMS operating system.

2. OpenVMS operating system VMS is used by in excess of 10 million people around the world. Digital changed the name from VMS to OpenVMS to indicate the compliance of the operating system with many of the Open System standards such as POSIX and XPG3. The change of name to OpenVMS also indicates the integration of other environments into the operating system and the ability the operating system now has to run on a wider range of hardware platforms: VAX and Alpha, which will be available to a number of vendors. It is important to remember that VMS applications running on VAX can today be converted to run on Alpha.

3. Open software licensing The traditional method of licensing VMS has now undergone a very significant change in line with the needs of the move to Open Systems, giving customers much more choice. Clearly one option is to license an unlimited number of interactive users, and another would be to license a particular number of interactive users.

4. NAS Networked Application Services are a key component of Digital's overall business strategy. NAS 200,300 provide the licences for DECnet/OSI and TCP/IP. NAS 300 and 400 includes licences for Rdb/VMS, Digital's relational database.

5. Enterprise network capabilities DEC TCP/IP Services for OpenVMS software V2 provides increased flexibility for the users of OpenVMS to interoperate and communicate with UNIX, IBM and PC-based systems using the *de-facto* standard TCP/IP protocol. Some of the new functionality supported by DEC TCP/IP Services for OpenVMS software V2 includes TCP/IP electronic mail, FDDI support, remote printing and network management.

6. Platform compliance Digital has more than three times as many X/Open XPG3 branded platforms as its closest rival.

7. ADVANTAGE SERVERS The new range of OpenVMS ADVANTAGE-SERVER systems are complete systems of balanced hardware services and software configurations offered to the market at a very competitive price. Initially these ADVANTAGE-SERVERS are available as sixteen different configurations ranging from the Desktop 3100 to the mainframe class 10000 systems. All these ADVANTAGE-SERVERS are bundled with NAS software integration products.

8. ACCESS SERVERS The ACCESS SERVER concept is a move by Digital to allow the interconnection of their hardware to other systems and databases such as DB2, IMS, VSAM, Oracle, Rdb/VMS and RMS, these running on their IBM and VAX or UNIX platforms respectively. In addition, access is also provided to different desktop systems running MS-DOS, Windows, OS/2, Macintosh, OpenVMS and UNIX platforms. Digital's ACCESSWORKS includes a MOTIF-based management console, enhanced SQL Services software with Novell support and enhanced interoperability with databases.

9. Peripheral storage systems for Alpha Clearly systems of such size and power will require a new wide range of disk and tape systems. For the desktop and the departmental systems there is the RF31T 381 Megabyte DSSI disk drive as well as the RZ36 1.05 Gigabyte SCSI disk drive. In addition, there is the TLZ06 4 Gigabyte SCSI 4mm DAT tape drive and the DECarray 300 cabinetry options. Moving up to the datacentre and mainframe class systems (the 7000 and 10000 systems), there are the TA857 18.2 Gigabyte and TA867/TF 867 42 Gigabyte SDI/CI tape drives and the DECarray 400 and 900 cabinetry options.

10. The Alpha ready programme Digital's Alpha ready programme means that for all new VAX customers purchasing a VAX system the following clear upgrade path to Alpha applies: from Alpha ready VAX to Alpha, VAXstation 4000-90 Desktop and Deskside Workstations, Micro VAX 3100-90 Desktop Server, VAX 4000-100 Desktop Server, VAX 4000-400 Departmental Server, VAX 4000-600 Departmental Server, VAX 7000 Datacentre Server (with board swap), VAX 10000 Mainframe-class Server (with board swap). Interestingly, the licences for layered software personal user licences will upgrade to Alpha at only one third more than the VAX list price. This is in line with my prediction earlier that the trend in the industry is for the application and layered software prices to follow (to some extent) the downwards move of the hardware prices.

Further Reading

'Architecture of the IBM System/360' *IBM Journal of Research and Development*, No.2 (April 1964).

Richard L.Sites (ed.), *Alpha Architecture Reference Manual*, Digital Press, Maynard, MA.

VAX Architecture Reference Manual, Digital Press. Maynard, MA.

CHAPTER 5

Strategic Implications of Alpha

5.1 Introduction

'So Alpha, so what?' This chapter looks at the way Alpha is likely to affect the different parts of the information technology industry in the short to medium term and offers some advice on the optimum tactics for all of the interested parties. I have split the industry into several sections:

1. Application developers
2. System integrators and system developers
3. End users

In each section I look at the strengths, weaknesses, opportunities and threats facing each of the parties if they take on Alpha as a strategic component of their operations. In addition, I start the section by considering the more general implications of a most powerful technology. I cannot predict the precise implications of Alpha on the industry. When I look at some of the more detailed market models of its impact I get very sceptical, especially since reading James Gleick's book (1987) on Chaos theory, which casts doubts on deterministic market models. However, there are a number of certain things one can say about the short to medium term (up to, say, 1998) that are very likely to be the outcome of Alpha strategies.

Perhaps one of the biggest changes for the industry will be in the balance of the market. Suddenly the real opportunity is in the development of value, not the slashing of prices, and the role of the systems integrator will become more empowered and important to the Digital community.

5.1.1 Structure of the Chapter

Basically the chapter is in four sections. The first looks at the more general implications of Alpha in the market. This section starts with a general view of the market and moves on to a consideration of the Open Systems sector and Alpha's positioning within it. Alpha is, of course, a microprocessor, and in many ways one of the markets Digital is now operating in is the general microprocessor market so I have spent some time looking at this in general (with some level of focus on Intel). IBM warrants a special note, especially since Digital may target IBM customers with Alpha systems. Will IBM buy Alpha processors?

The next four sections cover the market from the points of view of the application developer, systems integrators and systems developers, and, finally, from the end-user perspective. In each section I have used a standard strengths, weaknesses, opportunities and threats analysis to highlight the position. Throughout this chapter I have presented the key issues and some useful tactics to play in the face of weaknesses and threats attributable to the Alpha programme in the market. I have also set out one very essential strategy for all levels of the market, that of adding value and not just cutting costs by the exploitation of Alpha.

5.1.2 Issues Covered in this Chapter

I often ponder the question, 'How long can the IT industry survive in its present form?' I think that the industry is about to change dramatically for several reasons, the main one being the need to get more value from the sale of each system. The economics of many system sales does not make sense in the light of the manpower costs and the industry needs to look for ways of doing things better.

One of the key themes in this chapter is that no matter who you are, Alpha provides a sound platform, for good technical reasons, upon which such value systems can be built. Until now the power was unavailable to the mass market. The second theme in the chapter is that while Alpha is good news to all in some ways, it does bring risks with it and weakens the positions of various groups in different ways in the marketplace. For instance, the increase in competition caused by the open and available nature of Alpha is good news for buyers but not such good news for the old Digital-focused applications developers.

5.1.3 Questions Raised in the Previous Chapter

The three main questions raised by the previous chapter were on uptake, investment and customers. In this chapter, I will take these three outstanding issues as the platform and look at the strategic implications of the Alpha programme.

5.1.4 Example of Where This Chapter is Relevant

The chapter is relevant to four types of organizations:

- End users
- Application developers
- System integrators
- System developers

The chapter is aimed mainly at the commercial decision makers in these organizations. However, one of the key messages of the chapter is 'Make value from the technology, not price reductions' and therefore much of the content is relevant to those in a technical capacity, especially in the strategy and design areas.

5.1.5 Questions Addressed

I have listed below the kinds of questions addressed in this chapter:

End users
1 What are the risks in taking on Alpha?
2 What will be the effect on my business of Alpha?
3 How will my position in the market be affected?
4 What are the opportunities with the suppliers?

Application developers
1 How can Alpha help add value to my business?
2 What will the effect of Alpha be on competition ?
3 What opportunities in service open up with Alpha?
4 What account should I take of the different operating systems?

System integrators
1 How might I use Alpha in systems design?
2 What will the effect of Alpha be on my market?
3 How is my market going to change due to Alpha?
4 Where will the competition come from?

System developers
1 What are the risks of building Alpha-based systems?
2 What sectors of the market should Alpha be aimed at?
3 What new product opportunities present themselves?
4 Are there service implications in Alpha strategies?

5.2 Competitive Implications

Competition in the information technology market has steadily increased over the years. In particular the past five years have seen a fierce increase in the competition for various sectors of the business and this competition has been increasingly-based on price and commoditization rather than added value. Competition has been differently driven in the various sectors of the market. For instance, in the low-end personal computer market, the commoditization of the hardware and operating system has led to a purely price-based competition with little impact caused by the introduction of more advanced and efficient functions and features. Generally, however, this is a volume commodity market.

In contrast, the top end of the market, that of mainframe systems, has almost collapsed. Surrounded by smaller, faster systems which can offload more and more of the existing and future workload, the mainframes are no longer the lucrative market they used to be. Technology innovation has been the driving force in much of the industry. The power of systems has increased many orders of magnitude over the past ten years while the cost of the system to the end user has fallen in real and absolute terms. The implications of the falling revenues and margins for the players in the information technology industry are very severe indeed. Major corporations have foundered or are in difficult, embarrassing and potentially disastrous situations, and the competition heats up as the concept of Open Systems really starts to take off in a big way, following a gestation period that, it seemed, might never end. The implications of this for the industry are quite clear. On one hand, there has to be a concentration of power into a smaller number of larger players. This is true for all the players in the industry, from the manufacturers to the third-party sales channels. On the other hand, there has to be an ability in the industry to exploit smaller and more precisely defined market sectors. This requires a flexibility and expertise that are likely to be found in much smaller operations.

The picture of competition that emerges is of an industry driven broadly by the strategic operations of a few, very large, global corporations, but of a very large overall market-based on the activities of much more tightly defined businesses who essentially take general technologies and add value to them in the context of the end user. Digital's Alpha programme in general and the technology in particular represents both the commercial and technical response to the present and future challenges of this competitive market, one in which Digital intends to be a remaining big player.

The implications for applications developers, systems integrators, systems developers and end users are going to be significant. On the one hand, competition has fuelled lower prices, higher performance and more responsive operations. On the other, companies have failed, leaving end users high and dry, and applications developers have often struggled to fund development of new products in an industry that is short of cash and in which the conventional financial institutions are nervous of investing since the assets of the businesses are so nebulous.

5.2.1 A General View

The competition in the information technology industry is increasing at an alarming rate and, as I have said earlier, with many, often negative consequences. One of the major driving factors in the increased competition is the influence of Open Systems. In principle, Open Systems allows one to become fully independent of the vendors of all the components of the systems at one's disposal. This is an unachievable ambition but a decent enough overall principle to strive for at the technical level. Unfortunately, the messages of the Open Systems advocates have tended to be interpreted far too literally with a consequential mismatch of expectations and abilities.

The founding principles of Open Systems are really the standards used in the industry. These, over time, allowed some level of interoperability and interchangeability of system components, soft and hard, but generally in the more peripheral areas of the system. UNIX changed all that by entering the scene with a general-purpose operating system that was simple to port, and which supported a highly portable language known as C. The arguments became very heated when one school of thought believed that UNIX was equivalent to Open Systems while another felt that openness was purely a function of the supported standards on a system and that two systems were equivalently open if they supported the same set of standards. Clearly the answer to the problems raised by this dilemma falls somewhere in the middle. However, the competitive advantages of UNIX started to become apparent in the mid-1980s but were confined to the more technical markets. Over the past five years, however, UNIX has moved forward into the limelight and is now threatening the bigger and more proprietary systems directly. By doing this, UNIX has fanned the fires of the market, bringing the base systems elements into the commodity arena in the same way as the Intel-based personal computer and Microsoft MS-DOS earlier.

There are now a large number of Open System suppliers, a great proliferation of versions, many of them very different, of UNIX and a market that is ready for a real shake-out of the quality producers of UNIX systems. In this difficult situation, Digital had continued to increase its market and be successful in the area of its VMS operating system because the interfaces to the system were so well defined in terms of commonly adopted and often internationally recognized standards at every level and in all areas of the system. The standards rather than the standardization approach was Digital's way. Later, in the early 1990s, the 5000 range running ULTRIX and later OSF/1 made a name as a fast-selling, good-value system that would provide Digital with a growing market presence in the fashionable area of UNIX-based systems. Alpha was going to blow open the whole market, the assumptions and the balance of power just three years later.

Innovation was needed in the industry and needed badly at all levels but specifically in two key places: operating systems and base microprocessor hardware. In both of these areas, the offerings on the market were at least 7 to 10 years old and in some cases (like UNIX) having a lineage that went back over 20 years. Innovation was a real opportunity, a key to the way ahead and the place where Digital were to compete directly with Alpha and indirectly in conjunction with Microsoft with the Microsoft NT operating system running on Alpha-based systems. Together these would turn the situation round and unbalance a market in a stable but unattractive state. In the market, one corporation above all others typified the problems of the industry as a whole: IBM. In 1993 IBM made the biggest loss in global corporate history. The corporation, despite cutting deep into its workforce, was in a situation where it found itself unable to turn a declining business and a corporate culture set in the 1970s and 1980s into a responsive, growing business that could be a leader in the 1990s.

Many of the problems would seem to be cultural and structural. IBM is just too big and its culture too rooted in secure and conservative attitudes to match the needs of today. IBM can change, can be a success and can once again be top of the heap, but getting there is going to be very painful, expensive and full of massive risks for this ailing giant. Tied into the mainframe systems of the last decade and earlier, unable to move fast enough into the arena of Open Systems (what the market wants, even if it is not always the right thing), IBM are suffering badly. The industry has not, until now, moved fast enough to take the systems we have to work with, design and build, that are really capable of fulfilling the needs of the next 10 to 20 years. Systems need to do more, add more value and provide more capability. On the other hand, there is the issue of Microsoft and NT. This operating system is Microsoft's new offering in the mid-range server market and as such will have, in the market of today, to match the fast-growing sales of UNIX in this area. Remember, it has taken 20 years for UNIX to take off. Microsoft NT will take off much faster than this, but it will meet stiff opposition, especially now that its arch rival Novell has bought out AT&T's stake as major shareholder in UNIX Systems International, the body which owns UNIX System V and controls the future of the operating system in practice. Between Microsoft and Novell we will see a battle royal in the mid-range market between two fairly evenly matched corporations.

Microprocessors are the base issue of the industry, the main item that has come to drive all other innovations and commercial strategies. In this field the undoubted leader is Intel, who are shipping in excess of 2 million Intel microprocessors per month and spending over $2 billion per annum on new product design and development. Intel are the volume leaders, sadly they are not the industry leaders in processor performance and in many aspects, their processor range is not RISC-based but SISC.(The arguments around this are complex and very refined these days, but Intel does not really qualify as RISC-based for the i486 and are not perceived as such by the market.) Furthermore, there are no 64-bit true implementation microprocessors designed to be as open as one might like, that is, there were none until Alpha came along. MIPS are a real supplier of RISC technology chips, but they are not in the same league as Intel and they, like many others, lack the same level of openness that Alpha provides.

The power of microprocessors today gives us the opportunity that until lately we could not realistically take up. The war is on for power, performance, price and, above all, the place as the dominant player in the power server market. This is the sector of the market that is growing fastest and that has the best margins together with the biggest slice of the lucrative corporate market and the services budgets that accompany this. Far from solving the problems of the industry, Open Systems has created confusion, or, to be fair, confusion has been generated by the naive, the incompetent and the mendacious about the realizable benefits of Open Systems. People are fast buying into UNIX implementations on everything from IBM AIX, through Intel to Digital and finding out that one does not end up with a glorious electronic 'pick-n-mix'. Hardware, software and operating systems are not always compatible, switching is not trivial in many cases and there are hidden costs in systems implementation and maintenance that can eat up assumed benefits if one is not careful.

Finally, in the markets, legacy systems, like the Ghost in *Hamlet*, stalk the stage, unwilling to go away and needing to be decently laid to rest by the community that depends on them for the smooth running of their businesses. These legacy systems are a big market for the right systems approach and the right systems solutions. They have driven the market in downsizing and require more and more power to maintain them.

5.2.2 Open Systems Positioning

Open Systems are, as I have said earlier, a complex subject with an equally complex market. This market has generally split up into a number of reasonably well-defined sectors with their associated attributes. In Table 5.1, I have shown the basic structure of the Open Systems market as it looks today:

Table 5.1 Open Systems market attributes for UNIX-based systems

TYPE OF SYSTEMS		ATTRIBUTES OF MARKET	
Hardware	Operating System	Value	Other
Intel	SCO	Low	Commodity Intel systems from a number of small vendors
MIPS	System V/own-brand UNIX	Medium	Higher-value MIPS systems from a number of companies
Own RISC	Own-brand UNIX	High	High-end/high-value systems from the old proprietary vendors like IBM, DEC, etc.

Note

In volume terms, the Intel-based small systems running versions of UNIX like SCO are by far the largest share of the market. However, these systems tend to be in the small-server or single-user end of the market: they are rarely part of the main systems strategy for mission-critical system components. These systems are often made from standard components by small hardware companies and then assembled and marketed, locally or through very tightly defined sales channels. The systems are mainly single processor, though there is a trend towards small numbers of processors in some of these systems, though generally less than four. The total system values for these machines and their operating systems tend to be low, and the applications that run on them, while often quite sophisticated, are targeted at the small to medium-sized enterprise. (There is an exception to this with Intel but that is covered later.)

Next in the market comes MIPS with the 'R' series RISC processors. MIPS are the leaders in RISC microprocessors in terms of volume and the systems that are produced using the R series processors are sold generally into the medium-value market, the UNIX mid-range systems, though some of these can be quite large. Manufacturers, including Digital, have produced hardware-based around the R series processor, and it is fast, sophisticated, reliable and offers good value for money. Generally the organizations using MIPS processors are larger companies and corporations, and the manufacturers of the hardware tend to sell through defined sales channels and globally. The end users of these system range from the top end of the Intel type, hot box systems up to the top end of the mid-range server market.

These systems run a range of UNIX in the market. SCO is available, but more typically the sale includes either the manufacturer's own proprietary version of UNIX (like Digital ULTRIX), OSF/1 or often UNIX System V. These are systems for the larger organization, often used in a more mission-critical area and likely to be at the centre of a number of sub-servers. Unlike the hot box market, the organizations that buy this hardware are either looking to the specialised needs of, say, a CAD or technical operation or are medium to large enterprises.

Finally we have the market for systems that use their own proprietary hardware and the organization's own version of UNIX. IBM with the RS6000 range are a good example of this. The RS6000 range of systems uses IBM's own processor and run IBM AIX, the IBM version of the UNIX operating system and broadly-based on System V. These systems are sold to the larger enterprises or to those customers with proprietary system that are deciding to go to UNIX as a corporate standard (i.e. if an IBM customer goes from S36 to UNIX, they are more likely to stay IBM and opt for RS6000 and AIX than go to another supplier). The market value of these systems is relatively high, they pull in a range of services as part of the sale, and the market sector is similar to that for the MIPS-based systems.

Here I must point out that there are a number of corporations, the bigger companies like NCR and Digital, that have a range of systems-based on Intel (presently i486) processors and providing systems that compete in many ways with the higher-value MIPS and proprietary-based systems in the Open Systems market. For instance, the

NCR systems are scalable up to 4096 processors! These systems tend to run UNIX System V.4, but the operating system often has modifications, additions and extensions to cope with the technical and administrative requirements of the large number of processors. These systems are generally aimed at the higher-value sale and into the larger corporation.

The Open Systems market has some interesting characteristics. There are many more systems than I have included in Table 5.1, but these are the ones that influence the market and with which the major users have to operate. In the Open Systems market, Digital have worked at becoming a respected player for a very long time, and, if one takes the standards rather than the standardization view of Open Systems, then it can be reasonably argued that for a long time, VMS has been a fairly open operating system.

The market is demanding UNIX as the base for the systems now, though the precise version of UNIX that is required is not clear. All that is certain is that System V, the AT&T version of UNIX, is the base around which many other systems gravitate, that the Open Software foundation (OSF) has floundered and that there are a large number of variants of UNIX in the market today.

All this leads to a position where the market trends will drive the particular operating system or version of operating system that will be in favour for any particular period. Alpha, because of its design, will easily support almost any operating system that one might care to design and build. Because of this, the Alpha processor puts Digital in a very strong position.

First, OpenVMS really does allow the construction of open operating systems. Second, the initial supported range of operating systems includes OSF/1 (a version of UNIX System V essentially) together with support for Microsoft NT which, over time, may become a *de-facto* standard. Third we are very likely to see a port of UNIX System V to the Alpha microprocessor very soon by a third party, with a microprocessor that has unmatched power and functionality together with the added advantage of being able to retain almost all the VMS base. The Alpha microprocessor, and Digital's move to sell this throughout the industry, is likely to result in a system that makes most of the running in the top-end, high-value systems first. The main threat is to the proprietary systems of the vendors like IBM, ICL, etc. and to the top end of the MIPS and Intel markets (like the NCR 3600 series). Furthermore, the functionality of the architecture, with its capabilities to build true symmetric multiprocessing systems, to address huge amounts of memory and to be extensible for the next 25 years provides an investment protection second to none.

Let us look now at how competition in the Open Systems market is likely to take place with Alpha. First, the low-end systems will remain a commodity market, one in which the price is the governing factor, until such time as the power requirements of the systems at that level of use exceed the power available from the 32-bit technology on the market and start to require true 64-bit systems. This, at the low-end, is likely to take another 5 years, i.e. to the end of the century. In the mid-range, there will be two sorts of competition. For the likes of IBM with a proprietary system like the RS6000 running AIX, they will fight very hard to keep the client IBM-based. Interestingly, since the guiding philosophy of the Open Systems movement is the independence of the user from the vendor, this acts as a powerful force to weaken brand and supplier loyalty. Given this, the next issue is of the portability of the applications themselves. Now if an application supplier supplies primarily to the IBM market, they will take a lot of persuading to make their application available on other systems (not least because of IBM's possible reaction). Therefore the penetration of the market is likely to take place at the level of replacement systems or additional system components rather than, in the main part, displacement of existing systems.

Following on to the other market areas, the Alpha-based systems are likely to make a big impact in those areas that have the need for the sophistication and power together with those organizations who are keen to include longevity and the ability to expand a system as part of their overall strategy. Remember, a small Alpha box running UNIX and a huge, symmetric multiprocessing Alpha system running UNIX can both use the same application, with no need to recompile or alter the application. Competition at this level is on the basis of value and function. The response of the competitors is likely to be in the area of price initially since the technology changes required to compete on the basis of function and feature takes a lot longer. This puts the competition in a dilemma. If they drop their prices they have even less money to invest in the expensive exercise of developing new product functions and features.

Clearly the market is going to be hit from a number of directions, through Digital with its own branded Alpha systems and also through other hardware manufacturers based on Alpha technology. Later we are likely to see the Alpha microprocessors themselves licensed for production by other semiconductor manufacturers. The market will then see a very rapid rise in the availability of Alpha-based systems. Furthermore, these will now be going into some of the very high value systems like those supplied by Kubota Pacific and Cray Research. These will compete directly with the very top-end workstations from IBM under the RS6000 technology, the multiprocessing Intel-based systems from the like of NCR with the 3900 range and the best that can be offered by way of loosely coupled large networked server systems from other manufacturers.

The probable positioning trends will be for the Alpha systems to start to make the big impact at the top end of the market and then move into the mid-range. Penetration in the low-end will be slower due to the price sensitivity and the prevalence of Intel, though the power user and those looking for the top-end servers will be the first to come over from this section of the market.

5.2.3 The Microprocessor Market

Microprocessors are a commodity market. This is essential since the design, development and production facility set-up costs are absolutely massive. Digital have spent well over $2 billion on Alpha microprocessor design and development to date, and that is just what they can account for. The real figure is likely to be even higher.

The main player in the market for the volume microprocessor market is Intel, the company that grew so fast following IBM's decision to adopt the 8086 Microprocessor as the CPU for the (then) new personal computer. A few corporations (like Digital and IBM) produce their own microprocessors from design and development through to production. However, the number of organizations that do this are getting fewer by the day, leaving the main microprocessor market to the commodity specialists. The one problem with this is that if one is in the commodity market, then moving the technology on very far is difficult since one cannot afford to cut the existing user base adrift. An example of the Intel organization's power and size is given by the basic facts about Intel and its microprocessor programmes.

First, if one looks at the number of transistors on a microprocessor as a function of its power and sophistication, then over time, Intel have rapidly improved their product range as can be seen from Table 5.2.

Table 5.2 Microprocessor power over time measured by number of transistors

Year	1980	1983	1985	1991
Processor	8086	80286	80386	80486
No. transistors	29K	134K	275K	1.2M

Table 5.3 Relative microprocessor power over time

Year	1980	1983	1985	1991
Processor	8086	80286	80386	80486
Power rating	0.3	1.0	7.0	20 to 50

Clearly, on this scale of performance, the Intel range has driven upwards at a significant rate. From data such as this it is clear that the industry is power hungry. Unfortunately the CISC technology used to develop the Intel 86 range of microprocessors soon starts to encounter the theoretical limits of the technology. These are issues around the physics of the microprocessor and it is therefore going to require either symmetric multiprocessors or a different microprocessor technology to feed the business. This new technology is RISC.

A massive corporation like Intel has to spend enormous amounts of money to develop these products. From the period 1983 to 1992 the research and development spend in Intel has been huge, as Table 5.4 shows:

Table 5.4 Intel research and development spend 1983 to 1992

YEAR	1983	1984	1985	1986	1987	1988	1989	1990	1991	1992
Spend ($millions)	130	180	200	220	250	300	350	500	590	700

It is also clear that to make the kind of volumes required to justify the expenditure on such a scale there needs to be a similarly large capital spend to support the operation. In the following table the level of capital expenditure shows just how large Intel has to stay to keep in business:

Table 5.5 Intel capital spend 1986 to 1992

Year	1986	1987	1988	1989	1990	1991	1992
Spend ($millions)	160	305	500	460	680	980	1000

As I have stated, the volumes required to keep a corporation like Intel in business have to be huge. I have set out in the following table the approximate numbers for Intel and the competition shows some interesting features:

Table 5.6 Competitive production in 1991/1992

Who	What	Number shipped
Intel	i3/486	21,200,00
Apple	MAC	1,800,000
MIPS	R3000	80,000
IBM	RS6000	35,000

All this is very interesting. Intel have a huge business, it is unlikely to go away very soon and they seem to be doing well. My only concern is that they are nearing the end of their present technology generation, and they are now working on the next two generations of processor, the P6 and P7. It is not known what these processors will be, but it is a fair guess that they may be real RISC microprocessors. If that is the case then Intel will have a large maintenance load to carry for the existing CISC base together with a new processor to launch in a market that is already moving fast away from it on true RISC. Given the very high levels of investment required to achieve the desired goals, Intel could find itself in trouble if it falls foul of the power and RISC traps.

In comparison with the mighty Intel, MIPS are a much smaller operation. However, they are in a good position as one of the leading suppliers of RISC technology to the market. The one thing they do not have is the scale of production but they are doing very well and may yet outshine Intel in the long run. Again they suffer from a processor technology that, while advanced, is now (relative to Alpha) behind the leading edge and likely to fall back further.

Lastly, companies like IBM, who have developed their own microprocessor, have the great disadvantage of seeing it only available on their own hardware (except for badged products like the RS6000 systems sold by Bull). Therefore the huge costs involved in the development of new microprocessors (and these costs rise fast all the time) are unlikely to prove to be attractive in the long run except if the volumes are likely to justify the investment (since it is clear that the price paid in the market will never again do so for low volumes). One can therefore see that the market for microprocessors is getting more competitive, with a concentration of suppliers and very high barriers to entry by the way of lead times and cost. In the face of all this, Digital's Alpha technology looks to be an innovative system, able to grow over time, with the prospects of higher volumes. As a Digital-only product and able to outperform its rivals, this was possibly the last opportunity to enter the microprocessor market with any real chance of winning.

5.2.4 IBM

The mighty IBM stands like Everest, bigger than the rest and fascinating just for its size. Like Everest though, it has succumbed first to assault by large organizations using brute force and then to much smaller operations that could move very fast and avoid all that the colossus had to throw at them. IBM, once the leading giant of the computer industry, is in trouble, the main reason being cultural. It has been too safe and too secure for too long. The culture is resistant to change and slow to react to market conditions, being more concerned with ensuring the status quo than the market share. IBM need a vision and a fundamental change in its methods of operating. This will be very painful and is likely to see the reduction of the operation by a very significant margin indeed. Recently IBM turned in the biggest loss in global corporate history. In such a climate it is unlikely that they will be spending vast fortunes on the development of processor technologies that can only have small market shares. IBM are destined to fail or go to the commodity suppliers for the base microprocessors of their next generation of systems.

Digital are in the position of having a technology that could be of use to IBM. This would be especially the case if IBM decided to work with Microsoft and NT to provide a range of server systems. However, IBM are unlikely to go down this route. Even if they did get back into bed with Microsoft, they would be more likely to go with either a MIPS or a parallel Intel processor strategy than to work with their rival Digital. If IBM are going to do a technology turnaround, they need to move fast. They are in danger now of losing out badly on the UNIX market and they will find that their customers might be tempted away by the lure of a system as powerful and advanced as the Digital Alpha range, especially as they would still be working with a large and reliable organization.

One place in the market in which IBM have fallen far short of their potential is in the area of the desktop and small server systems. Having started out very well as the introducers of 'The IBM PC' it now seems ironic that they have to struggle against the odds. The real mistake was the move away from Microsoft and into the development of OS/2. Microsoft had such a large market share and growing power that only by including Microsoft could IBM have made a real success of OS/2. The competition now is Microsoft NT, an operating system similar in many essential features but much more sophisticated and likely to be the dominant player in the market.

5.2.5 Summary

The competitive implications of Alpha are wide ranging indeed. It is clear that the market is much more competitive than it was just five years ago, with a concentration of power as one key attribute and the emergence of a large number of highly specialized organizations with closely defined market sectors as the other. Alpha has a lot to offer, as it has been designed to meet the technical and commercial challenges of today and the next 20 years. The competition have a number of weaknesses in comparison. Intel is still heavily CISC-based though trying to move towards RISC. MIPS are a close technical contender but still a long way behind and will find difficult the massive capital investment needed to catch up. Competition in this market looks like remaining price-based in each sector while the MIPS, Intel and other competitors take time to catch up on a function and feature basis. Digital will meet this by overwhelming functionality now and price performance rises that will continue to leave the opposition trying to catch up.

Digital's positioning will start in the high end and at the top of the mid-range in terms of volume growth. These are the areas where Alpha-based system have the highest value to offer. Growth in the other areas will, by comparison, be slower and more dependent on the third-party relationships, like those with Olivetti, to move forward.

With the Alpha project, Digital has entered the arena of microprocessor manufacture in the public sense. The microprocessor market is one in which the competition is fierce and the barriers to entry very high in financial terms alone. Intel are the clear volume leader, though in the upper end of the mid-range the technical workstation market and the larger RISC-based systems, the closest competitor is likely to be MIPS (except for multi-Intel-based systems from companies like NCR).

The home-grown microprocessor strategies from IBM are looking shaky at present, simply on the basis of volumes and costs. I cannot see this policy continuing, especially in the face of such large corporate losses. Digital has a lot to offer in this market with Alpha. It represents a technology generation jump, is widely available and is designed to be compatible with the broadest range of industry needs over the next 25 years.

As we have seen, IBM have done badly in recent times. We also know that many IBM systems are in markets and with clients that Digital would value as converts. IBM have many problems to solve, some technical, but most commercial and managerial. With IBM in such a weakened state, Digital will almost certainly mount a sustained attack on its more vulnerable customers with Alpha systems. Most likely this will be in the Microsoft NT and small UNIX server end at first, the classic surround/siege tactics.

While IBM sort out their problems, one option would be to use Alpha processor-based systems. This is, however, very unlikely indeed.

Were Alpha a processor restricted to Digital alone, I would view the market implications very differently. My view would have to be restricted to Digital's customer base and some small additional growth (for the same reasons I view IBM RS6000 as a restricted player in this market). However, the fact is that Digital have decided to go public, to make Alpha freely available to many companies around the world, and this alters the situation significantly. Alpha may well change the perception in the market. It is not going to knock Intel or MIPS out altogether, but it will make a big impact and is certainly going to mop up a very high proportion of the higher-value and more mission-critical systems in the market over the next five years.

5.3 Applications Developer Implications

Applications developers are those organizations that have to develop software for the end user to operate on the system. This is a loose definition and intentionally so. As such, it is a catch-all that will include everyone from the developer of accounting packages through to the compiler developers. The message of this section of the chapter is that Digital's Alpha has some significant implications for your organization and the applications that you produce. In all the following sections I look at the strengths, weaknesses, opportunities and threats presented by the Digital Alpha technology and the Alpha programme as a whole.

There are two main classes of developer that will be interested in this section: first, those who are already servicing the Digital market at the moment. These are most likely to be VMS developers primarily, but perhaps with a smaller interest in UNIX or MS-DOS. Second, there will be the group of developers who are not working on software for Digital platforms today but want to consider doing so, or who are just interested in what Alpha platforms might mean to them and their markets. Both development groups are considered in the following section.

The technology used to develop software is also relevant to the discussion since this may mask the base system from the application to a greater or lesser extent. I have split the development technology into two broad groups. First, I look at the traditional developers working in third-generation languages (3GLs). These form by far the bulk of all software developers and include the school of object technologists, that fast-growing element in the systems engineering equation. Second, I have taken a separate look at the developers working in fourth-generation languages. Many recent applications have been developed using these tools and the problems and opportunities they face will be different in each case.

Finally, I have included notes where relevant on the different implications for the application developer of the operating system alternatives for the Alpha platform, namely OpenVMS, OSF/1 and Microsoft NT. These options offer a number of different functions, some cooperative and others competitive.

5.3.1 Strengths

For many software developers with an interest in Digital today, the introduction of the Alpha platform will be a welcome addition to the product range. However, it is also true to say that the introduction of the platform is not trouble-free as we shall see later. The great single advantage of the Alpha platform is that it gives the existing VMS users a migration path. This can be in two modes: either a translated image of the software can be run on the Alpha system allowing the software to run without being recompiled, or the software can be fully recompiled and run in native Alpha mode. The advantage of the first method is that it is quick, easy and does not require the availability of any of the layered products or the compilers on the Alpha machine in order to work. The disadvantage is that the performance will be considerably slower than in native mode.

The second method, of recompiling the software on the Alpha machine, while the best option and giving the highest performance, does assume that the compiler that one needs is available and that so are the layered products. It should be noted that compilers are not all available yet (but will be) but some of the older layered products are not scheduled to be brought across to Alpha at all (like TDMS). If the software you have developed is presently running on a Digital 5000 series system under ULTRIX version 4.0 or above, the translation to the Alpha system and to OSF/1 is going to be very straightforward indeed. This allows the 5000 user to move over to a newer technology and a power upgrade. As developers who until now have concentrated on Digital and most likely on VMS, the issues surrounding Microsoft NT will now appear to you as real opportunities in your markets. If you use Microsoft NT and Alpha then you have a first-class system with an excellent front end. For the existing users of VMS systems and of ULTRIX-based systems, I would suggest that you look at the positioning of your existing products and how this might be strengthened by the addition of an NT-based front end (see Figure 5.1).

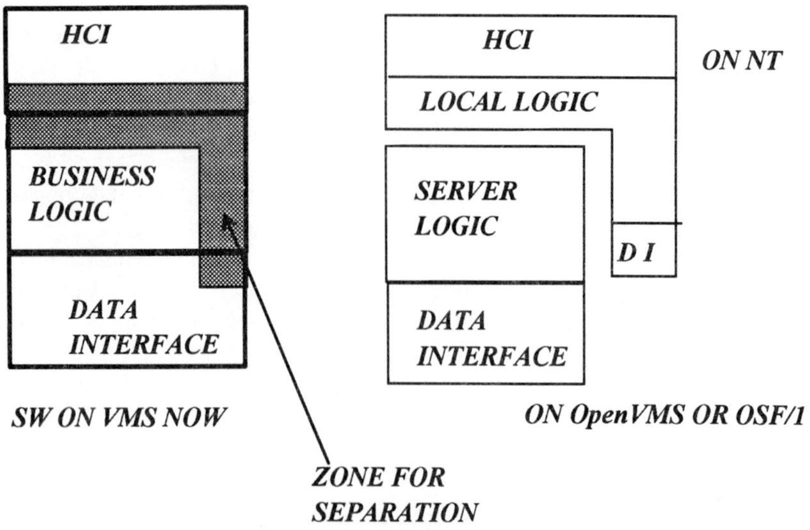

Figure 5.1

If you are a developer who does not presently operate on a Digital platform, the real question is what operating system to go for. If you are in the UNIX community today, then all three operating systems will be reasonably easy for you to move to. For instance, it is easier to go to OpenVMS from, say, UNIX System V than the other way round in general. Microsoft NT is also a platform that is worth considering from a UNIX system (see Figure 5.1). If one chose OpenVMS, then the whole of the existing customer base of VMS customers would be open to your applications. By coming into the Digital market from outside, one strength you have is a broader experience of systems use and customer expectation. By opting for an Alpha platform, not only will you be strengthening your applications portfolio but you will be also increasing your market. OpenVMS, for instance, really is a good system to work with. You might start by porting just the data management or communications components of your application to such a system. OpenVMS has sufficiently open interfaces to allow this with ease. OSF/1, on the other hand, is likely to be the place where most of the new system sales occur in the upper end of the value market, with Microsoft NT taking the lower-value and perhaps more peripheral server market on Alpha. This gives you the option of positioning the applications in the right sector and on a platform with the right operating system.

There are issues that relate to all types of applications developer. First, a note on 3GLs and 4GLs. Alpha will support many of these and on different operating systems depending on the language suppliers. The 3GL applications will be in a reasonably strong position in general. For instance, if C or Cobol is used as the implementation language, then so long as there is a compiler, even if this is different (like Microfocus Cobol or VAX Cobol) then portability from one platform to another can be achieved, albeit with some work. However, the developers using 4GLs have a problem.

They cannot go onto an Alpha platform unless it is fully supported by the 4GL vendor. Furthermore, the level of platform functionality that will be supported will be in the hands of the 4GL supplier. For instance, on the Microsoft NT platform, not all 4GLs will support the level of Object Technology supported in NT. In short, a 4GL system may go over to Alpha really quickly if the supplier ports the 4GL. In addition, what one can do on the platform, the level of value added to the application, may be limited by the supported technologies within the 4GL.

I said earlier that one of the really big problems in the information technology industry today was the rapidly reducing real and added value of systems in the market. Alpha can be used in one of two ways. First, you could see it just as a cheaper machine to run your application on. If this is the course of action do not be too surprised if the market reacts by pressurizing you to reduce your application prices in line with the market price of the hardware. A better strategy is to utilize the power of the Alpha technology to increase the delivered value of your application to the market. This is as true for the existing developers of applications for the VMS market as it is for those on other operating systems that are considering the Alpha technology from afar.

First, the additional power can be used to support additional functionality, things, for instance, that the older systems could not cope with given the performance. An example of this might be the inclusion of a number of 'what if' or alternative options within an application in the decision support area. Second, the Alpha platforms can be used to deliver features that are not presently available to you on your current system but which will in themselves bring added value to your application. One example of this might be the inclusion of a Microsoft NT front end to an application with the obvious power that such a sophisticated multi-user windowing system brings. Technology inclusion is now possible and practical where before Alpha it was not. Two areas well worth looking into are multimedia and AI, both of which are perceived by the market as adding a great deal of value to the system and to its use. One example of this is a client I recently talked to who until now needed a multi-user, multimedia system but could not afford one, Alpha makes this possible to average businesses now. My client is likely to swap an aged UNIX system and a PS2 with applications that now look dated for an OSF/1 system on Alpha.

Lastly, Alpha is a great development platform in its own right. If you are developing for a number of platforms (and for many application developers this is a real issue) then the sophistication of Alpha and OpenVMS or OSF/1 will provide a platform second to none for target-host development of large and complex applications. Alpha puts you in a strong position, either as an existing developer on Digital products or as someone considering the Alpha platform from outside the Digital community.

5.3.2 Weaknesses

As with any new technology, risks exist early on related to the technology and with all associated changes, the risks of the changes themselves are not inconsiderable. In this section I want to look at the weaknesses in moving to Alpha and in not doing so or not doing so quickly enough, and the internal threats that come from going to such a new technology.

1. Developers aimed at Digital today If you are presently developing software aimed at the Digital market today, there are some, albeit small, weaknesses in moving to the Alpha platform. These can be summarized as follows:

- You may need to strip out third-party and unsupported layered products to go to the Alpha platform in native form. By doing this you will be getting to a longer-term supportable position. However, the risk will be that you have two very different sets of code to support. Furthermore, this may be the case for a considerable time if you have a significant size of customer base. Supporting more than one code stream is costly and weakens your position in the market. In addition, the removal of the software dependencies from your application will require some level of up-front investment, the size of this being dependent upon your particular situation.
- Should you just take a raw application over on to the Alpha platform, one problem you will face is the expectation of reduced cost for the application on a per-user basis unless you can add value. In this sense, a raw port only exacerbates the spiral of faster hardware and lower per-user costs for a given level of performance.
- If you have been associated only with applications developed for the VMS platform in the past, there is a route for you onto OpenVMS with Alpha. However, the future sales of the Alpha platform into new accounts is far more likely to be-based on a UNIX operating system such as OSF/1 or System V. Therefore, the long-term survival and growth of your user base will have to reflect this and this raises the question of your application's suitability for porting over to a new operating system. In addition, the question of your credibility in the Open Systems market will become an issue. These are weaknesses in your strategic position that are highlighted by Alpha and which you must address in the mid-term (certainly by mid-1994). A lack of skills on the Alpha platform (particularly for the platforms running operating systems other than VMS) is a real issue, as is any undue dependence on VMS-specific features in your applications.
- The method of volume growth for the Alpha-based systems chosen by Digital is via third-party hardware vendors. In order to succeed in your market you will have to consider two things: first, that relationships may have to be formed with vendors other than Digital (and for many operations that have dealt exclusively with Digital this may come as quite a significant challenge) and second, you will now be competing with applications that were not operating in your market sector before.

For instance, if you worked on an application, sold it into a niche market, say in Italy on VAX, you may now come up against competitive applications on Alpha and Microsoft NT sold on a platform sourced from Olivetti. In general, the level of competition in the market associated with Digital will be on the increase for the applications development community. Those in the weakest position will be those with VMS-only skills and products to sell.

2. Developers considering Digital

- Breaking into a new market is never easy. If you are considering making your application available on OpenVMS there are a number of things that you have to consider. First, there is the application itself. While it is true that moving from, say, UNIX to VMS is easier in general than going the other way, it is not trivial. Terminal handling, for instance, is significantly different in VMS from UNIX and many functions and features of commonly used utilities vary between OpenVMS and UNIX as they do between one UNIX version and another. The second area of difficulty in breaking into the market is likely to be both the level of VMS facility that is used in the application or in the surrounding shell and the level of expertise you can muster to support the application.
- You will need to choose a vendor. If you are moving down the route of working with Digital but have not done so before, beware, they are very different from most other computing companies, especially IBM! The choice of vendor is a difficult one and will ultimately be dependent on the vendor's presence in the market sector you are operating in. For instance, Olivetti in Europe might prove to be a better choice in the office automation sector than Digital, while Digital would be a much better choice in Europe for a manufacturing systems market. It is quite likely that you will be drawn into multi-vendor relationships in this process since Alpha is a pan-vendor platform.
- All that I said previously about the need to show additional value on the Alpha platform and not allow it to become another turn in the downwards spiral of system prices and stagnant functionality also applies to this class of applications developer as with the previous class.
- To those considering Microsoft NT and Alpha the big weakness will be the level of competition. Almost all the vendors of applications on PCs see Microsoft NT as a method of getting into the more lucrative mid-range systems market. Many will be unpleasantly surprised when they realize that the level of support and quality required from this market is so much higher than for the PC market. However, the statistics indicate that there will be a flood of applications on the back of Microsoft NT. If you are considering this as a route forward, remember, the level of service that is expected is very much higher and the people who present the greatest threat to you will be the vendors of UNIX-based applications, since these will move relatively easily onto Microsoft NT and their vendors already have extensive experience of the mid-range market.

5.3.3 Opportunities

Alpha presents a whole range of opportunities to the market, partly because as a technology it provides an unsurpassed level of power and performance and partly because its design has been carried out to make the technology very portable indeed. However, it is true to say that some of the opportunity that arises from Alpha is-based not on the technology but on the associated sales, marketing and service programmes from Digital. In this section I will be looking at the main opportunity themes for the market and suggesting areas for exploitation.

It is clear that Alpha produces opportunities. Digital have an opportunity to succeed and at the same time, the competition have an opportunity to undermine the userbase. Change is always a time when threats and opportunities exist. Digital have to counter the threats generated by the change to Alpha at the same time as exploiting the opportunities created.

1. Developers aimed at Digital today The picture for the developer who operates today on VMS only, possibly with a recent move to the Digital 5000 series running either ULTRIX or OSF/1, is indeed one of opportunities. Alpha has provided definite areas of the market with the need, not just the option, of change, and from such needs business can be made, even in a recession. The main areas of opportunity associated with Alpha are:

- The first sets the pace and can mop up. Today Digital Alpha-based systems are new and that in itself is an area of opportunity. The first person in a market sector with the applications on the platform will be in a strong position (assuming the influential consultancies get to know about you).
- Good deals are available from Digital by way of hardware, software and services to the developer that wants to get onto Alpha-based systems fast. This will not last at such lucrative terms forever and so the smart developers will move fast onto Alpha platforms with as much assistance from Digital as they can negotiate.
- From my own experience in the VMS community, there is a very great deal of interest, and a certain amount of confusion, about the Alpha systems. This is a good climate into which new or newly ported products can be launched (this book, for instance!).
- While the cost of VAX systems has remained higher than the cheap, Intel-based, 'hot boxes', it is true to say that the prices of VAX systems has plunged over the past 5 years and along with it the end users' expectations regarding application and service prices. Alpha gives you a chance to move up the value chain once more, but this can only happen if you add value to the applications you have at present by the intelligent use of Alpha's functions and facilities.
- Alpha opportunities also impact the markets that you operate in or the sectors of the markets. For instance, your application might be suitable for all warehousing

markets but in the past the power of the VAX was not sufficient to make this a realistic issue. Alpha might change that and allow you to move up-market. Be aware that this does come into the scope of falling system prices bringing application prices down, so you should look at how you might add functions, features and hence value. Alternatively, you may have skills that allow the development of products for markets that you could not enter until now. For instance, you may be able to operate in the engineering market through the use of your stress analysis software and link this to other CAD software running on Kubota Pacific workstations. New markets, either driven by the technology or by the fact that the Alpha processors were included in the base hardware from a number of manufacturers, are opening up all the time, but getting in fast is the key.

- Including new technology gives other opportunities, adds value and improves the market perceptions of the application. For instance, in the field of decision-support systems the wide-scale use of Artificial Intelligence (AI) techniques is well known but restricted in practice. This is due partly to a shortage in skills and partly to the lack of available power in systems for small AI components to be included in the overall system. One might reasonably look to the Alpha-based systems to have the level of power and sophistication to allow the inclusion of usable AI components based on the use of languages like Prolog or Lisp, which until now have not been sufficiently efficient at run time to be considered for general use. In addition, technologies like free text retrieval databases will become more widespread for more general applications. In free text systems, the lack of database structure has until now prohibited their use in all but the most simple systems. At the user interface we are likely to see an explosion in technology from the use of stylus-based handwritten systems and voice command and recognition to the less esoteric application of Microsoft NT to the systems running UNIX and VMS today. All these activities are value adding to the base applications.

2. Developers considering Digital

- Perhaps the single biggest opportunity is that of choice. Those coming into the Alpha market from outside have a number of choices, first of operating system and then of hardware vendor. This level of option allows the application vendor to be in the fortunate position of controlling, at least to some degree, two of the variables in the marketing equation.
- The second opportunity is the VMS customer base itself. As a new entrant, it may well be that you have an application that is functionally superior to the present offerings to the VMS market. Clearly, the work required to move from, say, UNIX to OpenVMS may prove to be a worthwhile investment given the dominant position enjoyed by VMS and Digital in certain key market sectors.

The key message in this section is that Alpha systems may be worth investing in for the applications developers and that this investment is likely to pay better rewards if made sooner rather than later as the competition for the market hots up. In addition, the chance to show significant levels of added value exists for those with the imagination, skill and courage to do this. It should be remembered, especially by the present VMS community, that one company's opportunity is another company's threat based on a weakness. Alpha requires an escape from the myopic policies of many VMS developers in the past if they are to have a future.

5.3.4 Threats

All coins have a flip side, even Alpha, and for every opportunity there is a threat for some organization or another. Broadly, these can be defined as:

Developers aimed at Digital today and developers considering Digital

- Others getting there first. Quite simply, the organizations that move fast will be in with the biggest chances. Do not underestimate the speed of the existing customer base or the interest from the broader market.
- Erosion of your market share. The competition in the applications arena will increase, simply because the Open Systems market allows this to happen in general and Digital's Alpha system is a prime example of the Open System in the market. Threats from applications vendors will start soon and you need to counter these both by consolidating your applications customer base and by adding value faster than they can or by counter-attacking their base if possible.
- You will be seen as old technology if you do not move to an Alpha solution or at least offer one as part of the portfolio. Without such an asset, you will simply be regarded as a dead-end supplier by the market and probably by Digital and your competitors.
- Low-margin, non-Alpha business means that you may be short of funds to invest in your products. This investment is required if you are to compete in the Alpha market, so the Alpha change will threaten to put you in a self-perpetuating position unless you play a very skilful line in managing your company.
- Being late on Alpha may be seen as a real problem for one big reason: the recession. If it is ending (let us all hope) then the upturn will mean an upturn in capital investment by your customers. All the clients that I speak to in the VMS community are considering Alpha platforms as their next big investment. If you miss out on this, you miss out on the financial jump-start that your business may need. Furthermore, the whole market picture tends to get renewed in the information technology business after a recession, and this could result in latecomers being seen as 'also-rans' irrespective of your pre-recessionary position.

5.3.5 Summary

I have taken a brief look at the implications of the Alpha system for the applications developer, that broadly being anyone developing software for sale into the market, both working now with Digital and looking at the Alpha market from outside. The choice of application development technology is an important issue with big differences being apparent in the use of third- and fourth-generation languages. The rise of Object technology means that the popularity of fourth-generation languages is on the decline for the more advanced applications and the desire to use technology innovations faster than the 4GL suppliers can include them may well increase this trend. However, it is certain that the systems written in 4GLs will continue for the foreseeable future and for the less strategic, mission-critical or platform general applications, the use of 4GLs will continue to be popular with the Alpha systems providing a significant hike in performance.

Microsoft NT, that new and potentially explosive force in the market, is a technology that all the developers in the market should seriously consider since the level of functionality as a multi-user server is unparalleled by either VMS or any of the UNIX interfaces I have seen to date. In Alpha, the clash of three operating systems will be spectacular with the availability of Microsoft NT, OpenVMS and UNIX (OSF/1 now and System V soon). This allows a great deal of scope for the system designer, the customer and, if they have the skill and imagination, the applications developers. It is clear that the Digital Alpha systems offer an upgrade path for the existing VMS users of which there are in excess of 10 million. This may well prove to be an upgrade to more heterogeneous systems in the long run but initially the VMS user will only be upgrading to OpenVMS (with certain special exceptions). To those who invested in the Digital 5000 series systems in the past few years, the Alpha-based OSF/1 systems will provide an unparalleled power upgrade and systems that are fully compatible, so that small Alpha additions could be made, say, by using an Alpha file manager or an Alpha front-end processor running Microsoft NT.

Value is a critical issue for those in the information technology industry and the Alpha range of systems provides both opportunities and threats by empowering the addition of value to the systems in the market. Value can be added by the inclusion of functionality in the base application and by features and technologies that may have been previously impossible such as multimedia, AI, etc.

On the other hand, there are not a lot of Alpha systems out in the market yet and if you are moving an existing application to the Alpha platform (from whatever system) it is likely that you will end up with another code stream to support.

Relating to Digital is different to other corporate relationships. One has to understand the people more and the corporation less than, say, IBM. Digital is still a rather unique corporation to do business with and one in which innovative deals can be and are struck. My advice to the uninitiated is to invest a significant amount of time in meeting and understanding the people who you will have to deal with. Even if they move, they are a source of advice, information and help, that is the Digital philosophy (at least in part.)

The move to make Digital Alpha widely available will result in a lot of competition, as will the availability of a range of operating systems in the market. The big, slow, developers will be at a disadvantage in some ways since they will come up against the top end of the power PC market on Microsoft NT and the massed ranks of the UNIX applications developers both on UNIX and Alpha and on Microsoft NT.

With such a new system one has to ask, 'Is the technology stable?' and clearly the answer has to be 'not yet'. However, I know of no major problems, no big issues on the Alpha technologies on either OpenVMS or OSF/1 (NT is not released on Alpha at the time of writing this book). There are, however, a number of other risks. For instance, the availability of third-party or Digital layered products may make the move over to Alpha difficult or in some cases impossible.

Price is going to be a factor in the application market with the introduction of the applications on the new Alpha platform. One issue is the level of added value that the application can bring to the market given the power of the Alpha system. Another is the market sector itself that the application can exploit. These two issues need careful thought and management by the applications developer. Being the first or one of the first on the Alpha platform is important for the market as is the inclusion of lots of new technology features and, it has to be said, a clear plan to invest in the application for the further inclusion of other technologies, functions and features. Only by the addition of this value can the applications developers protect and indeed improve their margins and their range of associated service offerings.

Open hardware, or more specifically, the Alpha-based open hardware platforms, opens up a wide range of markets and therefore increases the competition in the market by the introduction of a larger number of competitive applications providers. Hence it is essential not to be seen as old technology or as the purveyor of systems that are in any way stagnating in the fast-changing cycle of technology innovation. Alpha is not a flash in the pan, it is a product designed for longevity, and this attribute should be seen as a significant selling point if you are providing your applications on Alpha-based systems. The greatest danger is that by staying on VAX or non-Alpha products, you will see the value of your applications continue to fall and the margin continue to be eroded, thus continuously reducing the funds available for investment in the applications, the technology and platforms.

Alpha is more of an opportunity than a threat, but the peak time to move onto such a new applications platform is early on its life. If one looks at similar revolutions in the information technology business, for instance the introduction of the personal computer by IBM, the applications that were on the platform early are the industry leaders now. Alpha means change, and perhaps one of the biggest changes is going to be the change in the business balance toward more services. Just what these services might be, how they are provided and what the likely shape of the service business will be in the future is uncertain. What I can say is that the value of an application will be enhanced by the addition of functions, features and enhancements that take the application closer to the business problem and that in the process of analysis of this problem, the acquisition of business-specific expertise should be regarded as an asset. Services that follow on and build from this base of experience assets will require a different set of skills and a different approach to the business at a fundamental level.

5.4 Systems Integrator and Developer Implications

First I will start with some definitions:

Systems integrator:

'Any organization that is involved in pulling together a number of disparate elements into a single working system.'

Systems integrators work across a range of hardware, software, operating systems and networks. Normally the set of these with which they operate is limited and in many cases is restricted to one or two suppliers for each component type.

Systems developer:

'Any organization that develops base system platforms including the hardware, operating system and software.'

Some or all these components may be bought in, and value is added in the specific systems architecture. An example of a systems integrator at one end of the scale might be NCR, who buy in a lot of their base components and at the other end we could look to IBM on the AS400 range as being almost completely self-sufficient in terms of the base design of the components (though subcontracting some of the production).

Applications developers are different animals altogether. System developers and systems integrators work a lot closer to the silicon and must have a much higher level of understanding of the base technology. This changes more rapidly than the upper layers of the system and generally the staffing profile of these two organizations reflects higher levels of skill than for the applications development community. This is not to say that systems developers and systems integrators are immune from the applications world. Quite the contrary, they are likely to have some of their own applications. In the case of the integration market, it is more often that the system integration capability arose from an existing applications business than conversely.

Alpha implications for these two communities are considerable and widespread. For instance, there is a very large number of architectural opportunities for the use of Alpha-based systems in the design of an overall systems architecture. From such a strong technical base the services that can grow are considerable, especially as one implication of the systems would be a much broader range of components going together to make up the complete system (hence Open Systems imply a significant need for a growing service business).

It must be remembered that players in the system integration market will enter the arena previously dominated by companies that until now were Digital systems-based. In addition, the move to making Alpha available on other vendor hardware, like Olivetti, will encourage the systems integrators from this market to come over into previously Digital-only markets. The systems developers, on the other hand, will need to be able to determine the markets they want to work with, if the answer is the higher-value end of the market. Then it is certainly the case that the Alpha processor is likely to make a very significant impact on this market soon and certainly by mid- to end-1994.

5.4.1 Strengths

Both systems integrators and systems developers have a lot of advantages to gain from a strategy that includes Alpha. System integrators who decide to adopt Alpha as a component of their platform and skills will gain the ability to improve the value of the systems that they design for any given end use. This is because of the range of technology that the Alpha systems can support as well as the significant number of system components that could usefully be constructed around the Alpha-based systems themselves. It must be remembered that if you are not in the Digital market today, acquiring Alpha skills as a systems integration operation opens a potential market of 10 million users to you around the world. If we look at the way in which the Alpha systems might be used we are limited only by the imagination. Four main areas are set out below as an example:

- *Hub systems* One common problem to be faced in the systems integration arena is the job of joining a number of systems or subsystems together. For instance, in a retail bank (high street bank) there are a number of systems. The tellers have a terminal of some kind, generally a PC on a local area network and including devices like cheque book printers, statement printers, swipe card readers and the like. In addition, the more intelligent devices like automatic teller machines (ATMs) may be connected to the branch office or central office or both. Finally there will be wide area communications lines into the retail bank from the central or divisional system (and most of this is SNA-based in banking). If we take an Alpha OpenVMS system, the wide area communications could be connected as well as the PC and device network and the intelligent devices. The advantage of this would be that the Alpha node could run software that automatically managed the PC network, possibly with the addition of applications and databases that the PCs could not cope with in native mode. The smart devices could be automatically managed and the retail bank branch could run a regularly updated local database offering some level of independence from the divisional system and hence better security and resilience. Furthermore, the local power and data would exist to allow the branch to market focused services to their local customers in a way that is difficult in British banking at present. Another example of a hub system would be where a stock control system is implemented to monitor the stock levels in a number of companies and re-order based on usage and projected usage patterns and on real need over the group and not just on the basis of the needs of one branch of the group. It may be that the systems in the group are all different following growth based on a strategy of acquisition and that the job of communicating with all these systems, then doing the stock re-order calculations followed by the stock level commitments to the systems at the branches is a very complex and disparate task. Again we would find that because of the very wide range of communications standards supported by the OpenVMS system and the power of the Alpha processor, the option would be open to the system architect to use, say, a pair of Alpha systems running OpenVMS and to give high resilience and provide the disparate communications (including, of course, a lot of EDI) that would link the systems together and act as a smart hub for the system as a whole. Many more examples abound, but I have to say that for the job of a central hub I would opt for the OpenVMS system unless there were very strong client preferences for a UNIX option, simply because of the standards supported and the sophistication of the communications products available on the Alpha systems under OpenVMS.

- *Front-end systems* The easiest way to demonstrate perceived value increases to the end user is to improve the human-computer interface (HCI). I am certain that for many of the systems that have to be designed by the average systems integrator, the Microsoft NT operating system provides the most comprehensive general solution to the HCI problems of today and for the next few years. There are organizations that have adopted a corporate standard like X-windows, OS/2 or even Openlook, but Microsoft NT gives a more powerful and sophisticated result for most general systems designs. Once such sophistication is coupled with the power of Alpha, then we have the option of setting up a series of front-end processors of amazing sophistication and power around a base that might be of any system (UNIX, VMS, IBM, etc.). Clearly this level of systems integration will be the one that should be targeted first since it offers the most apparent (hence easiest to sell) benefits across the board. I think that Microsoft NT is so powerful that it is likely to be the standard front end to many systems in the future, including UNIX and possibly Digital's OpenVMS.
- *Communications processors* The ability to communicate between systems has long been the strength and the hallmark of Digital, one of the key factors in the penetration of VAX into many other markets previously dominated by other players, and OpenVMS builds on that lineage. Furthermore, the growth of business transactions based on electronic communications is so rapid and sophisticated that the Alpha revolution and OpenVMS are both around at a point when the market could be counted on to be most receptive to them. In the systems integration world, the need to communicate to the wider world is now a standard item. However, this

needs to be done with varying levels of security and OpenVMS is the most secure option available on Alpha today. Therefore the systems integrator who needs to offload wide area communications to a specialized component must look seriously at the use of OpenVMS and Alpha as the most cost effective and technically efficient method of addressing the problem in a secure manner.

- *Applications integration platforms* The job of the systems integrator includes the task of taking a number of very different applications and integrating them together, sometimes on the same hardware platform and sometimes on a number of different platforms but being accessed by the same HCI. Since the Alpha range of systems and associated operating systems includes support for applications written to almost all the international standards accepted around the world as well as many *de-facto* standards (like Microsoft Windows 3.1 applications) then Alpha provides a good platform upon which to base the integration of applications. This is so if the applications all run on Alpha platforms on a network with each platform running a different operating system, or if the applications are all being ported to the one Alpha platform running just one of the available operating systems.

To the systems integrator there are a number of really positive reasons to move to Alpha. This is a super component for the integration of existing systems and for the addition of value as part of an overall systems integration exercise.

Moving on to the systems development community, Alpha has several key strengths to offer. First, the processor and semiconductor technology is second to none and offers systems capabilities both in the single- and multiple-processor configurations that are at the very top of the scale. Second, Alpha microprocessors provide a sound basis for systems development because of the longevity ensured by the design philosophy adopted by Digital in Alpha programme over the last three years together with the very open nature of the technology itself. This aspect of longevity is one well worth considering for the systems developer since most of your investment in operating system ports, customer base services and the like are at risk on the point of a major technology change (and likely to be duplicated for some time after the change, as in going from a proprietary system to UNIX for a vendor for instance, one does not simply dump the customers).

Thirdly, Alpha will become the standard processor for most of the high-value systems in the market, both from Digital and from the third-party systems developers. Lastly, as a systems developer you will always be looking for ways to strengthen your position in relation to the competition, Alpha provides this. By moving into systems that are so significantly powerful, you could move into the position of supplying higher-value systems to the more influential end of the market and by so doing produce a much healthier return on your capital than the suppliers of higher-volume, lower-value systems to the market. For a while at least, Alpha is a unique selling point but not a proprietary system.

5.4.2 Weaknesses

There is never a free lunch, and for the developers of systems and systems integrators there are weaknesses associated with the move to Alpha. Some of these will be transitional weaknesses and others will be longer-term issues.

First, the system integrators will have a lot of new technology to understand, at least three different platforms if they take the route of running with OpenVMS, OSF/1 and Microsoft NT. In addition to the base systems technology, there will be a level of value-added technology to become familiar with. For instance, EDI is a complex technology for the systems integrator to understand, as is Multimedia. The likely outcome will be the need for many specialist consultancies in highly defined areas working with larger, more general systems integrators. The need to form and manage relationships will also extend to relationships with the system suppliers themselves. For a systems integrator this is essential since the level of operation is so much closer to the technology base than for the application developer. It may be that until now your organization has had to deal with only one operation. Do not misjudge and underestimate the very significant amount of management and technologist time required to enter this market and to keep afloat, once in. In truth, one of the key attributes of multi-vendor system integrators is the efficiency of their relationship management with all their vendors and partners.

Another weakness that Alpha will bring to the systems integrators is that many organizations that previously did not operate in the Digital market will doubtless take the opportunity to advance into the territory, increasing the competition and bringing with them the likelihood of applications and service portfolios that will challenge the existing market order.

To make headway in the move up the value chain that the Alpha systems enable, your operation will need to examine closely the type, extent and provision of value-added services. One example of this is an organization I worked with who moved into the top end of a market with a very prestigious customer sale of an innovative (VAX-based) system. Unfortunately, they forgot to think about the service aspects of this. The customer wanted (and from examining the business this was obvious) 24-hour support, 7 days a week. Unfortunately when the organization got involved in this, they did not think out the cost of providing the service, the method of providing it or the way it might be staffed. This problem was a typical example of a company moving into a higher-value market, seeing the potential of the services and not realizing that they are needed as soon as the sale of the systems integration exercise is made (or before). In many cases the services will themselves be so specialized that they will inevitably have to be subcontracted out to the specialists by the prime systems integration company.

Systems developers, on the other hand, face a somewhat different set of problems. First, like the systems integrators, Alpha is another technology to learn. However, it is likely that the Alpha-based systems and the older ones from the systems developer will have both to co-exist for a longer period. Hardware companies that can switch to other systems platforms are therefore likely to be quite large (like Olivetti, Cray, etc.) in order to bear the set-up and parallel business expansion costs. Second, do not expect the markets that you operate in and the major players that are in it to react in anything but a very aggressive manner when threatened by an Alpha-based rival. Start attacking the IBM RS6000 base in any measure and you will find a very solid response, I am sure. This is likely to limit the market entry points and geographies somewhat for your new systems.

Lastly, I think Alpha will be the volume product in the mid-range server system and top-end systems and will be there sooner rather than later. I am less certain about Alpha as a replacement for the Intel systems on the desktop in any significant numbers, at least for the next 5 years. Thus your systems strategy needs to look at the value profile of your customer base. You could be producing systems they do not need or are unable to justify if you go down the Alpha route without very careful thought.

5.4.3 Opportunities

Opportunities, those chances to move forward, abound for the system integrators who chose to include Alpha-based systems in their portfolios of components for subsystem and system architecture and integration. First, the opportunity to include resilience coupled with performance in systems design is now possible in a way that was not economically possible in the past. By using multiple processor one can work with cold, warm or hot standby systems, in addition to which polled results can be used. These four system classes refer to systems that are available but not power up, systems that are powered up but need to come on line and share no part of the workload and systems that share the workload but could take more of it than their normal proportion (hot standby). Polled systems are situations in which, say, three computers carry out an operation and a fourth checks all three results. One might ignore any result that was different from any two others. If all three results differed then one might rerun the transaction. This kind of polled result system is useful in systems like those to be found in the space shuttle. They are also now a reality for systems that conduct financial transactions automatically like trading and dealing systems if Alpha is employed.

Clearly performance can be gained now that was impossible at the price in the past. Alpha is excellent at the Digital manipulation of images, for instance, and one can foresee a whole raft of applications that, can digitize design information and use pre-existing photographic information to add to it and produce a composite third made in full digital form. This might form the basis of applications in forensic science where the rules for the reconstruction of features of a skull could be used, together with accurate digital representations of a skull to both reconstruct a copy of the original features and decide if the features mapped to those of a photograph of a known person. All this has been possible for a long time, but at a price and for a performance that was never mainstream

Longevity is a really important issue in the integration of systems. Clearly the systems themselves are complex and, once running, the last thing that the organization commissioning them wants is the excitement and expense of going through the whole exercise again in a couple of years or so. Longevity in terms of the power and performance as well as in the design concepts that allow the support of a wide range of operating system and software is a real asset and one that you need to build around (and have procedures to support it).

The lot of systems developers is significantly different but no less strewn with opportunities. One that I particularly think will be a very interesting sector to watch is the market for specialized or even personalized systems. For instance, the Alpha processor is now so powerful that a whole raft of functionality can be included in portable devices that was impossible up to now. The ability to create instrumentation which is portable and which can perform very complex analysis such as stress structural analysis on real structures in real time from very large numbers of devices making a host of measurements is a whole field of opportunities in itself. Devices that are embedded into robotic systems can now begin to tackle problems of amazing complexity in the pattern matching field. The data space that is now usable is so large and can be manipulated so fast that world models as used by the robotic devices can now become several orders of magnitude more sophisticated. Perhaps one of the fastest growing areas for specialized systems will be the development of systems that improve the nature of the human-computer interface. Systems that begin to be built and use stylus-based computing, voice command and response and very high speed communications are a sector that has hardly been touched. True, there are PC-based systems today, but for the most part they seem slow and are not really powerful to do all the things one might like. Certainly this is the case with voice systems.

Areas of technical specialization for the systems developers, such as neural networks (Beale and Jackson, 1990), multimedia etc. are another opportunity waiting to be realized with the Alpha-based technologies. What is needed in this is imagination. Systems limits have gone back a long way and the use of the system must now match the capabilities. The integrators are in need of more specialized components that are very reliable and do their more limited functions very well, very fast and present the results in a consistent, standard fashion. Alpha can form the basis of this in the high-value end of the market.

5.4.4 Threats

For the systems integrator, the advent of the Alpha technology does bring with it threats as well as opportunities and strengths. The three primary threats that you will face, initially at least, will be:

- Digital itself. I have said earlier that Digital needs to make more revenue from the services side of their business for the same reasons that all in the information technology world must do this, namely reducing revenues and margins from hardware and software. One aspect of Digital's business which is fast growing and which must be very attractive to them for a number of reasons is the systems integration business. As a large, global player with a highly trained workforce, many of whose skills are in connectivity and systems development, they are in a very strong position, albeit one which is somewhat biased by their own products. It will be the case that Digital operates in a competitive manner to third-party systems integration companies. They will make great efforts to do this in an organised and agreed manner with those companies that they form relationships with, but compete they will, and they must. From my own experiences inside and outside Digital, their approach is generally well organized and professional but they are determined, and one can reasonably assume that they will be looking to work mainly at the larger, more lucrative end of the systems integration market, especially with the prospect of introducing Alpha-based components to any overall system. The only realistic counters to this threat are to agree a market policy with Digital, to have specialized skills, and to operate on a more efficient cost structure to provide for cost competition.
- Digital are not alone in having skills relevant to the Alpha systems. I have said that the OpenVMS variant of the Alpha systems, the Alpha AXP processors for instance, are ideally suited to the hub components and communications processor components of larger, more heterogeneous systems, so those with existing expertise in the VMS and VAX arena are in a good position to work with Alpha in systems integration exercises. If you are a systems integrator coming into the market and looking to acquire these skills from, say, a UNIX background, you will find that you are threatened by those from the VAX arena.
- Fragmentation. By this I refer to the rapid rise in the number of more specialized systems components that you will need to understand and keep pace with. As in much of the rest of industry, specialization and focus are important factors in the philosophy of market exploitation. I am confident that Alpha processors will be used to drive a large number of much more specialized and powerful devices than the average systems integrator sees today. Couple this trend with the desire of clients themselves to focus their own businesses more clearly, and one has a need and capability that must result in a rapid proliferation of products. My reason for thinking many of these will be Alpha-based is that the sophistication then possible, coupled with Alpha's very large addressable memory function, provides for a much lower electromechanical element in the overall make-up of such devices. For the systems integrator this can be a real threat, especially in a market where the number of components is likely to rise rapidly (like retail and manufacturing), since not only does the component itself require specialized technical knowledge but it predicates for a trend towards more and more specialized industry knowledge on the part of the systems integrator as well.

Systems developers, on the other hand, face a different set of problems:

- Alpha is great news for those wanting to go up the value chain, and it is set to take out some of the really high-value systems components. However, this is a problem in some ways for the system developer. I recently worked with a systems developer (who used Intel, not Alpha, as the microprocessors in their system), but I was unable to feel confident about taking them into large system sales simply because they were unable to run an efficient and effective maintenance service, especially by way of the spares operation. It is vital to remember that the higher price tag on a system that is aimed at the higher end of the market induces a much higher (disproportionately so) expectation about the levels of quality, back-up and service associated with the system. In this respect I have seen many manufacturers, some of them big names, come unstuck with new systems in the market purely on the basis of back-up service and production build quality.
- Competition gets to be two-way. As soon as you begin using Alpha processors as the basis of systems, then you will have to expect the competition to do the same and your market looks as lucrative to them as theirs does to you. This is one of the key driving factors towards system specialization, towards the need to add value to systems and the main reason that Open Systems, while being a philosophy that I, like all engineers, subscribe to, will never result in the absolute standardization of systems that many of its apostles claim. The real defences against the competition and the threat to your market are to concentrate on the lock-in mechanisms for the system, by specialization, functional or feature addition and by a tendency towards more proprietary and hence less open components as part of your overall systems design.
- Lastly there is the problem of hardware lives. As Digital know from their experiences on the PDP, hardware is very difficult to kill off once it gets into the community. Once down the route of using Alpha processors, your development budget for systems will need to be considerable. I would argue that the only way this can be fuelled fast enough in the modern economic climate is for your operation to be developing the kind of systems that your existing users will be prepared to upgrade to relatively quickly. The implication of this is that if they do not, the cost for your operation of supporting multiple hardware versions is going to be so great as to cause your business serious problems indeed. For this reason alone, most of the third-party vendors will be in the UNIX or Microsoft Windows systems arenas.

5.4.5 Summary

I have, in this section, used my own definition of both the terms 'systems integrators' and 'system developers'. While there are many definitions I could have chosen, the ones

I have used here fit the actual nature of most organizations in this category rather than their theoretical nature. Clearly, since these operations are working at the systems level, they are concerned with a broader and more detailed level of operations than the typical applications developer, though some will have their own applications to offer for certain industry sectors.

Most of the opportunities for these two sets of operations arise in the field or systems architecture, either of the overall system that the integrator designs or constructs from subsystems or in terms of the complete systems developed around the Alpha technology by the systems development operations. In both cases the implications for services, in terms of growth and value, are very significant indeed. The end result of Digital's Alpha technology for both the systems developers and integrators will be the introduction of a number of new players into a market that was, until now, the domain of Digital specialists. Above all, I think that this is the most uncertain area of the market since the number of influencing factors is so high. One thing is certain though, the level of competition will increase dramatically in the near future.

Strengthening of the position for the systems integrators will be achieved by the construction of systems with higher added values to the end users. The position of the systems integrator is further strengthened by Alpha since there are 10 million existing VAX users as a potential customer base for them. Probably the four most likely places to start with Alpha in systems integration exercises is as a central 'hub' linking a number of subsystems together, in the role as a front-end processor used to add functionality to the existing system components, as a communications processor to other local and wide area communications networks and lastly as a platform for the integration of a number of applications, an Open Systems target in some respects.

To the systems developer, Alpha presents a level of technology that is simply unmatched elsewhere coupled with openness and longevity that make the system an excellent investment protection base on which to build. Furthermore, Alpha is going to become the *de-facto* standard for high-value Open Systems which need performance, power and a long-life architecture.

Clearly there are a number of weaknesses that Alpha exposes during the transitional period and indeed beyond. For the system integrator, there are the issues of the additional expertise required, the need to form and effectively manage relationships with Digital if you do not already have them and the fact that other operations will enter this market aggressively. The system developers also have more technology to come to grips with, can expect a very robust defence of markets by those with non-Alpha-based systems and must realize, at least at first, that Alpha volumes are likely to be relatively low, so focus on the high-value end of the market is essential.

Opportunities abound and systems integrators can now design and provide levels of resilience and performance that have not been economically viable in the past together with long-lived systems that are capable of adapting to the challenges of the future because of their power and openness.

Systems developers have the opportunity to make more specialized, more focused systems that closely match specific market opportunities. At the HCI level, the systems developer can add a great deal. I think we have only begun to scratch the surface of what will be achieved with Alpha in this area as indeed is the case with AI components in systems.

The reverse side of an opportunity is a threat, and Alpha certainly introduces a few of these to the systems integration and development markets. Systems integrators will come up against Digital itself in the market. This is likely to be an increasing trend and will need to be carefully managed by them. Others will be in this market with skills from the VAX arena. If you are entering from outside, this may be a real problem for you, especially with existing VMS users.

Systems developers must expect the competition to work two ways. If you enter a market, so will the opposition. Second, you have to understand the need for quality and service from the higher-value end of the market. The expectations there are very different to the low-end, and finally you will end up supporting a number of old systems and your new Alpha range. I have seen this almost sink companies in the past. The only way to sort out the issue is to get the userbase up to the new systems, and that takes a lot of careful planning, marketing and selling to achieve.

The implications of Alpha on the systems integration and systems development markets is significant indeed, part positive, part negative, but in the balance the opportunities outweigh the threats. However, this is only true if the organizations understand and cater for the needs of the higher-value clients and show imagination in creating Alpha-based systems with real added value to the market and support them with equivalently robust service offerings.

In the next section I look at the implications of Alpha on the end-user community, both the existing users of VAX/VMS systems and the users of DEC 5000/ ULTRIX and OSF/1-based systems. As we will see, the marketplace looks very different if you are a user of Alpha-based systems from being either an applications developer, systems integrator or systems developer. The same type of analysis: strengths, weaknesses, opportunities and threats, is used but the perspective gained in the exercise is somewhat different. In the way of things no one of the views is, by itself, representative of the actual situation. They all show different aspects of the same complex set of interrelated issues.

5.5 End-User Implications

This is the group that really matters. The end users are the force that drives the market and the source of funds that fuel the innovation in the information technology business. My definition of end user is 'Those individuals or organizations that consume systems, applications, hardware, software and services for their own use and to add value to their own operations.'

In the market for Alpha-based systems, there are two classes of end user: first, that group who operate now on Digital platforms, specifically using VAX and VMS or

Digital 5000 systems running either ULTRIX or OSF/1. The second, class of end users are those who are thinking of adopting Alpha-based systems at some point but who presently run on other hardware and operating systems, and specifically this refers to UNIX (of many types), Microsoft Windows or proprietary systems.

In this section I have taken the point of view of the end user. In this respect the analysis of strengths, weaknesses, opportunities and threats relate to the position of the end user given that they adopt systems-based on Alpha, or are affected by the introduction of Alpha-based systems and with regard to the suppliers to the end users, i.e. system integrators, system developers and application developers. In some cases, especially for large commercial organizations and for local or national government agencies, some of these functions may be internal rather than the concern of external agencies.

5.5.1 Strengths

There is one immediate and obvious area in which Alpha strengthens the end-user position in the market and that is cost. Clearly an Alpha system with the same or greater power than an existing VAX is going to be cheaper to purchase and run. This direct cost reduction covers the system cost itself, the software and operating system costs, the power consumption (including air conditioning) and the space requirements. In all these important areas, the cost reductions on an average VAX installation will be between 15% and 60%. However, in the scheme of things, as I hope to show, these savings, while sizable and capable of being realized in the short term, are not substantial when compared to the added value that may well accrue from the use of Alpha-based systems. However, one last point on direct cost reduction: the longevity of the Alpha architecture does, in itself, bring substantial cost savings against potential expenditure in more sizable organizations. The indirect benefits of Alpha-based systems come from the improvements in the efficiency of the operation, for instance by the improvement of turnaround times or throughput of the business.

More important is the position a company could potentially get to using systems based on Alpha. First, the type and nature of businesses may be changed due to the capabilities provided by such systems. I can illustrate my point with the following two examples:

1. Manufacturing business. I know of a manufacturer who works in the market for subcontracted component manufacture for the aerospace business. By adopting Alpha-based systems, they are now becoming capable of moving further up the value curve in their business by carrying out both design and product research that was well beyond the scope of their old systems and far out of their reach in cost terms.

2. Commodity brokerage. Many commodity brokers are small independent operations without the resources of the large multinational corporations. I am aware of at least two who are looking for systems using advanced AI techniques to start to model the commodities market and the way that their top brokers perform with a view to developing small, affordable, commodity brokerage decision-support systems. However, until now the options were either very expensive or very slow. I have found out recently that one small operation in England is looking to service both clients by providing a system based on Alpha and OpenVMS. This would be a system to rival many in the larger corporations but at a fraction of the price.

In the first example, the operation concerned is making changes to the business, in the second the hope is that the efficiency (accuracy of buying and selling decisions) will improve over time providing a significantly better yield.

Another example of the improved value that can be gained by the use of Alpha is in the competitive edge a company can win. For instance, complex simulation tasks used in the design of a number of mechanical and electrical products were beyond the scope of computing for many operations until Alpha-based systems came along. This puts tools of great power within the reach of much smaller and more flexible and innovative operations than in the past. Examples of this might be fluid and aerodynamic modelling, molecular modelling, large numerical problems that one finds in engineering, physics, economics and medicine. These tools, once liberated from the large corporate structures, will have a very significant effect on the outputs from smaller companies. All this makes the end user a stronger operation and would not be possible without the Alpha technology and supporting programme.

Clearly, the decision by Digital to allow the Alpha processors to be used (and, in the future, possibly made) by other third-party companies is a real revelation in the market. One implication of this is the increased amount of choice that presents itself to the existing Digital user. For some considerable time, the OpenVMS systems will be available only from Digital. However, I expect this to change, and sooner rather than later. For the moment, however, the new range of Alpha-based, non-Digital systems may allow one to pick and choose the right product, at the right price, with the right application. This situation has never been possible before the Alpha programme. Existing users of VMS will now be in a stronger position, internally, financially, with their suppliers and technically, since they are able to have a route forward in most cases onto the Alpha platform.

5.5.2 Weaknesses

Most of the weakness in the end-user market occurs during the transitional phase from one systems platform to another and while the market moves and settles down again to a reletively stable position. However, Alpha can weaken certain end-user operations in the longer term under some circumstances.

First, there is the issue of change. Any change at the level and in such a dramatic manner as Alpha will bring about a level of risk. For instance, if one has a system on a VAX under VMS today, moving to the new Alpha platform may take a while. One will have to wait for the applications to be ported over by the vendor, for instance. Porting may require a level of code modification, and no matter how slight this is, the nature of software and its development predicate towards this exercise, increasing the likelihood of the introduction of errors into a system that might otherwise be in a stable reliability position. Changing systems takes up a lot of management time and money also and between the three, the changes add up to a weakening of one's position as a buyer, simply because the balance of power in the market has shifted slightly away from the buyer for a period of time.

One will need to get software migrated to the new Alpha system, but a decision has also to be made about the operating system to use. If you are a VMS user today, you are likely to want to stay that way, at least for the main application. This is where the power starts to move away from you. It is important that you look at the other operating systems and understand what they have to offer. For instance, it may be that by including Microsoft NT in the front end of your system you will improve the overall functionality. However, to achieve this one has first to get the systems integrator in and then rely on them for advice in the first instance. Following on from this, the change of an existing system through to a new system is one in which the work, the control of that work and the quality of the end result is largely out of your control. All this is a function of change rather than Alpha particularly. It is just that in this context Alpha is forcing the decision for some of the end users.

Next we have to remember that the suppliers have a potentially larger market for their applications. Their systems and their integration services on the Alpha platforms and the open nature of the platform make the market more open also. Given this, one's power is weakened. Essentially, the fish you are stays the same size, but someone has made the pond bigger!

Until now, you have been in the fortunate position of having a technical architecture that was constrained and defined (for many VAX users this is the case in fact if not in theory). However, now one has to make some decisions. The operating system is an option, the hardware supplier is an option and there is a very much larger range of organizations offering applications and services to choose from. Again, these issues weaken your position somewhat since the emphasis will be put on changing your options. It may be better (at least for the time being) to keep the core system on OpenVMS or even a VAX if necessary and work up a technical strategy and some experience in the other options.

Given the continued downwards pressure on the prices of hardware, software and services, the value each client brings to the overall turnover picture of a supplier becomes less over time. If you opt for the short-term cost reduction option, then inevitably, your value to the supply organizations will diminish as will the value of the system to your own business. Under these circumstances, your bargaining power and influence on the future direction of, say, any application's functionality will reduce rapidly over time.

5.5.3 Opportunities

The easiest opportunity to realize for the end user, in the short term, is to do a very nice deal with Digital, or one of the other Alpha systems suppliers, for a new system. It is essential when a new product is launched that this gets into the market in large numbers, partly for marketing reasons, partly for capacity in the manufacturing facility and partly for financial reasons. In the early life of a system, good deals can be done with vendors, especially if you are in some way prestigious ~ for instance, if you represent the first installation in a market sector or geography and especially if you are swapping out the opposition's hardware!

Another short- to medium-term opportunity is in the area of joint relationships with suppliers of systems and applications. If you are looking to be early into a market, say by taking their application onto an Alpha platform with them, this may be a chance to work with an application supplier to get exactly the application that you require for the job you do. The value added gives you the edge on others in the market and gets you there relatively early, if not first.

Due to the open nature of the Alpha platform and the associated business practices that it encourages, the choice of applications and systems vendor brings a wealth of experience to the market that as VAX users you were unable to tap. The experiences of this group can and should be used to add value to our business. They have products and services that could, in the right circumstances, not only add value to the business that you are in at the moment but also enable you to enter other, associated, businesses, as in some of my earlier examples.

As the reader may have gathered by now, my attitude to computing power is that it should be put to good use, to enable the end-user organizations to liberate the real potential in their businesses. Partly this may be through the adoption of methods and tools which until recently were out of the reach of your organization. Possibly the key lies in the store of data that you have in your business and that now can really be manipulated and managed in a way that can show trends, substructures and alternatives that have lain untapped before. An example of this is of a food company I know. They have a lot of data on sales of their different food lines going back for several years. They would like to build a sophisticated model to forecast trends in buying patterns and raw material pricing so that at any moment in time they are in a good position to make spot decisions on the value to their business of buying decisions for raw materials at spot prices and of the likely trends in product demand. This would have been an expensive exercise until now. They use a large Windows-based network and are ripe to swap this for a power Alpha system running Microsoft NT for many of the functions (the PCs are 286 based and running short of power). Not only would this be a functionally faster and more sophisticated system, it would have the power to drive the modelling and decision-support systems that they so desire, and at an affordable price for acceptable performance.

Markets around the world are getting more competitive, and in line with this your company needs to look for the individual market opportunities that can be exploited by close definition of (often short-lived) market needs. One example of this is the move by a Japanese automobile manufacturer to produce a limited edition of its early 1950s model car, but built in modern materials and with modern production materials. Using very powerful technology this was accomplished in just 20 weeks to production from design. Such sophistication and power are no longer the domain of the global corporations. These are now tools for the small to medium sized enterprise. By enabling you to exploit the highly vertical market sectors with your facilities and expertise, Alpha changes the nature of your business. Many of the application areas for the technology are in the domain of design and market manipulation or analysis. They are the high-value areas (in general) and most compatible with the high-speed, large-scale data manipulation.

5.5.4 Threats

Probably the most obvious threat to you as an end-user organization that is-based on Alpha is that of the future for VAX. Clearly Digital are not about to drop the VAX, stop investing in it or discontinue support in the near future. However, there will need to be a cut over to the new Alpha systems as the central strategic focus for the activities of Digital. Furthermore, while the VAX market is large and still a good source of revenue, the primary focus for the applications and system developers now has to be the Alpha-based systems since they are the growth area for value systems offering an open route. Therefore staying around for the long term on the VAX might not be too wise. Alpha has to threaten the future of the VAX and for highly VAX-dependent organizations (and there are some) this is a big problem.

The next threat to your operation created by Alpha is that of value and scale. Digital and all the other system developers and integrators are likely to want to concentrate on the value and prestige systems first. If you are not in this category, then you may find the selling response is less avid than one might like. Given that some of the larger operations are your competitors, you may be falling behind because of this phenomenon.

What is true for you is also true for your competitors. If they adopt the power of Alpha-based systems before you, add value to their operations first and make a better use of their assets and experience, then you will be competitively disadvantaged.

The final threat presented to the end user by the introduction of Alpha by Digital is caused by the increased competition that Alpha will fuel by virtue of its Openness. If you are dependent on a single organization for some critical element of your system, say for a bespoke application, then you are at greater risk of the supplier foundering in the rough waters that will be generated by such competition in the market.

5.5.5 Summary

To the end user, Alpha offers many potential rewards but not without risk or, in some cases, a weakening of the buyer's power in the market with respect to the suppliers. On balance, the greatest benefits, those that offer the most significant rewards in the medium to long term, are to be gained in the enabling aspects of the Alpha technology and programme. Short-term financial benefits are possible: one can simply downsize to an Alpha system from a larger one, either VAX or another, and the cost savings will be apparent for the same power. However, this short-term approach to technical strategy is rooted in the thinking of the last decade, in the era of 'smaller, faster, cheaper'. What really matters to the users of technology now is using the technology to add very significant levels of advantage to their operations. Part of this picture will be made up by companies that are in the small to medium-sized enterprises and who wish to use the same tools and methods for gaining competitive advantage as their global competitors but until now could not accomplish it. Part of the picture is made up by the innovative application of the technology to problems that until the advent of Alpha were impractical to solve for the mass market, such as sophistication in the human-computer interface and in advanced data management and modelling techniques.

In terms of the market position, end users will be in a slightly weaker position overall, but there are some short-term opportunities in terms of forming early relationships with Digital and associated suppliers that are worth exploring. If you are moving to Alpha, either from a Digital platform or another, the issue of software migration is one that requires careful consideration. It is true to say that software can just be translated from the VAX to the Alpha OpenVMS platform and run in translated mode. However, this is not a long-term solution and was only intended to provide an immediate path for migration under special circumstances. Many of the benefits of the Alpha architecture will not be available to you by going down this route so the best option, and indeed the only long-term option, is to translate the software. Dependence on the inclusion of third-party products such as compilers, databases, etc. and on Digital layered products will at least materially affect the schedule of porting and in some circumstances could require significant levels of rewrite to move over onto the Alpha platform.

In terms of the real impact Alpha-based systems could have on your operation, what is required is a review of your computing strategy with the emphasis on the added value that computing could bring to your operation if the power was available. By doing this you will then be in a position to enable the power in your business and take advantage of a broader range of opportunities by the adoption of new tools and methods. In all this you have to start pushing the suppliers to get the systems and applications you need. I have been consistently critical of applications in this book and for good reason. Many, though not all, lack any real vision and few show any imaginative use of technology to add value rather than to perform in a superficial way. However, in defence of the applications development community, they need to be better driven by the end user towards the areas you need improved for your business. True, as non-technical users, you may be in the position of not knowing what can be achieved, but you are in a position to ask for anything and then look, with the developers and suppliers, into the feasibility of delivering your request.

VAX is still a good platform and so is the Digital 5000 range. Inevitably, however, they are at the end of a lifecycle and any organization investing in applications and systems development must be in the position of changing the emphasis towards Alpha-based systems. Remember, what you can do so can your competitors, and not moving over to Alpha, not using its power but just riding along on its price performance, is likely to be the biggest investment mistake you are ever likely to make. All the major companies I work with that are on VAX and Digital 5000 systems today are not looking to decrease their system spend on Alpha relative to VAX, they are looking into the way Alpha can help their business. One company I am working with has an international network of interrelated warehouses and manufacturing companies supplying a very large number of retail outlets. They believe Alpha will allow them such sophisticated stock management and control that they could reduce their shelf stock levels by 30%. Not bad, considering that their rough estimate of shelf stock value today is in the region of $87 million.

The implications of Alpha are many and various. I look on the technology advance as one which will liberate the power of information simply because the manipulation that is now possible with these systems has never before been widely available and certainly not in such a flexible and open form.

5.6 Chapter Summary

In this chapter I have investigated some of the implications of Digital's Alpha programme and technology on a number of market areas together with giving a view on the strategies that are most likely to deliver real value from such innovations.

5.6.1 Main Chapter Themes and Issues

Markets are a balanced set of forces, some acting in favour of a particular player, others acting against. In this chapter I have used the simplest form of presenting the main market implications of Digital's Alpha technology and its associated sales, marketing and services programme, in the form of a strengths, weaknesses, opportunities and threats analysis for each of the main areas of the market. The main issues in this chapter are as follows:

Applications Developers My critical view of the status of the majority of applications in the industry today is based on a wide experience of what is on offer in a number of industries. The point I have made about adding value is absolutely critical if the applications are ever to match the capabilities of the hardware and not be swamped by them. Once you have a view on how your customers see the value of your application (i.e. what it does and does not do that makes it valuable to them as opposed to the price they paid for it) then you can begin to plan the way forward to adding value. If you take the other route, that of viewing Alpha as an even faster and cheaper machine than the Digital 5000 series, you will be making a very great mistake in the mid-term. Use the power and flexibility of the Alpha systems to integrate key technologies into your application, look at using Microsoft NT as the front end for your applications.

There are no absolutes about key technologies for the future. These depend so much on the industry sector, but the top runners I would strongly advise investigating are HCI improvements such as pen interfaces, voice and multimedia, data management and manipulation like Object databases, free-text databases, very large databases, database distribution and high-speed SQL access to data as an alternative to relational storage, artificial intelligence techniques such as neural networking, knowledge capture systems, heuristic editing and interfaces.

While applications developers want to sell lots of copies and updates of applications to the market, the market only really wants to buy one copy. The end result of this is that once an application is out and in use, it becomes an important part of someone's working toolset: they do not want to change it and they expect it to last a long time. Longevity of the application is therefore an important issue to the market and to you as applications developers. The important issue to consider is productivity against longevity and portability. For instance, if one has chosen a specific 4GL and Relational Database Management System as the implementation tool for an application, this will in the future restrict one's choice but produce great gains in productivity while developing the application. On the other hand, one might develop the application using good software engineering methods from each stage of specification through to the final code generation. On the whole, this is much less productive but a lot more portable since it (generally) depends only on the compiler. A mid-course is the facilitization of an application partly by the use of third-party products. This is fine but suffers from the same problems as using a 4GL without having the same level of productivity gain in general. Longevity in the application implies portability these days. One of my pet stories is of an application that is over 15 years old and written mainly in Cobol. While it started out on PDP it now runs on a mixture of VAX, Alpha/OpenVMS, IBM RS6000, HP UX, Intel-based systems running UNIX System V.4 and Prime. The catch in the story is that being written in Cobol, not only is it portable, but the application vendors do not have to pay high runtime licences to a third-party when they sell it!

Systems Integrators Perhaps the most important thing to remember as a systems integrator is that systems containing Digital's Alpha processors will initially be most successful in the mid- to high-end systems. Characteristically, these will be running either VMS today or in the UNIX arena. The Microsoft NT offerings will take another 12 months to make an impact (i.e. not before quarter 2, 1995). Given this move to the higher-value systems, you will need to ensure that your service offerings are up to a level, quality and coverage that fits the needs of this sector of the market.

In terms of the use of Alpha-based systems in the overall systems design, the most obvious places to consider them in terms of power and value are as hubs between subsystems, communications processors to networks, front-end processors, applications integration platforms. In all these areas, the Alpha systems would produce excellent results. Remember though, that one of the companies you will come up against in the high-end of this market is Digital itself.

For systems integrators, applications developers and systems developers, one key issue is that of the services that you offer and their quality. The industry will continue to move towards services, but the budget for these is finite and therefore the competition is increasing. Specialization and quality are the best tactics here.

System Developers The section in this chapter on Intel says only a tiny amount about one of the most remarkable hardware companies in the world. Like NASA, Intel impresses not just by results but by numbers, and big numbers throughout. Intel will continue to own the mass market for volume microprocessors for the foreseeable future, and they will be fitted to systems whose price and added value will continue to fall and where availability is likely to increase to very remarkable levels indeed. With the exception of the companies like NCR, who use multiple processors in their offerings, Intel will be outstripped by both MIPS and Digital in the higher-value systems for the next five years (to the end of 1998), with Digital taking the most market share in this sector. Given this, Alpha-based systems are all about value and not volume for the first 3 years (to 1996) at least.

As a direct result of specialization in the needs of the market, I would recommend that systems developers look at the specialized areas and modes of use for Alpha-based systems. My view on the front-running areas to look at would be HCI, voice, multimedia, pen interfaces, data engines, high-performance datastores, mass-storage controllers, communications, high-speed communications processors, high-security encryption devices, image processing, robotics, standalone systems, navigation devices, environmental control, biomedical, and leisure systems. Specialist systems are going to be a growth area for the systems development community, and the only limit is the imagination of the engineers.

End Users The real key to getting to grips with Alpha is in understanding what you would ideally like to use automation and information technology to do in your business and then work with the applications and systems developers to get it. The hardware now has the power to do what you need. Remember, a 64-bit system does not store and manipulate just twice the data of a 32-bit system, it works with 4 billion times as much data. That, in a nutshell, is a lot of scope for advanced systems.

Expect lots of changes in systems design on the Alpha platform, especially in the front-end processing area (the HCI). Do not be satisfied with technology in applications that is old hat, look at what systems like Microsoft NT offer by way of functionality, for instance, and think about how this would empower your business. Look for lots of functional changes-based on the manipulation of data, lots of trend and what-if analysis made possible by the very high-performance processor in that AXP system.

I have said repeatedly that the Digital Alpha processors are Open, and that so is OpenVMS and OSF/1 and (to a lesser extent) Microsoft NT. Do not have any illusions though, Open does not mean you can take RPG II code from an IBM AS400 and put it on a Digital Alpha AXP system running OpenVMS and see it run. It will not and it is never likely to! Open is a relative term. I like to say that 'Open Systems are not so much Open as slightly ajar.' Realistically the industry still has a long way to go. Interestingly though, Alpha systems may allow levels of automation in software engineering that have not been realistic in the past. We may yet see a little more light at the end of the tunnel.

5.6.2 Questions Raised by this Chapter

The key questions for each of the market areas concerned in this chapter are as follows:

Applications Developer

1. How and where can you use Alpha to add value?
2. What competitors will enter on Alpha?
3. How are portability and longevity to be addressed?

Systems Integrator

1. Where can you use Alpha to greatest effect?
2. How will you get the skills?
3. What are the implications for services?

Systems Developer

1. Are your volume expectations realistic?
2. Can you move to specialized systems on Alpha?
3. Are your services sufficient and of high enough quality to move up value with Alpha?

End User

1. What could Alpha be used for that adds real value?
2. What areas of present systems are least satisfactory?
3. Are my present suppliers going to fare well or ill with Alpha in the market?

5.6.3 Conclusions of this Chapter

The competitive implications of Alpha are wide ranging indeed. It is clear that the market is much more competitive than it was just five years ago, with a concentration of power as one key attribute and the emergence of a large number of highly specialized organizations with closely defined market sectors as the other. Alpha has a lot to offer, designed as it has been to meet the technical and commercial challenges of today and the next 20 years.

The competition have a number of weaknesses in comparison. Intel is still heavily CISC-based though trying to move towards RISC. MIPS are a close technical contender but still a long way behind and will find the massive capital investment needed to catch up difficult to raise. Competition in this market looks like remaining price based in each sector while the MIPS, Intel and other competitors take time to catch up on a function and feature basis. Digital will meet this by overwhelming functionality now and price performance rises that will continue to leave the opposition lagging behind.

Digital's positioning will start in the high-end and at the top of the mid-range in terms of volume growth. These are the areas where Alpha-based systems have the highest value to offer. Growth in the other areas will, by comparison, be slower and more dependent on the third-party relationships, like those with Olivetti, to move forward. With the Alpha project, Digital has entered the arena of microprocessor manufacture in the public sense.

The microprocessor market is one in which the competition is fierce and the barriers to entry very high in financial terms alone. Intel are the clear volume leader, though in the upper end of the mid-range, the technical workstation market and the larger RISC-based systems, the closest competitor is likely to be MIPS (except for multi-Intel-based systems from companies such as NCR). The home-grown microprocessor strategies from companies like IBM are looking shaky at present, simply on the basis of volumes and costs. I cannot see this policy continuing, especially in the face of such large corporate losses.

Digital has a lot to offer in this market with Alpha. It represents a technology generation jump, is widely available and is designed to be compatible with the broadest range of industry needs over the next 25 years. As we have seen, IBM have done badly in recent times. We also know that many IBM systems are in markets and with clients that Digital would value as converts. IBM have many problems to solve, some technical, but most commercial and managerial, with the big blue in such a weakened state that Digital will almost certainly mount a sustained attack on its more vulnerable customers with Alpha systems. Most likely this will be in the Microsoft NT and small UNIX server end at first, the classic surround/siege tactics. While IBM sort out their problems, one option would be to use Alpha processor-based systems. This, however, is very unlikely indeed.

Were Alpha a processor restricted to Digital alone, I would see the market implications very differently. My view would have to be restricted to Digital's customer base and some small additional growth (for the same reasons I consider IBM RS6000 as a restricted player in this market). However, the fact is that Digital have decided to go public, to make Alpha freely available to many companies around the world, and this alters the situation significantly. Alpha may change the perception in the market. It is not going to knock Intel or MIPS out altogether, but it will make a big impact and is certainly going to take a very high proportion of the higher-value and more mission-critical systems in the market over the next five years. I have taken a brief look at the implications of the Alpha system for the applications developer, that being broadly anyone developing software for sale into the market, both working now with Digital and looking at the Alpha market from outside.

The choice of application development technology is a vital issue. clearly the type of implementation language used is of paramount concern here. Very significant differences and issues surround the application developed in a third- or a fourth-generation programming language. The emergence of new technologies in general and of object technology in particular implies that the use of fourth-generation languages will decline for more advanced applications. The desire to use technology innovations of the platforms and operating systems faster than the 4GL suppliers can support them will increase this trend. However, it is certain that the systems written in 4GLs will be popular for the foreseeable future especially in the less strategic, non-mission-critical or platform general applications. The use of 4GLs will continue to be popular with the Alpha systems users since the platform provides a significant hike in performance at minimum cost.

Microsoft NT is the new and disruptive factor on the market. Microsoft NT is a key technology which all developers in the market should seriously consider. The level of functionality as a multi-user server is unmatched by either VMS or any of the UNIX interfaces I have seen to date for the price. With Alpha, the competition between the three operating systems will be significant given the availability of Microsoft NT, OpenVMS and UNIX (OSF/1 now and System V soon with System 5MK on the way). There is a great deal of scope provided for the system designer by this situation. Customers and applications developers are also faced with significant opportunities. Clearly Digital Alpha systems offer an valid upgrade path for the 10 million or so VAX/VMS users. This will surely be the first part of an upgrade to more heterogeneous systems in the long run. The first VMS user to move will only be upgrading to OpenVMS (with certain special exceptions).

Those users who invested in the Digital 5000 series systems (based on the MIPS technology) in the past few years will find the Alpha-based OSF/1 systems provide a power upgrade. Since these systems are fully compatible small Alpha platform additions could be made, say, by using an Alpha file manager or an Alpha front-end processor running Microsoft NT to an existing larger system.

Financial value is the key issue for those in industry today and the Alpha range of systems provides both opportunities and threats in this area. Value addition can be accomplished by the inclusion of functionality in the base application and by using features and technologies that may not have been previously possible. This view has to be balanced against the fact that there are relatively few Alpha systems in the market today, so if you are moving an existing application to the Alpha platform (from any system) it is very probable that your firm will have another version of application code to manage and support. Working with Digital is substantially different from other corporate relationships. Because of the ethos, success is dependent on personal more than corporation relationships in the traditional sense (as would be the case with, say, IBM). The big problem is knowing where to start. The best advice I can give is to be prepared to invest substantial amounts of time in building personal relationships with Digital employees.

The wide availability of Digital Alpha will definitely result in an increase in competition. This is also true for the availability of a range of operating systems in the market. The secret is to be fast and reactive, the slow developers will be at a significant disadvantage in many ways. As they come up against the top end of the power PC market on Microsoft NT and the massed ranks of the UNIX applications developers on UNIX and Alpha and on NT they will have to defend rather than attack.

With any new system one the question 'is the technology stable?' has to be asked. Clearly the answer is 'not yet'. As I write this I know of no major problems, on the Alpha technologies on either OpenVMS, Windows NT or OSF/1. There are many other risks though. Perhaps the most significant of which is the availability of critical third-party or Digital layered products. This will make the move over to Alpha platforms difficult and in some cases impossible.

Price is a key factor in the application market with the introduction of any applications on the new Alpha platform. One influence on the price is the level of added value that the application can bring to the market by using the power of the Alpha system. A second factor on the price is the market sector itself in which the application can be sold. These two issues certainly need careful consideration and management by the applications developer.

Being the first or one of the first on the Alpha platform is a critical issue for the applications developer. However, the market is also sensitive to the inclusion of new technology features and a clear plan to invest in the application for other technology functions and features. I fell strongly that it is only by the addition of this value that the applications developers will protect and improve their profit margins and the range of associated service offerings.

The Alpha-based open hardware platforms, provide opportunities to exploit a wide range of markets and by doing this increases the competition in these markets by the introduction of a larger number of competing applications. It is therefore vital not to be seen as dependent upon an old technology or as the purveyor of systems that (generally through lack of investment and vision) are static in the fast-changing world of information technology innovation.

Alpha is not a quirky, Digital only technology. Alpha is a product programme designed for longevity and this attribute is perhaps its strongest selling point. If you are providing your applications on Alpha-based systems you can afford to look at the platform as protection for your investment in the application with minimum risk. The worst thing to do is to stay on VAX/VMS or non-Alpha products. The consequence of this will be that the value of your applications continue to fall and the margin will be fast eroded. Such a situation of continuously reducing the available funds for investment in the applications, the technology and platforms will mark the start of a downward spiral from which it is very difficult to recover.

Alpha presents an opportunity more than a threat. The optimum time to move onto such a new applications platform is early in its market life. Similar situations in the business, for instance the introduction of the personal computer by IBM, show that the applications that were on the platform early on are the industry leaders now. Alpha generates change, and perhaps one of the major changes will be that in the business balance toward more services. Exactly what these services might be and how they are provided in the future is uncertain. What can be said is that the value of any application will be increased by the adding functions, features and enhancements that take the application closer to the business problem. The process of analysing of this problem and the acquisition of business specific expertise must be regarded as an appreciating asset. Services which follow on, building from this base of experience will certainly need a different set of skills and a modified approach to the business.

In this section, both the terms 'systems integrators' and system developers have related to a loose definition. Clearly, since many of these companies are working at a base systems level, they will be concerned with a broader and more detailed level of operations than the typical applications developer. Some of these companies will have their own applications to offer for specific market sectors. The greatest opportunities for these two types of organisation come from the systems architecture.

Digital's Alpha technology has implications for both the systems developers and systems integrators and this will be the introduction of a number of new players into a market that was, until now, the sole province of Digital specialists. This is the most uncertain area of the market given the number of factors. The level and nature of competition will change very considerably in the near future. The position of the systems integrator will be strengthened by the development of systems with much higher added value. This position is further strengthened by Alpha when one considers the 10 million existing VAX users as a potential customer base.

The best places to attack with Alpha in systems integration exercises are:

- In the role of central 'hub' linking a number of subsystems together
- In the role as a front-end processor used to add functionality to the existing system components
- As a communications processor to other local and wide area communications networks
- As a platform for the integration of a number of applications
- As Open Systems target

The systems developer must realise that Alpha represents a technology that is unmatched elsewhere coupled with both openness and longevity making the microprocessor technology an excellent investment base on which to build. Alpha will become the *de-facto* standard for high-value Open Systems which need performance, power and a long-lived architecture in most significant markets. There are a number of weaknesses that Alpha causes during the transitional period and for some time to come. The system integrator, has the issues of finding the additional expertise required, the need to form relationships with Digital (if you do not already have them) and the problem of other competitors entering the market. The system developers also have the technology problem but can also expect a robust defence of markets by those with non-Alpha-based systems. This problem is made worse at least at first, because Alpha sales volumes will be relatively low.

Systems integrators can now design and provide levels of resilience and performance that have not been economically viable at the smaller end of the market in the past. In addition, systems can now be designed that are capable of being adapted to the challenges of the future. Systems developers now have a major opportunity to make more specialized, market focused systems.

At the HCI level we have just begun to scratch the surface of what can be achieved with Alpha in this area. Part of the problem with Digital has been its confused channel management in the past. Sadly I see little sign of this improving in practice and systems integrators will often come up against Digital itself in the market. Others will be in the market with skills gained in the VAX arena. If you enter the Alpha market you have to understand the need for quality and service from the higher value end of the market.

The implications of Alpha for the systems integration and development markets is very significant and on balance the opportunities outweigh the threats. This is only true if such organizations understand the needs of the high value clients and show imagination in creating Alpha-based systems with significant levels of added value to the market.

In the next chapter I will look at the implications of Alpha for the end user market. The marketplace looks very different to a user of Alpha-based systems.

Alpha offers a lot of potential advantages to the end user but not without risk. On balance, the most significant advantages in the medium to long-term, come from the enabling aspects of the Alpha technology programme. The short-term financial benefits are easy to spot:

- One can simply downsize to an Alpha system from a larger one, either VAX or another,
- The cost savings will be apparent for the same power.

Unfortunately this short-term view of technical strategy is based on the thinking of the last decade, where value was just a function of 'smaller, faster, cheaper'. What really must matter to the users of technology now, is using that technology to add very significant levels of advantage to their companies.

Part of this section of the market will include the companies that are small to medium sized enterprises and who need to use the same tools and methods for gaining competitive advantage as their larger competitors. Part of the market is driven by the innovative application of the Alpha technology to problems that were impractical to solve, such as sophistication in the human computer interface and in advanced data management and modelling techniques.

End users will be in a somewhat weaker position, but there are some short-term opportunities in terms of forming early relationships with Digital and associated suppliers that are potentially very worthwhile. If you are moving to Alpha the issue of software migration is one that needs very careful consideration and planning. Software can just be translated from the VAX to the Alpha OpenVMS platform and run in simple translated mode. However, this can never be a good long-term solution and must only be considered as an immediate path for migration under certain circumstances.

Many of the benefits of the Alpha architecture are not available by going down this route, the long-term option is to fully port the software across. Dependence on the inclusion of third-party products such as compilers, databases, etc. and on Digital layered products will at least affect the schedule of porting and in some circumstances will require significant levels of rewrite to move over onto the Alpha platform. The main impact Alpha-based systems will have on your operation can only be assessed after a review of your computing strategy with the emphasis on the added value that Alpha could bring to you. It is essential that you start putting pressure on the suppliers of applications and systems to get what you need.

I have been consistently critical of applications throughout this book and for good reason. Many, though not all, lack any real vision and few show any imaginative use of technology to add value rather than to perform in a superficial way. However, in defence of the applications developers, they need to be better driven by the end user towards the areas where improvements are required for your business.

VAX is still a good platform and so is the Digital 5000 range. Inevitably, however, they are at the end of a lifecycle and any organization investing in applications and systems development must be in the position of changing the emphasis towards Alpha-based systems. Whatever you can do so can your competitors, and not using its power but just taking a short term view of price performance, will be a big mistake. All the major companies I work with that are on VAX and Digital 5000 systems today are not thinking of decreasing their system spend on Alpha relative to VAX. Instead they are looking at how Alpha can add value to their business.

Further Reading

R. Beale and T. Jackson, *Neural Computing: An introduction,* Adam Hilger: Bristol, 1990.

J. Gleick, *Chaos: The making of a new science,* Cardinal: London, 1987.

CHAPTER 6

Alpha in the Market

6.1 Introduction

In this chapter I look at the likely performance of Digital's Alpha-based products in the marketplace. The timeframe I have taken is split into three phases:

1. The first 3 years (1993 to 1996)
2. The next 4 years (1996 to 2000)
3. The long term i.e. > 7 years, (2001 and beyond)

6.1.1 Structure of the Chapter

The chapter is divided into four main sections covering:

1. Key industry perspectives
2. The prospects for Alpha
3. Future developments
4. Alpha perspectives.

The first section gives a summary of the outlook for Alpha in four key industry areas: discrete manufacturing, petrochemicals, telecommunications and research. In the following section I consider the prospects for Alpha from a time-based perspective. This has been divided into the introductory phase and then the short and long term. I finish this subsection with a brief review of operating systems. Future developments is a look at how systems trends, communications needs, the competition and legacy systems might all impinge on the success of Alpha in the longer term. This section also considers the areas that might best benefit from the technology in terms of added value.

Finally, I have taken a number of differing perspectives on the Alpha programme, those of other consultancies, existing Digital users, applications developers and Open System users.

6.1.2 Issues Covered in this Chapter

This chapter summarizes the position and prospects of Alpha today. Its main focus is the likely performance of the Alpha programme in its first few years in the market and from a number of differing perspectives. Clearly the markets that I have chosen are not an exhaustive review of the opportunities for the programme and its products and services. However, the choice does cover a wide range of industries and sectors and in so doing it is a good example of the classes of problems that are amenable to a solution using Alpha-based systems.

6.1.3 Questions raised in the Previous Chapter

The previous chapter put a number of issues before the users of Alpha technology, from the end user and applications developer through to the systems developer and systems integrator and systems developer. In this section the questions raised in the previous chapter will be put into a market context.

I hope that from this, the innovative developer of systems and applications and the end user seeking possible areas for application of the technology will get some idea of the place for the technology in the industry context.

6.2 Some Key Industry Perspectives

The industries that I have chosen for this section represent the major wealth generators in the world economies. Clearly there are a number of areas that have not been covered, but this key group of power industries (in which you will note that I include research, an often-forgotten industry in the Western economies) are representative of the wider picture for Alpha.

6.2.1 Discrete Manufacturing

Discrete manufacturing has been quick to realize the potential benefits of automation, with the result that there are virtually no new systems to be sold in this market sector, and business here is replacement only. The implication of this is that there has to be a significant motivation for the end user of a manufacturing system to change from what they have to something else. There are two basic reasons for a user wishing to change:

- costs of keeping present system
- capabilities of present system

Costs are seen as being high for many of the systems in the installed base at the moment, both in terms of the system maintenance costs, which for the larger proprietary systems can be very considerable indeed, and for the application support costs. (It must be noted that the cost does not necessarily reflect the level of quality of the end result: often the relationship can be inverse.)

The cost of application support is linked to the cost of the application which in turn is often a function of the system price. As the costs of systems have fallen there has, to some extent, been a similar movement in the application costs.

Capabilities of applications in the field of discrete manufacturing can be divided into two separate but related items:

- Manufacturing technology capabilities
- Information technology capabilities

Manufacturing technology has changed significantly over the past few years and continues to move very quickly. No longer is materials planning and scheduling enough for industry. Complex methods like Just In Time (JIT) and others are now considered essential to the running of any competitive manufacturing business. Information technology offers features to the manufacturing industry which can provide a significant competitive edge based on reduced operating costs in the business and increased efficiency of the organization.

There have been manufacturing systems in the industry for a long time, but in the mid-range market the picture of market share and trends is complex, as can be seen from Table 6.1. This summarizes the information over the period from 1990 to 1992 and for the main systems vendors in this sector of the manufacturing market.

Table 6.1 Percentage market share for discrete manufacturing (mid-range)

Manufacturer	1990	1992	Change
IBM	31	35	4
Digital	13	11	-2
Appolo	9	7	-2
ICL	6	6	0
Prime	6	5	-1
Others	35	36	1

As can be seen from this table, the bulk of systems are disparate in type and this trend is increasing, fuelled by the increase in the number and the diversity of 'open' systems. The key value in these systems today is in the manufacturing data on the systems, and the secondary value is in the area of the business rules which have been captured, either in the applications themselves or in the bespoke elements of the system.

The main areas of spend in the discrete manufacturing industry are:

- Manufacturing control
- Shopfloor control
- CAD (electronic and mechanical)
- CAM

From 1990 to 1992 the expenditure on these areas changed as shown in Table 6.2.

Table 6.2 Percentage changes in manufacturing system spend 1990-1992

Area	Change
Manufacturing	6.6
Shopfloor	21
CAD	23
CAM	-10

It can be seen from this table that the manufacturing industry spend is increasing most in the area of two technologies: device integration and networking (shopfloor control) and complex data manipulation for compound data (CAD). These are two key areas to which I will return later.

Another interesting trend is the change in the software type used in the discrete manufacturing industry in terms of products and bespoke software, as shown in Table 6.3.

Table 6.3 Percentage change in bespoke and product software for MRPII in discrete manufacturing 1990 - 1992

Type	1990	1992	Change
Bespoke	14	14	0
Product	19	22	3
Accounts	22	28	6
None	45	36	-9

The picture painted then is of an increase in the penetration of product package software into the mass of manufacturing companies. Bespoke software has changed little in the period covered between 1990 and 1992. The likely reason is that the problems involved in switching from the bespoke to the product system are so severe that the end users are unwilling, due to insufficient perceived benefits, to go ahead with such an exercise. The uptake of technology throughout the manufacturing sector is itself uneven, with automotive leading the race followed closely by the electronics industry and the rest of the businesses some way behind.

One of the key areas for consideration is that of shopfloor data collection. In the years from 1990 to 1996, the penetration of automated systems into the collection of shopfloor data looks impressive as shown in Table 6.4.

Table 6.4 Percentage shopfloor data capture 1990 - 1996

	1990	1991	1992	1993	1994	1995	1996
Market penetration	8	11	13	18	23	29	37

As with all other applications software, there is a mix of bespoke, product and other software on the machines of the discrete manufacturing industry. The best information available at the time of going to press suggests that this mix is approximately as shown in Table 6.5. From this it is clear that the level of penetration of applications is very variable in this market.

The greatest share of the market is still in the bespoke systems area, though many of these have some element of product as their base. MRPII is the fastest-growing part of the market with more systems being installed as the working practices to support their use in the industry become more prevalent. In many cases this has in fact accelerated under the competitive and financial pressures of the recession. However, bespoke systems will be around for a very long time to come. This further reinforces the argument for a number of disparate systems in the market all needing to be integrated, all operating on a wide range of devices, networked in local and sometimes wide areas and using different networking technologies with, to complete the set, different user interface technologies.

The driving force in the discrete manufacturing industry is that of competition. This manifests itself in tactics for competing, namely the control and reduction of costs, the reduction in time from design to market and general improvements in process and product quality (this includes environmental concerns).

One of the simplest ways to improve the profitability of a company is to be more efficient, and a key to efficiency is quality. In an effort to improve quality in discrete manufacture, Alpha systems can add value through the whole life of a product from design and simulation through robotic manufacture and inspection to final test and into the diagnostics during service (for instance, in aircraft simulation or in-flight data-capture and analysis).

Table 6.5 Shopfloor data capture software by type

Type	Total in use (%)
Unknown	11
Spreadsheet	9
Dedicated package	22
MRPII	28
Bespoke	32

Another attribute of modern discrete manufacturing business is the globalization of the workforce. To operate efficiently in this environment, corporations need to be able to interchange a wide variety of complex engineering data and multimedia information, all of which is very intensive on computational resources.

Perhaps the most important of all the attributes of the discrete manufacturing market is that of shortening development times. In order to compete in the global market, there has to be a significant level of computational resource committed to the design and simulation phase of new product development coupled with increasingly high levels of robotics in the manufacturing process itself. There is no longer time or money to build a long line of prototypes and get things right by trial and error.

The role of the systems integrator in the industry is becoming essential as are long-term vendor relationships with suppliers of discrete components and information technology products and services. This is essential in the discrete market since the need for specialised engineering applications coupled with technologies that are certain to come from a range of suppliers predicates towards systems integrators who can manage the needs of the industry in the longer term. Naturally, most of the companies in the manufacturing business have systems today, but many of these are less than satisfactory, add low and diminishing value to the overall business of the end user and are legacy systems that have a great wealth of design and product performance data on them. This is a real asset to the company, whereas many of the older systems are a liability, since proper access and manipulation of the data stored on these systems are often impossible or impractical.

Digital's Alpha-based systems must be seen as providing the power and sophistication that enables the support of geographically diverse workcentres by, for instance, data, image and graphics file compression and translation between CAD and CAM system and at very competitive prices. Many of the leading applications will move over on to the new Alpha platforms soon. Essentially this will be a standard port to the new platform, but all the major players (I am pleased to report) are promising to include new functionality over time that really makes use of the power, and not the price performance, of Alpha, adding value and not just competing on price in the design and development area of the discrete manufacturing business,

Alpha-based systems will transform the industry, essentially by giving the engineer today the power of a supercomputer in a workstation with all the implied ability to design, construct, model and simulate that will liberate the design teams of many companies around the world. A good example of this is the wide scale availability of systems to manufacturers who can now, perhaps for the first time, perform finite element analysis on their design solutions, or at least to perform these early and in-house. While all this sounds nice in theory, is anyone in the discrete manufacturing market going to buy? The answer seems to be yes. Digital are close to announcing supply and support of 500 Alpha AXP workstations to a major global manufacturing company, based in Europe and operating concurrent manufacturing in four continents.

The electronics industry is one of the main sectors of the discrete manufacturing market that promises to do well from the use of Alpha. Like the other sectors in discrete manufacturing, design to manufacture times are under a lot of pressure and the complexity and sophistication of electronic products is increasing at a very high rate. One of the main problems faced by the electronics industry is the need for very powerful computational machines to simulate and test circuit designs. The Alpha AXP machines are prime candidates for resolving this problem, adding value to the business by shortening development times and helping to improve quality.

The biggest of all the discrete manufacturing sectors is the automotive manufacturing sector. We have all seen the impact of high-quality Japanese methods and are well aware that many of the plants in Europe are driven by design teams back in Japan. Digital's Alpha AXP systems will enable the engineer to use incredibly powerful 3D modelling, design and simulation together with much-enhanced analysis tools. One example of this is that early prototypes of a vehicle can be crash-tested as simulations without the very high cost of building and using real vehicles for the purpose. The resultant reduced costs, increased quality and improved time from design to market are real added values that Alpha promises to bring to the automotive industry. These benefits also apply to the existing products of the industry, allowing improvements to products in the field today together with the capability to access, manage and manipulate the very large datastores in the corporate legacy systems for yet more value from this often-untapped source of innovation and information.

One of the most expensive parts of the discrete manufacturing industry is the aerospace business. Here the design and development costs of new products are massive and the time to revenue typically 5 to 15 years from design. If you think the automotive industry eats computer power, just imagine the needs of an aerospace manufacturer simulating the stress on an airframe in a turbulent airflow.

Only now are the supercomputer facilities available where they are needed, on the desks of the design team using Alpha technology. This will make for definitely better design and much-improved time to market for the final products. Finite element analysis and fluid dynamics can now be used to evaluate the effects of changes in the design of an aerospace structure in a few minutes on the engineer's desk whereas before this may have taken days. It should also be remembered that the data volumes and storage times for those data are very great for the aerospace manufacturers. These records can go back over 25 years.

A list of some engineering applications that are available on the Alpha AXP system is included in the section summary. Clearly, in these few examples of the manufacturing industry I have shown just a very little of the value that Digital can offer. As you will see in the other industry sectors, Alpha promises to provide a very real level of power to the market all round and to change many of our views on the speed (and possibly life) of a product in the modern marketplace.

In the discrete manufacturing sector there can be a lot of benefit from Microsoft NT running in server mode on Alpha platforms. In particular, the benefits to the systems used for the management and control of discrete manufacturing will be in the areas of integration and enhancement rather than for the removal of bespoke development work in the short to mid-term. Initially the high-value data in the existing systems will most likely stay on these systems in the short term. Applications that can therefore access the data on a number of different systems as well as on the native Microsoft NT database will be at a distinct advantage.

6.2.2 Petrochemicals

Petrochemicals, gas and oil represent very significant components of the industrialized world's most lucrative businesses. Furthermore (and especially in the case of petrochemical industrial products), the number, type and range that are produced are increasing fast with many products being increasingly specifically designed for highly specialized purposes in finer and finer niche markets. This sector of the market has some special implications and, the nature of the products is more fundamental to society than for many others in several ways:

- As a source of energy
- As the source of bulk industrial materials
- As the potential source of major ecological problems

These factors make the petrochemical, oil and gas industries more closely linked to the major economic, social and environmental issues of the day. Changes in these industries and in their products and by-products can have a major effect on the lives of many people in a short period of time (for instance, the changes in oil prices, new plastics and agrochemicals, etc.). By their nature these industries are in for the long term, the investment required to set up is very large indeed and the time to profit can be very long. However, the profitability of the industry is subject to many factors outside its control such as climatic conditions, political changes, geographic and geological problems, global markets for the products, tendency to price movements and legislative changes, especially regarding the environmental impact of the industries.

To make better use of the resources at their disposal and to protect and improve company financial performance as much as possible, the petrochemical, oil and gas industries are investing heavily in the use and applications of information technology. Areas of prime application include:

- Production and exploration
- Refining and marketing
- Environmental management
- Corporate management information

For many of these areas, the applications required fit (as we shall see) well into the capabilities of Alpha-based computing solutions. The base materials for these three industries share one thing in common: they are (in human timescales) non-renewable. These are industries that are defined and built on exploration and extraction in geographically dispersed and often remote and hostile areas. The substantial costs of exploration and extraction are therefore one significant potential cost saving for the industry. However, to do this requires computers of great power which are cheap and, more importantly, portable.

By the application of supercomputing power as provided by Alpha systems at a level that is now portable, the exploration and extraction process will improve its success rates by better analysis of seismic data. In addition, the computer simulation of the oil and gas reservoirs will assist in increasing the achieved yields from existing fields. Due to the initial costs of exploiting the resources, it only takes a small percentage increase in the effective extraction to make a substantial improvement to the profitability of an oil or gas field. The oil and gas exploration business has existed extensively for a long time and the companies doing this work have massive datastores of old records, many relating to data collected in the field and all needing sophisticated and computer-intensive analysis.

These are a potential source of new resources if more fully analysed. By the adoption of Alpha-based systems, this huge pool of old data can itself be analysed with a view to finding reserves that in the past have been missed. This is a massively data and computationally intensive task, one ideally suited to the large Alpha systems, especially the multiprocessor versions. For newer explorations, the companies can now afford to set up seismic exploration analysis centres in local areas linked to the more remote exploration sites by satellite link to give very fast results and analysis of the data.

As in any complex commodities-based market, the models for performance, the methods used to make buying and selling decisions and the management information systems that back this all up are becoming increasingly complex. In the petrochemical, oil and gas businesses, the models used are complex but constrained by the affordable power on the market. By the use of Alpha-based systems the market analysis and forecasting applications used by the decision makers in these industries can now become very sophisticated indeed. For instance, not only can very large data sets be handled (making management aware of global trends, for instance) but they can be used to represent many more dimensions in the models than were otherwise possible.

For instance, the impact of a greater range of economic indicators, industrial or political factors can be taken into account. AI can be employed to make decision support systems more valuable to managers whose rate of decision making will increase, as will the need for accuracy of decisions in this increasingly global and competitive market. Because of the complex interaction of the global economy with the market for these products, more sophisticated models will need to evaluate issues like alternative sources of supply in times of crisis, sudden changes in the needs for certain products and the implications for the overall mix of products in the refineries, longer-term market and production forecasting as well as automated market-trading systems.

Refinery operations can also benefit from more computing power. First, in the design stage it will now be possible for the industry to model much more accurately the actual efficiency of a designed refinery or petrochemical products plant. In addition, the ongoing management of the refinery can be much more effectively managed from input and process through to output and scheduled maintenance. Clearly one of the major implications for this application of affordable supercomputing is in positive environmental benefits. By more accurate management of refineries, of energy input and output and of matching production to the needs, the overall impact on the environment has to be significantly improved.

As with the other market sections in this chapter, a list of key applications and their developers is included in the summary section. All the issues in this section are workable on non-Alpha solutions, but in practical and affordable terms they are not. Certainly many of the areas of application require a long-term computing strategy and a supplier relationship of quality and durability with a system that is capable of growth over decades. In the industry today, only Alpha can offer this.

6.2.3 Telecommunications

Telecommunications is the high-growth area in all the industrialized economies of the world and in many of the emerging economies also. As an example, the market for telecommunications equipment and services in Europe is expected to reach $200 billion by mid-1995. The existing networks in Europe are less than ideally managed. Over 200 million PTT main lines are defined, recorded and, to some extent, managed on paper-based systems. Recently it has been estimated that approximately 10% of these lines are 'Lost' because of lost records and poor management of the information.

To this picture one has to add the industrial and socio-economic trends of deregulation in many of the world's major markets (for instance, Europe, and the old Eastern bloc countries) the implication of which is higher competition on a products, services and technology basis. The general trend in the telecommunications market is driven by the fast-growing information needs of the end-user organizations.

The old view of the telecommunications market as typified by national PTTs has died, being replaced by continental and global views of the markets, their infrastructures and technologies (it has to be said that the slowest part of the whole process is the political and legislative changes), with one of the fastest-growing components of the telecommunications market being that of mobile communications. Many of the problems faced in the telecommunications market are technology-based (for instance, the need for the increased bandwidth which requires fibre optic rather than copper networks).

The need to move to digital telecommunications and exchanges and the requirement for very high speed data compression and decompression coupled with intelligent network management systems leads to a situation where the data volumes in the telecommunications industry are growing very fast and where they need big, powerful systems to make sense of this ocean of data.

The need for accurate management of the network facilities, the billing systems and the customer services points towards the requirement for small, fast and very powerful systems running in a transaction processing environment over a distributed systems topology. There is an increase in the type of data being transmitted also. Voice and data together with fax are all well known, but other more complex compound data is being moved around, the main problem being the bandwidth of the networks. For instance, it is felt that multimedia would grow as a market a lot faster if the bandwidth existed for the systems to use this or if the systems themselves had the power and speed to perform very high speed compression and decompression of large volumes of data for multimedia applications. All this adds up to a fast-growing management problem at all levels, from the network, through the finances and into the technology.

Telecommunications are now becoming technology driven in many respects and Digital's Alpha systems have the power to help in a number of areas, most notably:

- Network modelling and network management including the use of AI
- Real-time management of vast volumes of data
- TP-based information from distributed systems
- Software development and maintenance
- Public and private switches-based on Alpha
- Asynchronous transfer mode (ATM) video, voice, graphics and data for video alternative to Email.
- Very high speed compression of image data on limited bandwidth lines
- Automated directory assistance (for example, Digital and Telecom Ireland are marketing an OSF/1-based system called CDS running on an Alpha AXP system).

The telecommunications market is one in which Digital's Alpha product will be able to provide a level of capability to the new network systems such as processor power to the intelligent switching devices and also augmentation of present network facilities such as the compression and decompression of complex data. Telecommunications and the other industries are all interrelated with telecommunications being the hub that joins the other companies together around the world.

Digital's Alpha systems will be the enabling technology that drives the use of systems far forward. Much of the complex data processing that gets shipped up the line in many industries will now be able to be performed at source. Network bandwidth is therefore likely to be taken up more with added value data (image, multimedia, etc.) and with data from remote collection points (retail, manufacturing, etc.). All in all, Alpha will change the use and the technology of telecommunications significantly.

6.2.4 Research

Research is at the heart of all the industry and all the services and products considered in this book. My definition of research covers all corporate research and education and training (academic and industrial). The undoubted intrinsic value of research and of education makes it another motherhood statement. We all sign up to needing research but the risky and indefinite nature of the results make it something that intrinsically goes against the grain for many businesses. In these recessionary times, the budgets for training and education have been ravaged, oddly, since it is the very research and education that is likely to help pull the Western economy out of trouble in the long run. What is certain is that many, if not all, research activities can and do benefit from some level of information technology but have now begun to question the value of this technology for reasons of price, performance and usability.

The general trend in research is for focus, specialization and cost effectiveness, and computing has to offer value in this as any other industry. The big gains in research areas that Alpha can immediately contribute to are in the computationally intensive areas and those requiring data visualization. These include but are not limited to:

- High-energy physics
- Genetic research
- Chemistry
- Astrophysics
- Meteorology
- Geology
- AI

These are the areas that have eaten up computational power over the last decade with some programmes taking up to 10,000 times the computing resources that they did in the 1980s. Clearly, return on funds invested has to be significantly improved or these projects will simply end up on the rocks. In addition to the power requirement, the need for large information technology departments is a drain on resources. These are now under scrutiny and the demand is for more usable computing resources, systems with more powerful and flexible user interfaces.

All this is driven by the industrial demand for innovation in products and materials. One of the keys to more efficient research and education is the sharing of information across national and linguistic barriers and in the delivery of this information using a variety of methods, including multimedia.

Digital's Alpha AXP systems can offer a lot to this market. For instance, the entry level AXP workstation costs less than $20,000 and yet has the equivalent power to a Cray-1 supercomputer. This puts power on the desk of the research that was previously only available to the most affluent departments. It is also true that the democratization of computing will be pushed a lot further now with many of the world's poorer countries able to compete in research areas denied to them in the past. By allowing the development of much more powerful and flexible forms of HCI, such as voice and pen interfaces, the systems themselves will empower the researcher in a way that is not possible today.

When it comes to the value that can be gained from the information archives around the world, applications on Alpha-based systems could facilitate the access to indexed journals of research locally or over wide area networks. Cost effectiveness will be improved by using Alpha-based systems by a number of routes. First, the basic power performance for the price of an Alpha system is unbeatable. Second, the effectivity of the researcher will be significantly enhanced as will their independence from other computing expertise for many of the basic activities. Third, Alpha's longevity and openness are in themselves protections of the investment in the systems and in interoperability that are essential for the research and educational community

The research community will find the value and the power of Alpha-based systems a real enabling technology to their work. Already a number of institutions are adopting these systems for their work both in industrial and academic circles.

6.2.5 Financial Services

Banking and financial services are major users of computational power and data management. The move to global trading in equities and foreign exchange together with the desire to focus the selling of products into the retail banking and insurance markets predicate towards significant opportunities for powerful applications and computers. However, the recession has hit the financial services and banking sectors as hard as any other and the focus on value for money is just as severe. Banks and financial institutions around the world are beginning to question the value of many of their older information technology investments and to doubt the efficacy of some of the more esoteric systems that have sprung up. It is true to say that many of the projects in this industry have suffered from having the right ideas but a complete lack of computing power to deliver them in a satisfactory manner to the end user at an acceptable price and performance.

Some of the areas that the Alpha-based systems can impact in the retail banking area are to do with intelligent automated teller machines and services (for instance, the development of voice recognition-based telebanking and the effective and efficient development of product markets based on customer account records). In the high street, electronic funds transfer and point of sale systems may soon be available using biometric recognition to avoid fraud, (e.g. retina scans or fingerprint image matching). At the local level banks will also be able to manage the customers' investment, insurance and financial portfolio on a more intelligent and automated basis.

In the non-banking side of the financial markets such as commodities, mutual funds, equities, foreign exchange and bond trading Alpha again has a lot to offer. These are the markets where a great deal of information is moved around and has to be analysed so that massive investment decisions can be made. Of all the areas that are likely to improve, the analysis and modelling functions of the markets will probably be the biggest users of Alpha as will the automation of trading itself. Part of the decision support structure will be the same applications at those used in research and mentioned above, that of powerful indexing and searching facilities across huge data libraries and new services. Moving to the more infrastructural side of the market, the systems used to keep track of the deals and transactions will be another ideal area for the application of Alpha such as in the reconciliation and registration of transactions.

The financial services and banking sector also have a lot of mainframes and legacy systems that are ripe for downsizing to Alpha-based systems over time. All in all, this is going to be a sector that price, performance and added-value applications will penetrate easily on Alpha platforms.

6.2.6 Summary

I set out in this section to look at the key industries and the likely perspective for Alpha given the issues facing them at the moment. The general functionality of the Alpha platform is relevant to the different markets in a number of areas as follows:

HCI and graphical presentation of information. This covers the Alpha power to use bitmapped and vector graphics for multimedia, three-dimensional modelling and ray tracing. The key industries affected by this will be automotive and aerospace, electronics and civil engineering by way of engineering and discrete manufacture; molecular modelling, biomedical research and chemistry in the petrochemical, oil, gas and pharmaceutical industries; network planning and management, end-user information presentation and systems design in the telecommunications industry; and finally general representation of research findings and information together with a more friendly HCI in the areas of research and education.

Computational power and mathematical functions. Alpha's power here can be put to good use in the scientific and engineering community (for instance, in fluid dynamic modelling, aerodynamics, stress calculation, dynamic simulation and real-time computation and pattern matching). The industries most affected by this would be aerospace, automotive manufacture, electronic manufacture and the exploration side of the oil and gas industries. Defence is also a clear market for pattern recognition and real-time computing systems. Mathematical modelling power is also very useful in the analysis, forecasting and finite element methods areas. These relate to banking and financial services, advanced discrete manufacturing (aerospace, automotive and civil) and to scientific research such as high energy and astrophysics as well as economic modelling.

Data management and manipulation. With their massive 64-bit architecture, Digital's Alpha systems are capable of manipulating very large amounts of data vary quickly. As well as manipulating a large conventional database, this functionality is very useful in the manipulation of less structured information such as images, handwriting, voice, natural languages, knowledge bases and unstructured textual databases. The industry sectors that will be able to apply this most usefully are the petrochemical, banking and financial sectors. Clearly the structured information in the other industry sectors will be a good target for Alpha's data management and manipulation. Research and education will benefit most from unstructured textual data management and manipulation in the first instance.

For each of the industry subsections, here are a few companies or organizations signed up to Digital's Alpha at present.

Discrete manufacturing The following is a list of engineering applications committed to run on the Digital Alpha AXP system:

Developer	*Application*
Adra Systems Inc	CADRA-III
Applicon	BRAVO 3D
CIMLINC	LINKAGE
Cisigraph	Strim-100
Computervision	CADDS5
EDS	Unigraphics II
HKSI	Abaqus
MacNeal-Schwendler Corp.	MCS/Nastran

Manufacturing and Consulting Services Inc.	ANVIL-500
Matra Division	Euclid-IS
Parametric Technology Corp.	Pro/Engineer
PDA	PATRAN
Structural Dynamics Research	I-DEAS
Swanson Analysis Systems	ANSYS
Cadence	Verilog
	Veritime
	Cadre
	Teamwork
i-Logix	Statemate
	Express
	VHDL
Synopsys	Design Compiler
	ECL Compiler
	HDL Compiler
	HDL System
Taradyne	LASAR
	Viewlogic
	ViewDraw
	ViewSim

In the oil, gas and petrochemical industries the applications committed to the Digital Alpha platform are in the following categories:

Production and Exploration
Advance Geophysics Corp.
Applied TerravisionSystems Inc.
Data Processing and Transcription Services
Dynamic Graphics Inc.
Environmental Systems Research Institute
Genetek Earth Research Corp.
Geophysical Microcomputer Applications Ltd.
Inter Information Technologies/ECL
Triangle Ernst & Young
Western Atlas Software

Engineering
Aspen Technology Inc.
EA Systems Inc.
Parametric Technology Corp.

PDA Engineering
Swanson Analysis Systems Inc.
MacNeal-Schwendler Corp.

Refining
Chesapeake Decision Sciences Inc.
Dynamic Matrix Control Corp.
Oil System Inc.

Other Areas
Fisons Instruments/VG Laboratory Systems
Gemsym Corp.
GTI-IA
Ross Systems Inc.
SAP (UK) Ltd.
Scion Energy Inc.
Setpoint Inc.
Texas Instruments - Process Automation Division

Research The premier research and development operations working with the Alpha systems at the moment are:

CERN. They are the world leader in high-energy physics research and employ over 4000 scientists in Europe. Since April 1992 CERN and Digital have jointly worked on CERNLIB, CERN's extensive applications portfolio. The CERN benchmarks on the ported applications show that the mid-range Alpha AXP workstation (priced at $30,000) has a performance equivalent to the top of the range IBM 9000 (single-processor model) and twice that of the HP 9000/720 workstation.

EMBL. European Molecular Biology Laboratories have 15 member states and 320 scientists and are using Alpha AXP systems as a platform for key molecular biology applications.

INFN. This high-energy physics institute is working with Digital to develop an Alpha-based board for use in a new generation of data-acquisition systems.

PVM. Parallel Virtual Machine software is public domain software ported to Alpha AXP now and under test at a number of sites.

RAL. Rutherford Appleton Laboratories have purchased an Alpha AXP for use both by its own research community and for connection to the UK academic network.

The products being produced for the Alpha system or ported across are as follows:

Vendor	*Product*
Biorad	CSEARCH
	IR/VAXsearch
Campus America	POISE CIS
CERN	HEP libraries
	Concentration Pheonics
Computing Resource Inc.	State
GCG Wisconsin Pkg.	Helix Systems ResearchStation
IMSL	IMSL Libraries
	C/Stat Libraries
	C/Math Libraries
	Exponent graphics
	For C
	IMSL/IDL
	ISU GAMESS
	OSF
Large Scale Biology Corp.	Kepler Software
Millipore	BioImage
	BioImage
NAG	NAG Fortran Libraries
	NAG Graphics Libraries
	NAG C Libraries
	AXIOM
	IRIS EXPLORER
	NAGWARE f90 Compiler
	GLIM-4
	Genstat 5
Object Design Inc.	Object Store
	QCPE CompChem SW
	Semichem AMPAC V4.0
	UCSF AMBER 4.0
	UT Knoxville PVM V2.4
	Waterloo Maple V
	Wavefunction SPARTAN
Wolfram Research Inc.	Mathematica
Xybion Corp.	PATH/TOX
	IMSL
	IMSL Libraries

6.3 Prospects for Alpha

The world likes winners, and the questions are, how will Alpha do in the market, will it win and how will it perform over time? In this section I am going to take a view of the likely market performance of the technology across industry sectors over time. As you will see, Alpha is likely to be a force that changes some market sectors considerably at different times.

It is certainly true that in the past Digital has had dramatic failures in sectors of the market that it should rightly have dominated. One example of this is the desktop, where Digital had more than one fiasco. I believe that the corporation are quite as capable of ruining this opportunity as many of their others, and the biggest risk facing them (as many other corporations) is that of restructuring. If there is one thing I have a great concern over it is the chances of Digital doing a severe and radical enough job of structuring the corporation to fit the needs of the future. If they fail in this respect then it will force the corporation to review the ongoing investment plans for the product. The other high-risk area is in the sales channel. Digital have had a poor record of channel management and in the case of Alpha, the primary channel for the movement of the product will be outside the direct control of the corporation.

6.3.1 The Introduction Phase

This is the period up to the end of 1993 and in some ways can be considered as part of the short-term view. I have separated this section because the introduction phase, more than any other, is likely to make the biggest impact on the success or failure of the Alpha technology in the marketplace. While the Digital Alpha-based systems have been around since late 1992, the period up to the end of 1993 is important for this will see the Alpha systems introduced into the real market and not just the development, academic and test user communities. This is the period that lays the foundations for the future and from which the shape and structure of the Alpha-based business will emerge. During this period, Digital's marketing has to sustain the excellent momentum it achieved in the early Alpha marketing programme. This is partly to keep the client interest alive and partly to ensure that the sales operations are taking place in a climate that has been opened up to the more complex implications of the Alpha programme.

Perhaps the most important of all the activities in this initial period is the relationship management of the new third-party signings with Digital such as Olivetti and the rest. The number of these has to be controlled in the early stages but there are sectors of the market and the world that Digital have to address through this process that have not yet been addressed. One example is the market for systems in certain countries such as Japan. The Alpha presentation level functionality is perfect for the complex problem of language display and translation in Japan as well as in China.

Another example is the market for laptop systems which is presently not addressed using Alpha from either Digital or Olivetti but which potentially could represent a high-value market in personal power systems. The main battle to win is with the applications developers themselves. As IBM found out to their cost, if the application developers are slow to come across (as was the case with the OS/2 venture) then the Alpha project will fall far short of its market potential. Digital have, by making the Alpha systems very open (for instance, launching them with a range of three operating systems), given themselves the largest potential market and are therefore likely to attract a very large number of applications developers and systems integrators.

At the time of writing this book, the worst of the world recession seems to be at an end, though the climb out to economic growth seems uncertain and painfully slow. In this rather flat economic climate, Digital have to develop a product market, and this section of the book deals with the likely performance of the Alpha programme in the short and longer term, a time, one hopes, of growth in industry generally.

6.3.2 Short-Term Prospects

At the end of the 1980s, supercomputers were the expensive tools of the more esoteric parts of the scientific, research and corporate engineering communities and represented the investment of many millions of dollars. Alpha brings that power to the market now and in this section I will be covering the short-term prospects for Alpha-based systems.

The best estimates of the market for scientific and technical uses of supercomputers is in the region of $6-7.5 billion per annum in the period 1993 to 1995. The market for commercial supercomputing (in large databases, transaction intensive systems, etc.) is between $26 billion and $34 billion in the same period. These figures are based on the present price of supercomputing and do not take account of the likely impact on the budget forecasts used in their preparation caused by the great improvements in price and performance that systems like Digital's Alpha technology bring with them. The scope, in terms of markets and segments, is enormous, but I feel that the two main market segmentations that can be viewed as the main potential areas of primary growth for Alpha-based systems are:

- Existing VAX VMS installations
- Higher-value systems.

From an industry point of view, the applications for Alpha cover the manufacturing and service sectors of the market equally. The two particular methods of application of the Alpha technology will be in :

- Visualization including multimedia and voice
- Data manipulation including data mining.

Data mining refers to the activity of taking an existing data bank and then analysing it for any new trends or interesting features, an activity that on any sizeable amount of data was beyond the scope of all but the most powerful and expensive systems until the introduction of Alpha. For instance, I have already given examples of the use of data mining in the oil and gas industry exploration business on seismic records, but there are other applications. One example of a data mining application would be the re-examination of stock trading records in a stock brokerage for trend analysis on a multidimensional basis. Another might be the detailed examination and correlation of medical records in pharmaceutical trials: the examples are endless. Data mining essentially liberates the potential value of an organization's data history and suddenly puts a high value on that data.

Broadly, the immediate opportunities for the Alpha systems fall into five classes:

- Applications on servers, workstations, etc.
- Downsizing of legacy systems
- Embedded systems. These are defined as: applications on servers, workstations etc. or basic applications built on the standard hardware platforms from Digital in the form of Alpha AXP systems, Olivetti systems containing Alpha and running Microsoft NT and the specialist systems from Kubota Pacific and Cray. However, this does not include systems needing special hardware developments.
- Downsizing of legacy systems. The market for porting software from old mainframe systems to smaller, more functional systems like Alpha. Clearly some of the larger VAX installations fall into this class.
- Embedded systems. Systems where the Alpha processor is a small part of a larger overall system such as in voice processing units for larger systems or controlling automatic analysis devices in a petrochemical plant.

In the short term, the market growth for each area will probably be as follows:

- Applications on servers, workstations, etc. Likely to account for more than 65% of total sales at the end of the first three years.
- Downsizing of legacy systems. Likely to account for 25% of total sales at the end of the first three years.
- Embedded systems. Likely to account for 15% of total sales at the end of the first three years.

Table 6.6 summarizes the position for the period 1993 to 1998 based on my data and assessment of the industry. It must be noted that this is a worldwide prediction and certain areas (such as Europe) may go slowly as they emerge from recession.

Table 6.6 Market growth by sector for Alpha-based systems in the period 1993 to 1998 shown as a percentage of overall volume (number of processors shipped per year)

	1993	1994	1995	1996	1997	1998
Applications	50	50	52	52	55	60
Downsizing	48	45	38	35	30	25
Embedded	2	5	20	13	15	15

Industry sectors While the Alpha systems will be invaluable in all areas of industry, there are definite instances where they are likely to do well at different times. Initially the performance of the Alpha systems is likely to be strongest in the manufacturing sector and weakest in the services sector.

1. Design and manufacturing Manufacturing and design-focused industries (architecture, civil engineering, etc.) will immediately benefit from the visualization capabilities of Digital's Alpha systems. In addition, the numerically intensive areas of design, such as stress analysis and mathematical modelling in general, will be areas of rapid uptake for Alpha systems with their supercomputer performance and highly scalable architecture.

Demand in these industry sectors will start high immediately and remain consistently high for the whole five-year period.

2. Banking, Insurance and Financial Services The main functions that are of interest in these market sectors are those related to the numerical capacity of Alpha-based systems, the data management and handling capabilities and the value that these systems can bring to the complex areas of data management, analysis and modelling in the banking, insurance and financial services sectors. The use, for instance, of very large-scale neural networks in the financial markets is thought to be very likely, and Alpha provides an excellent vehicle for this.

The banking, insurance and financial services sectors of the markets tend to be a little conservative in bringing in new technologies and at first the penetration will be significant but not as heavy as with the manufacturing industry. This is due partly to the number and type of legacy systems in this market sector and partly because the financial markets have had a bad time in the recession and the money is just not there to invest in new information technology systems.

Another factor is the apparent disillusion that is felt in this sector with many of the investments in information technology that have happened in the past and their failure to bring the promised returns on investment. Banking, especially retail banking, is likely to be a sector of the market that looks at Alpha-based branch server and district server systems, and the high transaction processing load would be a good match for the Alpha capabilities.

3. Public utilities I have taken telecommunications out of this section, though in many countries the governing body is the local PTT which is government owned or regulated. This leaves water, energy and transport functions. The single greatest factor in these markets is likely to be for cost savings, but the drive towards higher quality, better matching of demand and more planned use of limited resources all fall in as drivers in the equation.

Alpha will take off in the public utilities, especially in North America and the EC. One energy sector that is likely to buy Alpha very early is the nuclear generating section of the market. Gas (as I covered earlier) is also a big potential market. The move in these sectors presents some good opportunities from mid-1994 onwards. The main moderating factor will be the utilities themselves, as these are always slow to change and are often subject to corporate and governmental policy decisions.

4. Telecommunications As I mentioned earlier, telecommunications using either standalone Alpha AXP systems or special hardware developed, and with Alpha processors on the boards, will be a big growth area. The highly sensitive nature of the telecommunications market and the critical part that telecommunications plays in modern society mean that the lead time from design to implementation of these systems or system components is likely to be quite long. My best guess is that telecommunications will not be a volume market for Digital's Alpha microprocessors much before the end of 1995.

5. Health Health is a big market, partly because so much of the biomedical research is carried out within this market and partly because the highly visual nature of much of the information makes it an ideal market in many respects for the application of desktop supercomputer power.

However, these market areas do take a long time to penetrate (for many of the same reasons as the utilities, plus the length of time to get applications developed), simply because the period from first investigation to final application of the technology in some areas is dependent on the clinical efficacy of the systems being used. In addition to the direct application of technology to the health systems, there is the view of health as a large manufacturing and distribution market. However, I have taken all these areas into account under the health heading.

The initial uptake into the market is likely to be slow, addressing only point opportunities in the first place and supplying in systems for research and product development. Moving on from this, we can see a very rapid growth of the Alpha microprocessor systems in the health market both in the standalone workstation and server systems and in the application of the technology in the embedded form in clinical devices such as scanners and automated analytical units

6. Research and Education The capacity of certain areas of research to use all the computing power available and then some is legendary. Many difficult problems in high-energy physics, quantum electrodynamics, meteorology, fluid dynamics and molecular biochemistry require a very significant amount of computing power to solve or investigate. Supercomputing on the desktop is a reality with Alpha. This does not now mean that the biggest Alpha-based machines will sit idle in the research departments around the world while the mass of the work hits the local servers. Rather, the tools at the disposal of the average scientist and engineer are now many times more powerful, making for a more productive research community.

All research and education establishments around the world have funding constraints, and this in itself will lead to the slow take-up of Alpha in any significant volumes in the first two or three years. However, by 1996 it is expected that the opportunities for the introduction of Alpha into this market will be significant. Most of the applications of the Alpha technology will be in the data manipulation and numerically intensive computing fields rather than visualization which, while important will be a subsidiary benefit to the systems. Perhaps one of the most exciting areas that the Alpha systems opens up in the research and education fields is that of the data manipulation. Data mining for new research trends from patterns hidden deep in mountains of data is now a real possibility.

A second area where the potential for Alpha systems to liberate information from data is a significant issue in the research community is in the area of database searches. It will soon be possible to use very large databases of published research material in a more efficient and effective manner, linking ideas together and searching libraries of information across a very wide area indeed. The ability to link ideas together, to identify associated work in different areas, is the key to much research and an excellent way to speed up research while reducing the costs. Only supercomputer levels of power can accomplish this and Alpha, by putting this on the researcher's desk or in the department or library, will transform the breadth of information and the sophistication of filtering this information.

Databases themselves can now afford to change as well. Relational or indexed databases have been at the heart of all computing and for many applications will remain the ideal method of data organization. Some applications, however, do not fit neatly into structures, require almost infinite numbers of indexes to classify them or simply need an unstructured method of interrogating the database.

One approach to these types of problems is the free-text database in which the documents are not stored in any order or structure. Information searches are then conducted on all the text in all the documents in the database (possibly with some delimiters on document age or other classification). Clearly this kind of application eats memory and processor power but fits well into certain styles of work, especially research activities. Alpha now makes this type of database a practicality for many businesses, one example being the law. Being married to a lawyer, I am all too aware of the complex nature of the enquiries that have to be made for precedents and cases. Large, fast and cost-effective Alpha-based data stores with free-text retrieval systems mounted on them would be an excellent application in a research activity with real-world implications.

7. Retail and distribution From a retail point of view Alpha will take off fairly slowly except at the transaction processing level for telesales and as a multi-storey server in the electronic funds transfer and point of sale network environment. In distribution and warehousing there will also be opportunities but in general this will be a slow market for Alpha since many of the installed systems for the larger players will fall into the legacy systems category. The longer-term market for Alpha in the retail and distribution market looks better, though not on the same scale as for manufacturing or banking and finance.

8. Petrochemicals There are immediate opportunities for Alpha in this market for the reasons I described earlier. It is likely that there will be initial interest in the use of Alpha for the evaluation of mining-related information either in the analysis of seismic records or the simulation of oil and gas field reserves with a view to the more efficient extraction of materials from existing sites. The market will initially be attractive but again slower than for the manufacturing, banking and finance markets until around 1996, when the market for Alpha in the oil, gas and petrochemical industries is predicted to take off (this is partly linked to the expected upturn in demand for these products around that time).

9. Military Applications Military applications of Alpha fall into three main classes:

- Development platforms
- Command and control systems
- Embedded microprocessors

Already Raytheon have signed up a licence agreement with Digital Equipment Corporation that allows Raytheon to produce military versions of the Alpha architecture. Raytheon are to have a main position in the militarization, marketing and manufacture of Digital's Alpha architecture to the US government's customers and contractors. Raytheon have for some time been doing the same kind of things with Digital VAX-based systems. Interestingly, the licence agreement with Raytheon includes technology transfer from Digital and Raytheon will adopt the Alpha architecture and designs to develop and produce computer systems that comply with military specifications.

Military applications for development platforms will mean that Alpha systems will be used as platforms to develop software for a number of other computer system targets. This will reduce the inefficiency in some of the development projects and increase the consistency and quality of the end results. The needs of any command and control system are a good fit with Alpha's capability in both visualization and computation. Capabilities for the management of large numbers of signals, the very fast processing of signal data and the computation of options and scenarios are all essential in modern command and control systems. Alpha gives the supercomputer the mobility and reduces size and weight that now make it possible to deploy such systems in the field in large numbers.

Embedded microprocessor systems are an essential component of all modern weapons and surveillance systems. Functions such as very fast pattern recognition, signal processing, data matching and encryption or decryption are all functions that Alpha-based systems have the capabilities to handle at a speed, size and weight never before possible for onboard computer systems. It is likely that the uptake for the architecture will be very rapid in the military systems market with large numbers being shipped in the long term but not short term. (The largest numbers are likely to be in embedded weapons and surveillance systems, which take around 5 years to develop and produce.)

Table 6.7 Short-term potential volume predictions 1993 - 1998

	1993	1994	1995	1996	1997	1998
Design & manufacturing	M	M	M+	M+	H	H
Banking, insurance, etc.	L+	M	M+	M+	M	M+
Public utilities	L+	M	M+	M+	H	H
Telecommunications	L+	M	M	M+	H	H
Health	L	L+	M	M+	M+	H
Research & education	L	L+	M	M+	H	H
Retail & distribution	L	L	L+	M	M	M+
Petrochemicals	L	L+	M	M+	H	H
Military applications	L	L	L+	M	M+	H

Note: h = high, L = low, M = moderate, + = rising, - = falling,

6.3.3 Longer-Term Prospects

Longer-term in this section refers to the period up to the year 2001. In this section I predict volumes for sales of Digital's Alpha processors related to the period 1997 to 2001 in each of the industry cases.

1. Design and manufacturing The market will start to recover with the industry as the worst effects of the recession are left behind. In addition, the applications vendors themselves will have made significant investments in the software to fully exploit this technology in the period up to 1996.

2. Banking insurance and financial services The natural conservatism of this market will mean a relatively slow place for the Alpha systems to really make an impact. In addition, there will be a need for the Windows NT viruses UNIX situation to be sorted in the market. Due to the high levels of investment and the large numbers of (often bespoke) applications, I do not feel that Alpha will make the highest levels of impact for around 5 years.

3. Public Utilities Most public utilities are going to find the funding of any new investment more difficult than conventional industry. Existing applications and hardware will need to be replaced slowly and this is a sector of the market where specialist applications are few indeed. For this reason, I feel that the take-up of Alpha, relative to the rest of the market, will be slow.

4. Telecommunications Once Alpha is truly integrated into telecommunications, for instance in intelligent switches and digital video devices, then the market will run away with this excellent microprocessor

5. Health All biomedical applications are long-term investments. Clearly the development of applications and systems capable of using Alpha technology will take at least three to five years.

6. Research Despite the lack of funds claimed in many educational and research establishments I feel that Alpha will do well and continue to do so. Part of the reason is the short time required for applications development, part is because of the cost effectiveness of Alpha and partly the reason is based on Digital's educational discounting policy.

7. Retail and distribution This is not an area in which Digital have ever been a major player. Alpha makes a number of applications available on a Digital platform that where hitherto based on IBM, HP, etc. However, I doubt Digitals ability to effectively manage the relationship issues in this area and hence my slightly pessimistic view of the product performance.

8. Petrochemicals From my research in this area it seems that there are many petrochemical applications already being ported. Having said this, the timeframe for write-off of existing hardware and replacement with Alpha is around 3 years. Given this, Alpha will make volume market share only through innovation in the application domain and not by just replacement of old systems (as is indeed the case with all market sectors).

9. Military applications Cost is now an issue in the military spending of the world, but technology is still key to driving future generations of weapons and battlefield communications. For this reason, Alpha will gain wide acceptance in the military market and will remain strong (especially in the United States of America).

These views are summarized in the Table 6.8:

Table 6.8 Long term volume predictions for Alpha 1997 - 2001

	1997	1998	1999	2000	2001
Design & manufacturing	H	H+	H++	H++	H+
Banking, insurance, etc.	M	M+	H	H++	H+
Public utilities	H	H	H	H	H
Telecommunications	H	H	H++	H+	H++
Health	M+	H	H+	H+	H
Research & education	H	H	H+	H++	M
Retail & distribution	M	M+	M+	H	H
Petrochemicals	H	H	H++	H++	M
Military applications	M+	H	H++	H++	H+

6.3.4 Some Views on Operating Systems

As a technologist I want to see standards in the industry. They make things simple and easy, they allow us to know what to do and they set a boundary inside which we can play safely. Unfortunately, they also take a long time to agree. Of late, the diversity that was UNIX has started to move slowly towards a single set of standards and chances are that in just a few years the final standards will be in place to cover the majority of issues surrounding the unification of UNIX systems and software. This is not the same as saying that there will be only one UNIX, far from it, but it is true to say that by the mid-1990s, just 30 or so years after it was born, UNIX will be self-consistent in all its flavours.

Or will it? The present effort in standards continues to provide standardization that is some years from the cutting edge of the technology, yet the rate of technology change gets greater, and this implies that the backlog of standards is becoming larger and the applicability of these standards to the industry is diminishing. Perhaps Microsoft NT will offer a way out of this problem by presenting the industry with an operating system controlled by one organization (and therefore consistent) across a range of microprocessor options. I tend to think that if NT can take off in a big way and get the backing of the main applications developers in all the key industries, then it does stand a very good chance of initially becoming the *de-facto* standard for the interface and object management level in industry and then going on to be the basis for a more general set of standards. This implies that there will have to be a general acceptance of just one organization as the predominant supplier of operating systems, and middleware associated with these systems, to the industry at some level. In essence, we would see a greater degree of verticalization in the operating system market itself if this were to happen, with a move to the object management and user interface clients being provided by Microsoft together with the compiler technology to support this, and the back-end data management systems from IBM, DEC and the UNIX houses. A third element in this picture that is likely to be important is the supplier of the pan-platform functionality, things like the TP monitor for a number of operating systems that allows the interworking of applications on a scheduled resource basis from an NT client to a UNIX server then to a VMS server and returning to the NT client via an IBM AS400.

No one company could or should ever own all this picture. The new picture of an operating environment (I use this term to replace operating system as it has a more generic scope) is likely to be one that is built up of components from many organizations. The sting in the tale is that to achieve this requires standards, just the principle that is slowing down the present industry. However, there is hope, by the inclusion of only a small number of organizations in the development of the functionality of an operating environment, that the standards issue is likely to be resolved more quickly than we see at present in, for instance, the Open Systems standards area. Furthermore, the standards themselves are likely to represent the needs of the technology in the market and not an image of this from some time long ago.

There is a cultural need for a new operating system at work in the market. First, like the UNIX users of the academic world who influenced the shape of the industry today, our academic base needs to make its mark. There is a real desire in the undergraduate community to be at the front of something new, to have a technology that represents the future and not the past and to be the practitioners of a newer wisdom. Any new operating system would have been a candidate for this, but one as cheaply and freely available as NT is in the prime position at this point in time (interestingly, the NT developers kit is, in real terms, about 30% of the price of UNIX as it used to be sold from Berkeley in the 1970s). Second, the need for an interface to an object-based system designed to operate in a client server environment in a truly pre-emptive multitasking mode exists as a reflection of the state of applications in the real world.

The applications that are in existence today were, generally, designed for the industries they targeted three to ten years ago.

The effect of the applications on the industries they serve is to make them different in a number of ways, thereby changing the requirements of the industries for the applications. This positive feedback loop has, in many places, led to users desiring functionality that cannot be economically provided from the existing technology base. At the top of the list is the need for the user interface to be smarter while allowing the applications to live longer or be recycled. Both requirements are fulfilled by Microsoft NT.

The industry is set for something of a war. IBM are continuing to back OS/2 as their operating system for the mid-range multi-user systems to compete with MS Windows and DOS. Alliances between IBM and, for instance, Apple will make the task of winning over existing IBM users to a new, non-IBM operating system difficult. On the other hand, there are a number of players who will be providing Microsoft NT on hardware platforms as diverse as NCR and DEC. These organizations will be pitching powerful price-performance and a new operating system into a market that was just starting to settle down. By doing this it is highly likely that existing sites with OS/2 may be forced to consider their options for the future. As mentioned earlier, NT allows the migration of data to the system with relative ease from an OS/2 application. Therefore, if the end result is more powerful than existing OS/2 offerings (which NT is in its first release) then there will be a strong reason for at least seriously considering the place of NT in an organization.

I have painted a picture of two systems, balanced in the marketplace by technical and commercial forces and eventually reaching a market equilibrium until this is disturbed by the advent of some new, far-reaching change in the networking arena of the industry. I think this is a highly probable scenario and the stable situation is likely to come about in the next 5 years or so. In the systems constructed with a UNIX or proprietary mid-range centre and a Microsoft NT outer, the management of the central system will eventually be done through the Microsoft NT layer and using the tools provided therein. The system style and appearance will be based on Microsoft NT and not on UNIX or the proprietary mid-range. End users will use Microsoft NT. This, however, is not a situation the other operating systems manufacturers will sit back and allow to happen without a fight, which is most likely to be in the standards arena where the present incumbents wield the most power. It is therefore clear that NT will have first to gain and then consolidate its position in the front-end client role within the client server architectures of this and the next decade.

6.3.5 The Strong Position of UNIX

UNIX used to be a dirty word at Digital. Clearly the corporation came to the UNIX market slowly, late and in a badly organized fashion. The market they face is interesting and competitive. For instance, UNIX System V has a 79% market share of the Open Systems marketplace. Digital, like IBM have suffered from the arrogance of the proprietary systems vendor and the blindness of an organization to the facts of the market. IBM, like Digital have this problem but IBM do not have the Alpha chip. As I write this book Alpha faces an even more confused market with the advent of NT.

Is this all bad news for Digital? The answer is 'not necessarily'. Microsoft Windows NT is not getting the rapid take-up of applications vendors that it needs to compete with UNIX at present. In addition, I have very few clients or contacts in industry who are actively moving substantial applications over to Windows NT. Partly this is a lack of expertise and partly it is a need for more powerful processors. Of all the systems I have seen NT running on, the Alpha_AXP systems are the best.

Clearly, Alpha based systems have a lot to offer if we look at them as a hardware platform for other peoples products. UNIX is not dead and is going to compete head-on with Windows NT over the next few years, Novell will ensure this is so. Alpha running System V or even better System 5MK (the soon to be released microkernel version of the UNIX System V operating system) will be a very attractive platform on which to work given its clearly standard base from which to generate other versions of applications for more esoteric versions of UNIX.

Furthermore, UNIX has a strong position in a number of the key markets in which Alpha is set to do relatively well in the period up to 1998 such as: manufacturing, health and education. The biggest danger here is Digital itself. I am still of the opinion that people buy from Digital rather than Digital selling to them. The 'meetings' culture is still prevalent (it is not uncommon to be told people from marketing are unavailable for days as they are in meetings). The Alpha technology could end up being the best microprocessor the industry never adopted if Digital does not have a real shake-out in sales and marketing soon.

Alpha is the technology the UNIX market has been waiting for. It is clearly essential that there is support for full SMP hardware in the early versions of the System V and System VMK operating systems on this platform or much of the potential market will be lost.

There are a large number UNIX systems in the market today with UNIX system V.4 being seen as an industry standard. It is certain that the future looks secure for the moment, with the prospect for collaboration between USL and its industrial partners continuing to be good, and more functionality is going to be provided in the next few years most importantly the microkernel version of UNIX System V.

6.3.6 The Challenge for Microsoft NT

Clearly UNIX is well suited to the role of the operating system for the mid-range servers of today and for the next few years. How can Microsoft attack this position with its NT operating system and how and where will NT compete in the market? To answer these questions, I will look at how Microsoft NT compares with UNIX in the chosen market of the mid-range server system-based on the criteria laid down in the UI-ATLAS roadmap. The areas to look at are:

- A framework for systems management.
- An definition for transaction processing management.
- Distributed computing environment (DCE) support
- Enhanced networking functionality
- Enhanced desktop functions for UNIX System V

UNIX International's view of the change in role for the desktop computer in the mid-term, based on flexibility with information as the focus is shared by Microsoft. Like UNIX International, Microsoft seem to view the main components as flexibility, interoperability, connectivity and distributed processing. Also like UNIX International, Microsoft see multimedia as a fundamentally important component of the desktop in the close future (to such an extent that Microsoft are buying up the rights to books and films and producing their own multimedia CD databases by publishing them themselves). This therefore implies a need for the operating system to be based on object-oriented technologies to support this datacentric approach. Given the history of UNIX, the operating system is being adapted to fit the needs of an object-oriented computing environment by the addition of APIs and tools. However, it is true to say that UNIX itself was not designed in a world where object orientation was present.

Microsoft NT, on the other hand, has taken object orientation as a fundamental truth in computing and as such has integrated the principles of object orientation thoroughly into its design and development. Part of this is via OLE (Object Linking and Embedding). OLE allows data portability between applications in a way that reflects the needs of business. For instance, information from production figures or from a spreadsheet can by moved with the mouse into a completely different application like a graphics or spreadsheet application to which this data would be foreign under other circumstances. This level of object orientation via OLE is specific to Microsoft at the moment. If your application does not use Microsoft Windows or Microsoft NT, then OLE support does not help, yet. It is fair to say that almost all major vendors of Windows (and NT) based applications presently support OLE, although some (like Lotus) go much further.

In response to this challenge, Microsoft are launching an upgrade to OLE1 known as OLE2, which includes a number of tools that allow the easier manipulation of objects outside their native application. Moving further on from OLE2 we find (not too surprisingly) OLE3. Codenamed 'Cairo' by Microsoft, OLE3 is a move towards true object engineering and includes support for heterogeneous platforms, the development of gateways and utilities for object conversion. This level of functionality will therefore allow the users of a Microsoft Windows application to use object modules from non-Windows-based applications running on other platforms. When OLE3 finds itself included in Microsoft NT, the operating system will be able to outstrip UNIX significantly in the real race for object leadership on the desktop.

The main problem that Microsoft will face is the weight of opinion of the Object Management Group. This is the standards body, made up of over 280 other companies and organizations, who administer the definition of object technology standards. OMG members make little secret of their opinion that OLE is proprietary to Microsoft and not fully compliant with their definition of the Object Request Broker, which is much less platform-specific in definition today. However, Microsoft has on its side the knowledge that shipping more than 1 million copies of an operating system per month gives it a certain industry weight through penetration alone.

Compared to UNIX International's drive towards a desktop with an object-based metaphor, independent look and feel, fault tolerance and distributed systems management, Microsoft NT achieves many of these things well but, above all, it achieves an acceptable level of object management and good look and feel today and not some time in the next two years. Furthermore, Microsoft are, as the main volume shippers of GUI technology, in the position of leading the end-user's expectation in the market. Microsoft NT is well placed to take this *de-facto* standard into the realm of the multi-user desktop system and compete well with UNIX (of whatever flavour) due mainly to its dominant HCI as a *de-facto* standard and to the pragmatic use of object technology in the form of OLE.

It is essential for servers to interoperate both with proprietary and Open Systems. The approach taken for Open Systems will be similar to that by Microsoft by supporting distributed object technology through using systems services, and to do this without needing modification to the installed base. However, Microsoft have already achieved this with the release of their OLE1 and OLE2 standards and system services. Furthermore, there is a realization among the applications developers that there is no free lunch. Some of the applications will not be able to use OLE just as some will be unable to use the object technology to be available under UNIX. To this end the tools being developed by Microsoft to support more powerful manipulation of objects puts them ahead of UNIX in a key area. Lastly, OLE3 (Cairo) which will come out in 1993 with NT support gives a true object file system.

A number of other functions are also essential for such servers, and top of the list is security. Microsoft NT has C2 security, making it fully capable of performing in all but the most unusually high security environments. Data integrity functions are also well addressed by Microsoft NT with data integrity being achieved by the NT operating system using its own file management system called NTFS. This adds a transactional log that records each disk access to speed up recovery following a system crash. The NT operating system is also capable of reading and writing OS/2 and DOS files.

Distributed systems management in Microsoft's approach is integrated with communications services. These are required by the server for an application to interoperate with other applications on remote systems The communications services are at a number of levels and available across a range of network types and standards. Networking is the key to the market and Microsoft are going to hit a number of other topologies, especially PC networks such as Novell, Apple and UNIX as well as IBM by supporting:

- Co-existence with NetWare
- Links to IBM's NETview
- Support for TCP/IP
- Support for SNMP (including VI and II of MIB)
- Macintosh Client support
- LAN manager users may log on concurrently on more than one network.
- Lanmanager X is the UNIX end and is developed by AT&T
- Full AppleTalk protocol support planned
- Full SQL server

It is worth noting that Microsoft have allowed the management functionality of IBM's NETview to be available in their system.

Mission-critical data in the corporate environment, must be managed in a very secure and efficient manner and UNIX System V must provide better methods of doing this in the future. Fault tolerance in a real UNIX system is achieved today through the inclusion of a TP monitor such as TOPEND or TUXEDO. Such TP monitors are presently not available for Microsoft NT and therefore the systems developed on an NT base will not have as much resilience as those developed using a TP monitor on UNIX. I have not been able to find a supplier of TP monitors who is willing to commit to Microsoft NT support at present, therefore one has to assume that this functionality will, at least in the early days of Microsoft NT in the market, be unavailable. The alternatives are to develop one's own two-phase commit protocol (which, using objects, is not a difficult exercise) and perhaps then to add some level of rollback mechanism to this giving the most basic level of TP monitor functionality but without resource-need balancing.

UNIX International's plan for a distributed heterogeneous environment (transaction management, transactional processing in symmetric multiprocessing environments, fault management, security and capacity planning) is matched by the capabilities of Microsoft NT at most levels. The question of success is answered by looking at how fast the industry leaders sign up to Microsoft NT and compete with those signed up to UNIX.

Clearly the operating system for the mid-range servers of today and for the coming years must be well suited to the role and to the technologies emerging as key. Microsoft can attack this market with its NT operating system and compete well with UNIX, especially in the area of object technology and networking. As the main producers of GUI-based systems Microsoft are able to call the shots when it comes to setting and exceeding user expectations.

UNIX does seem to have the upper hand in the area of fault tolerance, but this is primarily due to the use of transaction processing monitors like TOPEND or TUXEDO. If this functionality is provided to the Microsoft NT world, perhaps by extending an existing TP monitor into the Microsoft NT system, then technically the two systems will be closer matched in the area of fault tolerance but NT would still be ahead in object technology at the real rather than the theoretical level.

6.3.7 The Joint Future for UNIX and Windows NT

As systems price performance continued to improve over the past two years, UNIX has been able to gain ground into lower and lower levels of the market. In addition, the attractions of UNIX-based server systems and desktop systems when compared to the relatively simple Microsoft Windows technology were still able to win in the serious corporate sale and for high-volume, transaction-critical applications. This game is now significantly changed by Microsoft with the introduction of the NT operating system. While those users who have invested heavily in UNIX on the desktop will not be likely to change in the short term, they will undoubtedly be attracted to the power and sophistication of Microsoft NT. It is likely that for any given market sector where the applications are available (and this is an important qualification) then Microsoft NT is likely to be a strong contender for mid-range server business. UNIX is most likely going to trade on its reputation as being mature and therefore reliable plus the resilient aspects of transactional systems that can be supported through the use of TP monitors.

It is likely that the lead that Microsoft NT will have over UNIX will allow it to enter market sectors presently being addressed by UNIX, these specifically being in the small to mid-range server sectors and in the networked desktop. In this last sector the main problem for Microsoft will be the Novell networks of PCs rather than UNIX systems.

UNIX has a long and fascinating history which works both for and against it. I stated earlier that one of the main reasons for the take-up of UNIX in the commercial market was that the expectations of those coming out of higher education had been set by the power, flexibility and, above all, familiarity of UNIX. The same is now true of MSDOS and MS Windows. Most students of computer science have a DOS and Windows-based machine, and like their UNIX-trained predecessors their expectations have already been set and these expectations and prejudices will strongly influence the market in the future. Once the Microsoft NT operating system with its embedded object technology takes off, the offering will be all too tempting to miss for those who have grown up with the principles of object orientation. Above all, Microsoft has a great strength, it is one organization and that makes it flexible and responsive in a way that the larger corporations and the corporately sponsored standards groups can never be. I have often thought that the information technology industry has many of the attributes of a biological system. Perhaps the dominant and specialized nature of UNIX is now threatened by the faster, predatory generalization of Microsoft NT.

6.3.8 Summary

The range and number of factors that impinge on the likely performance of the Alpha technology are very large. Perhaps the most crucial of these is the ability of Digital to control and manage its own marketing and sales operations in a way that suits a very new style of business. The most distinct change in this respect when the new Alpha-based business is compared with Digital's previous offerings is the reliance on third-party sales channels. Never before has such a key component of the Digital corporate portfolio been put out to the market in this way. The task of managing the channels is a very different one from the traditional role of managing the VAR/Distributor type of arrangement. For this component of the Alpha strategy to succeed, it will require a clear match between the commercial and the technology aspects of the programme. In doing this, the problem of confusion between channels is one that dogs all such operations. In the traditional area of the VAR/Distributor, Digital have had some notable disasters with channel confusion, and I have some doubts as to their capability to manage such a new level of complexity in this area. This is the reason I think the technology may be slower to take off than the technology alone would tend to suggest: simply that getting the sales channel right is no easy job.

As with all major new technology platform innovations (such as UNIX in the past and Microsoft Windows NT now), there has to be adoption of the technology by the applications development community if the technology market potential is to be realized. Part of the problem here is that the technology itself could lead to pressure downwards on applications prices (due to the comparison between the applications and the system pricing). The only way to combat this in the long term is for the applications to add much more value (in terms of total or specific functionality) in order to justify to the users the increased applications to system-price ratio. The problem with this line of reasoning is that it implies that there has to be investment on the part of the applications development community for this to happen. Investment itself has to be funded out of operating revenues, debt or equity injection, and in the present economic climate, raising funds by any of these means for the software business is no easy task. However, on the positive side, the power available from the Alpha technology for the end user means that there will be significant opportunities for new classes of applications based on the assumption that real power in the field of visualization and data manipulation is affordable to the mass market at last. Clearly the fields associated with these applications domains will be the ones to watch for the high-value installations on the Alpha platform.

The break with the traditional link with VMS is one that Digital has finally made. This is not to say that VMS is dead, far from it, but the future will be elsewhere for the mass market. The big battle is going to be between UNIX and Microsoft Windows NT, and I have covered this in detail. Suffice it to say that UNIX will not be dislodged without a real fight, one that will last for many years.

In the end, the biggest threat to Digital is Digital itself, if it fails to restructure severely enough or to reorganize in a way that would be appropriate for the new business it has to become. Like IBM, Digital is too big to just disappear, the danger is that it will just get damaged by not taking on board the lessons of the past, the main reason being that small and fast is better than big and slow, and the other being that the geography issue for a global corporation can be the most expensive luxury.

6.4 Future Developments

Alpha. The word is synonymous with the concept of beginning, and for Digital, Alpha is not the end of the VAX but the beginning of a new era. In this section I will look at some possible developments associated with this exciting new technology.

6.4.1 The Trends in Systems

Distribution of functionality and of the data in an organization continues to be the predominant factor in the architecture of new systems. Certainly the Alpha system will influence this in that the processing power, once distributed, will be considerable. This in itself will lead to more powerful and highly specialized applications distributed on these processors. One interesting implication of the power of the systems is that once data is on the local system, the need to transfer the data to and fro will be minimized since the system itself has most of the power to perform functions locally. In this respect, Alpha systems will allow a short- to medium-term reduction of pressure on the bandwidth of many local and wide area networks. In the long term, and for some more interactive applications, this trend will be reversed, with Alpha systems causing significant loads on existing networks.

Visualization and the whole area of the human-machine interface is another area where the Alpha technology is set to make a very significant impact. No longer will the processor power be a limiting factor on the sophistication of the interface. Voice- and pen-based systems will stop being the crude and rather slow toys they are at present and will finally become the *de-facto* method of interaction with a number of devices by the use of embedded Alpha-based systems in the new ranges of input and output devices. All in all, the trend will be for the person to have a means of communicating with a system. In this respect the system will not be unlike a telecommunications network and the personal communications device will resemble the role of the personal phone. In my view of the future, however, the Alpha-based personal interface to the system will have the processing power of a Cray and the sophistication in terms of type and style of interaction that we can only dream of today, When we see this personal Alpha-based assistant, we will really be witnessing the dawn of a really new method of computing, one in which resources are just a commodity (like network time) and which we use on an as-required basis.

An implication of this trend is for the growth in the availability of remote connectable computing and data resources to feed a market hungry for *ad hoc* power and information. This market becomes blurred as the facilities we look at fit as well into the leisure sector as into the business sector (in much the same way as cable networks do now).

Alpha is set to grow as a technology and as an area of application. Clearly the competition will be trying to catch up but there is one thing for certain: being first is the most important thing.

6.4.2 Communications

Communications with high-performance systems requires high-performance networks and protocols to drive them. Years ago X.25 was thought to be hot stuff, then along came Frame Relay, and now Asynchronous Transfer Mode looks like the way forward. However, all these systems have a limitation when it comes to the transmission of visual data. On the horizon, most of the promising research is coming out of the AI and neural networking areas, especially those associated with human sight and perception (since we perceive a lot that we do not constantly see, for instance).

The introduction of large numbers of Alpha-based systems into organizations will cause some problems in the long term with regard to available bandwidth (fibre optic being the only reasonable physical medium to consider). However, there are a number of other issues relating to the use of Alpha within a network that have some interesting consequences.

The first of these areas is the dynamic gathering of information in real-time from a network. By the use of the massive power of the Alpha systems, it is now possible to gather information on, say, telephone networks as they are being used. One use of this information would be to provide real pictures of the patterns of use of a large telephone system throughout the working day. This information would then have a number of uses:

- Form the basis of network testing
- Used to develop more efficient topologies
- As the basis for market analysis and service pricing
- To dynamically reconfigure a network

These things are done to a limited extent today but in no way are they possible within real-time or to any level comparable to the cost-efficient solutions offered using Alpha-based systems.

If we now turn our view to another area in which Alpha offers significant advances in the future of communications it has to be as a network processor managing large databases on a distributed system. Communications services are following the trend for industrial globalization. The consequence of this is that the information that corporations use is stored on networks spanning many parts of the world. Present technology makes the cost of storage and processing of such information prohibitive for all but the largest corporations if the data volumes are significant and the processing overhead sizeable.

Very soon the Alpha technology will bring these data networking systems within the reach of many small operations. An example of this is an automotive company I have been speaking to. They have a number of small subsidiaries around the world and are looking to use Alpha-based systems to manage databases of CAD and engineering data for all products in all countries. The reasoning behind this is interesting. They do not know how they are going to use this mass of information yet, but they are sure the engineering potential of such information in the development of new and innovative products will outweigh the moderate costs involved.

Communications has to encompass human communications too and this is my third and last example. The ability to add significant value to the process of communications by the use of Alpha-based AI systems in the translation of first written and then spoken language from one to another and from one language to another will soon be a matter of course. Already there are a number of corporations around the world researching the development of products to achieve this.

6.4.3 Will the Competitors Catch Up?

I stated earlier that there was a big advantage in being first. That is very true but sooner or later the other guys catch up! None of the major microprocessor manufacturers will be sitting on their hands while Digital steam ahead with the Alpha. The nearest in performance to the Alpha is the R4400 from MIPS, and even this is no real match for the Alpha processor. The real trick is going to be the speed at which the applications and systems vendors adopt the Alpha systems and the rate at which migration tools can be developed. It has to be remembered that for almost all the main vendors, the move required to catch up to the Alpha is going to require a significant change in architecture, and that implies a lot of migration for the applications and the operating systems.

Undoubtedly the competition will succeed through the engineering activities in catching up to Digital. The real issue is, will they have missed the boat commercially? In the end it would be nice to think that Digital will lead the pack and win hands-down leaving the other runners behind. I am of the opinion, however, that through its own efforts this may not happen with Digital. The key has to be in the alliances that the corporation strikes up in this critical period of market penetration. If they play their cards right, they may achieve in the 1990s what Intel did in the 1980s. One thing is for sure: they will not achieve this alone. It is reasonable to say that Digital is ripe in many ways for a merger or acquisition of a key partner. In the next 3 to 5 years the rest of the pack will catch up technically, Digital have other innovations up their sleeve though, and the pack do not seem to be taking this into consideration when one looks at the way the futures are being forecast by the major players.

6.4.4 Legacy into Asset

Many corporations used to look at the cost of keeping all that old data, (for instance, 7 years of accounting records). Data was in many cases just a costly issue. Suddenly the power of Alpha has really transformed that into a potential asset. For once, the power is affordable to take an Alpha-based system and to create an ordered and valuable set of information from a disorganized pile of data.

At the software level we also see the impact of the Alpha architecture, inasmuch as the new lease of life that is available to the software once the porting process has occurred. The ability to extend both the functionality of the application and the interfaces to the data and to the real world are significantly improved due to the speed and flexibility of the architecture. Initially the VAX/VMS-based systems will likely stay at the VMS level. However, a significant trend is emerging for systems to be ported across to the Alpha processor and also to UNIX at the same time. The combination of the speed and flexibility of this port makes an old application competitive once more at the performance level. Once we layer on this the ability to increase the data and human interface values by the addition of, say, an SQL back end and a GUI front end, then we see the applications that have the real power to solve the basic business problems being turned round to cope with the requirements of a more discriminating market.

6.5 Alpha Perspectives

This section looks at the differing perspectives on the Alpha programme. In particular, it covers:

- Consultant opinions
- User attitudes
- Developer views

6.5.1 What the Consultants Say

Most of the consultants feel that the Alpha technology is a real advance in the field of microprocessor design and they share the view that this may be the salvation of Digital. In general the scepticism surrounding the future is based on the corporation's ability to cope with the commercial and not the technical part of the operation. The following are some consultants' views:

- 'If the figures are correct, Digital has moved, in one year, from last to first in hardware technology.' Marc Schulman, UBS Securities (USA)
- 'This technology should place Digital in front of Sun and HP's chips and in front of their next generation as well.' Harry William, Sanfor C. Bernstein (USA)
- '... It is definitely the most powerful chip available in the whole world today ...' Martin Hingley IDC (UK)
- 'In the constant leapfrog race Digital has definitely taken a giant step ahead of the competition with Alpha ...' Lars Miertz, Technology Investment Strategies Corporation Ltd (UK)

6.5.2 Existing Digital Users

Digital users are a little bemused by so much happening so fast, though this is changing as the marketing machine gets the message across better to the smaller users. Having talked to many, the following checklist is worth going through if you are a Digital user and are considering going over to Alpha:

1. For those using VMS today, the question is whether to add Alpha to the existing topology or to replace the VAX processor base with the Alpha. The answer depends on the systems you have and the ease (or otherwise) of porting to the Alpha platform. Addition is always a good starting point. This then allows the older VAX dependencies to be gradually reduced
2. For users of a form of UNIX on DEC, for instance either system V or more commonly Ultrix or OSF/1, then the real question is should you stay with Digital or move to another supplier? The answer to this depends on your view of dependency in a supplier relationship. From a technology point of view, there is no doubt that staying on Alpha from, say, a VAX or MIPS base is the best option.
3. For Digital users looking to move to Open Systems, the Alpha really gives the performance, if coupled with a form of UNIX and/or the addition of Windows NT servers and workstations. The resulting topology is as open as one might reasonably be able to find. The question to ask in this case is the same as in item 2. For strategic reasons do you want more than one supplier of the base technology?

6.5.3 Applications Developers

The applications developer has some particular requirements, and these can be summarized in the following views, taken from a number in the field:

1. Alpha is yet another platform to support
2. Alpha weakens the VMS base
3. Alpha strengthens the Digital sales message
4. Digital have just added a lease of life to a threatened base.

Now this is a really broad set of views. The real issue is that Alpha offers a very competitive edge to the applications developer only if the end user buys into the platform. If this is not the case, then the applications developer has to make sure that the applications performance will be acceptable on lesser platforms. This then reduces the scope for the addition of compute-intensive features. Alpha in this sense acts against the commercial implications of the Open Systems movement in that it reduces the viable options for the platform for those brave enough to use the power of Alpha to good benefit.

6.6 Chapter Summary

In this chapter we have looked back at the rest of the issues raised in this book with a view to the future performance of the Alpha technology. It is clear that the move to this technology by the Digital Corporation has been a very bold one and that this has also been the subject of a great deal of speculation.

The risks to the programme are all-based on the performance of the corporation in the commercial arena and not in the respect of the technology. Digital is a hugely successful technology innovator, hampered only by a need for a matching sales and marketing performance. From the initial signs in the market, it appears that the corporation have learned the lessons of the past and are able to move forward with this innovation and to capture the high ground once more.

The competition is already fighting hard to keep up and Intel have announced plans for a successor to the Pentium programme. Digital have the lead and are moving fast to get the Alpha family of processors out and available in a manner that will flood the high-value end of the market. It looks like they may just have a huge winner on their hands.

The fate of the Digital applications and systems houses is dependent on the innovation they can bring to the problem of how to use the Alpha. It is not enough to use the system as a method of reducing the applications and system bundle price. Intelligent use of such power assumes the integration of associated technologies of visualization, speech, pattern recognition, data management and a whole lot more into the base of the applications portfolio.

I have often criticized applications vendors in this book. I do this only because I see the market moving in ways that threaten the future of such businesses. In the long term it is essential for the applications to be more valuable in a very real and measurable way. The climate and technology are now right for this to happen and let us hope that the applications vendors make this so. Digital urgently need to attend to these relationships, the key to the success is in making other people rich, do that and your success is assured. Today it is sadly true that Digital still have a long way to go in selling, marketing and third party relations. As always, their technology far outstrips their commercial ability.

The last word on Alpha is that it is fast. It is an impressive technology that is really capable of taking on the world and becoming the equivalent of the ubiquitous 86 series from Intel. I hope that Digital wins, but in this business the next innovation is just around the corner.

Index